Economic Sanctions

Economic Sanctions
Ideals and experience

M. S. Daoudi and M. S. Dajani

Routledge & Kegan Paul
London, Boston, Melbourne and Henley

First published in 1983
by Routledge & Kegan Paul plc
39 Store Street, London WC1E 7DD,
9 Park Street, Boston, Mass. 02108, USA,
296 Beaconsfield Parade, Middle Park,
Melbourne 3206, Australia, and
Broadway House, Newtown Road,
Henley-on-Thames, Oxon RG9 1EN
Set in Press Roman 10 on 12 point by
Hope Services, Abingdon
and printed in Great Britain by
Robert Hartnoll Ltd, Bodmin, Cornwall

Library of Congress Cataloging in Publication Data

Daoudi, M. S.

Economic sanctions, ideals and experience.
(International library of economics)
Bibliography: p.
Includes index.
1. Sanctions (International law)   I. Dajani, M. S.
II. Title.   III. Series.
JX1246.D34 1983   341.5'8   83-4572

ISBN 0-7100-9583-X

To our parents, and to May, Muhsen and Walid,
whose love and support are our
driving force

Contents

List of Figures and Tables

Introduction

In 1966 Dennis Austin observed that 'the literature on sanctions is surprisingly thin despite the interest aroused in the problem in the 1930s and again today.'[1] Since the 1965 UN sanctions against Rhodesia and the Arab oil embargo of 1973, the controversy over the use of economic resources as instruments of international politics has intensified. It has been observed that 'in contrast to traditional international politics, partnership, beneficence, and threat are more likely to be conceived, perceived and evaluated *economically* rather than *militarily*.'[2] The literature on economic sanctions and their role in the international system is expanding rapidly. Industrial nations, as they experience severe shortages in some vital raw materials and moderate shortages in others, are giving raw material supplies more and more serious consideration and higher priority in the shaping of their foreign policy. The policymakers' attention is focused on short- or medium-term supply limitations, not in terms of resource exhaustion, but rather in terms of possible political cutbacks or sabotage of production and distribution facilities. The situation is exacerbated when vital raw materials are located in politically unstable areas and when there are no practical substitutes for the imported commodity in question.

'International security, once defined and preserved by military might, had suddenly been threatened by the uncertain availability of critical economic resources,'[3] Robert L. Paarlberg has written. 'Nations seemed in a position to struggle for dominance over one another by offering or refusing access to increasingly scarce primary commodities and raw materials. In one view, the most dramatic aspect of this struggle was to occur between producers of food and oil.'[4] Paarlberg discusses 'agripower' as opposed to 'petropower' and dismisses earlier predictions by a number of American officials that food power can serve as a natural counter to oil power: 'Exportable oil has indeed become a prime ingredient of national power in the contemporary international system, but food has not.'[5]

This study examines the power of economic sanctions to act as effective countermeasures to politically or economically motivated interruptions of supplies, given the new emphasis on producer–consumer relations since 1965 and 1973. Of the five different types of sanctions, the moral, diplomatic, financial, economic, and military, it focuses on the economic sanction. In this type of sanction there are at least five kinds of embargoes: (1) an embargo on exports of arms, munitions, and implements of war; (2) an embargo on imports; (3) an embargo on raw materials; (4) an embargo on technology; and (5) an international boycott. We are concerned here with the last four kinds.

This study is not intended to provide answers to particular questions. Rather, it aims at broadening our views and perspectives by providing new ways of viewing political events. Nor is it intended to forecast or predict the future; its goal is to bring to our attention the lessons of the past in order to understand the complex issues we presently face.

While there have been some thoughtful and well-informed books on economic sanctions, in none of them is the objective of economic sanctions clearly stated and extensively explored. Most studies have assumed that the objectives of economic sanctions were to return to the *status quo* that prevailed prior to the perceived act of aggression which brought the sanctions about. In reality, the aims of economic sanctions have consistently been less ambitious: they have aimed to influence the perspective of the target elites so as to force them to conform to a desired pattern of behavior, a change that may not result directly, during, or immediately after the implementation or lifting of sanctions. To rectify this discrepancy which has led to disillusionment as to the efficacy of sanctions on the part of many analysts and observers, this study aims at appraising the use of sanctions in terms of their double objectives — declared and implied.

Definition of terms

The terms 'boycott,' 'embargo,' and 'sanctions' are difficult to define precisely. A number of writers have tended to use them interchangeably. For the purpose of this study, it is important to clarify the differences among them.

Webster's New International Dictionary (2nd edn, 1957) gives the following definitions:

Boycott: (From Captain *Boycott*, a land agent in Mayo, Ireland, so treated in 1880)
1. To combine against (a person, as a landlord, tradesman, employer, etc., a group of persons, or a nation) in a policy of nonintercourse, esp. for political reasons; to withhold, wholly or in part, social or business intercourse from, as an expression of disapproval or means of coercion, often with deterrence of others from holding such intercourse.
2. To refrain by concerted action from using or purchasing (certain classes of goods or services).

Embargo: (Spanish, from *embargar*, 'to embargo,' from (assumed) Vulgar Latin *imbarricare*, from *barra*, 'bar.')
1. An edict or order of the government prohibiting the departure or entry of ships of commerce at ports within its dominions, called a *hostile embargo* if laid on an enemy's ships and a *civil embargo* if on domestic ships.
2. Any prohibition imposed by law upon commerce either in general or in one or more of its branches.
3. A stoppage or impediment; a prohibition.

Sanction: (French or Latin; French *sanction*, from Latin *sanctio*, *-onis*, from *sancrire*, 'to render sacred or inviolable.')
1. Formerly, a decree, especially an ecclesiastical decree.
2. *Ethics.* Any consideration, principle, or influence, which impels to moral action or determines the moral judgment as valid. According to various theories, pleasure and pain, or the findings of conscience, or the principle of the golden rule, or the goal of perfection constitute such *sanctions*.
3. *Law.* The detriment, loss of reward, or other coercive intervention, annexed to a violation of a law as a means of enforcing the law. This may consist in the direct infliction of injury or inconvenience, as in the punishments of crime (*punitive sanctions*) or in mere coercion, restitution, or undoing of what was wrongly accomplished, as in the judgments of civil actions (*civil sanctions*). A sanction may take the form of a

reward (*remuneratory sanctions*) that is withheld for failure to comply with the law.

Webster's New Collegiate Dictionary (1977) adds the following definition for sanction:

> 4. An economic or military coercive measure adopted usually by several nations in concert for forcing a nation violating international law to desist or yield to adjudication.[6]

Once outlined in front of us, the differences between the three terms emerge. A boycott is carried on by individuals, groups, or organizations. It implies no force of law and carries no coercive tones. It is a question of breaking relations with others, withdrawing patronage from them, and urging others to do so also. It is a form of ostracism where one or more members of a community are temporarily excluded from certain privileges. De Crespigny and McKinnell compare the definition of the term 'boycott' found in the *Encyclopaedia Britannica* — 'the refusal and incitement to refusal to have commercial or social dealings with any one on whom it is wished to bring pressure' — to that of the *Encyclopedia of the Social Sciences* — 'a concerted effort to withdraw and to induce others to withdraw from economic or social relations with offending groups or individuals.'[7] They note that both definitions emphasize

> the element of incitement as a feature of boycott. They differ, however, in two respects. The former definition includes the notion of 'bringing pressure to bear,' which is absent from the latter. A second difference is that the former refers to 'the refusal . . . to have commercial or social dealings . . .' whereas the latter refers to an effort 'to withdraw . . . from economic or social relations.'[8]

They propose the following definition: 'the refusal and incitement to refusal to have commercial or social dealings with offending groups or individuals.'[9]

In his book *Law Among Nations*, Gerhard Von Glahn defines the term 'boycott' as it is used in international affairs as 'a modern form of retaliatory action involving the suspension of business and trade on the part of nationals of the injured state with the citizens of the offending state.'[10] Governments, however, may be involved in boycotts.

'Embargo' is a somewhat stronger term, since it is a prohibition of trade by government order and thus carries the force of law. It is a form of reprisal which in its early form 'consisted of the detention in port of vessels flying the flag of the offending state in order to coerce the latter into remedying the wrong done.'[11] In modern times, the term has been used to refer to 'an action by a single state or as a collective act of a number of states, to prevent an alleged or potential aggressor from increasing its stockpiles of essential war materials and supplies.'[12] In *Black's Law Dictionary* (4th edn, 1957) embargo is defined as 'a proclamation or order of a state usually issued in time of war or threatened hostilities, prohibiting the departure of ships or goods from some or all parts of such states until further order.' More recently,

> embargoes in the form of export prohibitions have been undertaken, individually or collectively, to force countries to cease assertedly illegal or undesirable activities or to prevent them from utilizing certain categories of goods, mostly war materials, for purposes objected to by states instigating the embargoes.[13]

A 'sanction' is a collective action against a state considered to be violating international law taken to compel that state to conform. It may involve diplomatic, economic, or military measures. Eric Partridge in *Usage and Abusage* explains that

> sanction has four main senses: two that are antithetic — 'reward' and 'punishment'; a neutral sense — "authority (official) permission"; and a political sense, this being a specialization of the "punishment, penalty" sense. This last, short for *punitive sanction*, has, in the main, been — or issued from — the League of Nations usage.[14]

The American Political Dictionary explains:

> Under the United Nation Charter (Chapter VII), when the Security Council determines that a 'threat to the peace, breach of the peace, or act of aggression' exists, members may be called upon to invoke military or nonmilitary sanctions against the lawbreaking state. Since the adoption of the Uniting for Peace Resolution in 1950, the General Assembly is also empowered to levy sanctions against an aggressor by a two-thirds vote. Sanctions may include such actions as breaking diplomatic relations, embargo or blockade, and the use of force.[15]

President Franklin Roosevelt desisted from using the term 'sanction', describing it as 'a terrible word.'[16] Instead, he preferred to use 'quarantine,' a 'euphemism for blockade, or one-sided embargo,'[17] which later became established in the American political lexicon as 'a kind of stern but peaceful act risking dangerous involvement in a good cause.'[18]

William Safire's *On Language* gives a vivid description of the term:

> The word 'sanction' is one of those rare terms (like 'sanguine') that mean the opposite of themselves.
>
> 'Sanction' means 'official approval,' from the same root as 'sanctify' and 'saint'; as a verb, it means 'to give permission.' At the same time, 'sanctions' have come to mean those actions, usually economic, used to punish a nation. In one sense, the word means 'permission,' to be coveted, and in the other sense, the word means 'penalty,' to be abhorred.
>
> Strangely, nobody seems confused by this contradiction. Here's why . . .: The plural turns the meaning around. When a sanction becomes 'sanctions,' its meaning switches from approval to restriction. This is not always the case — if you start to examine each of the sanctions, the individual sanction takes the negative meaning of the group.[19]

Another definition which focuses on the retaliatory effect of sanctions is that of John Austin, whose definition is 'the evil which will probably be incurred in case a command be disobeyed.'[20] Similarly, in *International Sanctions* (1938) the term is defined as 'action taken by members of the international community against an infringement, actual or threatened, of the law.'[21] This definition emphasizes function.

A definition that focuses on the deprivatory effect of sanctions is that of Arens and Lasswell (1964), who define them as 'deprivations or indulgences of individual and group norms for the purpose of supporting the primary norms of a public order system.'[22] In a later article Lasswell and Arens emphasized behavior conformity, defining sanctions as 'measures employed to encourage conformity or to discourage non-conformity.'[23] Donald L. Losman, who uses the two terms 'economic sanctions' and 'embargo' interchangeably in all of his writings, defines economic sanctions as 'penalties inflicted upon one or more states by one or more others, generally to coerce the target nation(s) to comply with certain norms that the boycott initiators deem proper or necessary.'[24]

But it is Johan Galtung who provides us with a particularly useful general definition of economic sanctions in which he combines both the retaliatory and the deprivatory effects. According to him, economic sanctions are

> actions initiated by one or more international actors (the 'senders') against one or more others (the 'receivers') with either or both of two purposes: to punish the receivers by depriving them of some value and/or to make the receivers comply with certain norms the senders deem important.[25]

Richard Olson suggests sharpening the definition by replacing the word 'receiver' with the word 'target' and making 'coercion' interchangeable with 'sanction.'[26] This modification, Olson maintains, would 'capture more of the element of threat in these situations,'[27] and move the definition 'a bit further away from legal terminology.'[28] The final version of this definition would be as follows:

> Economic sanctions (coercion) are actions initiated by one or more international actors (the 'senders') against one or more others (the 'targets') with either or both of two purposes: to punish the targets by depriving them of some value and/or to make the 'targets' comply with certain norms the senders deem important.

This is the definition of 'sanctions' used in the present book.

Two more terms need to be explicitly defined: 'oil weapon' means 'any manipulation of the price and/or supply of oil by exporting nations with the intention of changing the political behavior of the consumer nations,'[29] and 'oil power' means 'the power which stems from the dependence of the consumer nations on oil.'[30]

In discussing economic coercive diplomacy, it is important to be aware of the distinction between 'economic sanctions' and 'economic warfare.' While the first represents a milder form of coercion employed in peacetime to coerce or inflict punishment on a selected target, the second represents economic coercive measures employed during wars as part of the general military effort to inflict as much havoc, destruction, and deprivation as possible on the enemy. Professor R. L. Allen defines economic warfare as 'the conscious attempt to enhance the relative military and political position of a country through foreign economic relations.'[31] But it is Professor Medlicott who provides a clear distinction between the two concepts:

> Economic warfare is a military operation comparable to the operations of the three Services in that its object is the defeat of the

enemy, and complementary to them in that its function is to deprive the enemy of the material means of resistance. But unlike the operations of the Armed Forces, its results are secured not only by direct attack upon the enemy, but also by bringing pressure to bear upon those neutral countries from which the enemy draws his supplies. It must be distinguished from coercive measures appropriate for adoption in peace to settle international differences without recourse to war, e.g., sanctions, pacific blockade, economic reprisals, etc., since unlike such measures, it has as its ultimate sanction the use of belligerent rights.[32]

Trade wars or *monetary wars* are also used as part of the escalation process, either as substitutes for or adjuncts to war itself. The high level of economic interaction in the last two decades has prompted many nations to rely on economic coercive policies to pursue foreign policy goals. Quincy Wright in *A Study of War* (1965) notes that 'increased trade increases vulnerability to commercial retaliation and blockade and so may increase the sense of menace.'[33] Geoffrey Blainey points out in *The Causes of War* (1973) that 'the very instruments of peace — railways and international canals and steamships and bills of lading — were conspicuous in the background to some wars.'[34]

For clarity and consistency's sake, the terms 'sanction,' 'embargo,' and 'boycott' are defined here as follows:

Sanction   Penalty attached to transgression and breach of international law. Sanctions are punitive actions initiated by a number of international actors, particularly a world organization such as the League of Nations or the United Nations, against one or more states for violating a universally approved charter, as inducements to follow, or refrain from following, that particular course of conduct and conform with international law. Examples of such measures would be the League's sanctions against Italy in 1935 and the United Nations' sanctions against Rhodesia in 1966.
Sanctioner One who is applying sanctions.
Sanctioned One against whom sanctions are imposed.

Embargo   Prohibition by a country or countries of the export of certain kinds of goods as a reprisal action designed to coerce political policy shifts or to injure a target nation for taking a certain political stand. Such actions by senders (producers) take the form of curtailments or stoppages of production and export of a commodity in demand, and they are executed either individually or in concert. Two such examples would be the postwar Strategic Embargo by Western nations against the communist bloc and the 1973/74 Arab oil embargo.

Embargoer One who is applying an embargo.

Embargoed One against whom an embargo is imposed.

Boycott Whereas an embargo is a policy in which the sender takes action to cut or curtail his production and export, a boycott is a situation in which the receiver refuses to hold commercial relations with a target nation or opts to stop or curtail his imports from a sender, on account of political differences, so as to punish that nation for a political position it has taken, or to coerce it into abandoning it. In this situation one or more nations are quarantined by others and the target nation's exports are interdicted in the hope that such economic pressure will cause fissures in the regime which will eventually lead it to submission or collapse, as was the case with the Western powers and Iran in 1951–3 or with the United States and Cuba since 1961. Boycotts may be limited to one commodity as was the case with Iranian oil, or they may be more extensive as in the case of the US and Cuba, or they may involve curtailment of all commercial intercourse, as in the case of the Arab states and Israel.

Boycotter One who is applying the boycott.

Boycotted One against whom the boycott is initiated.

General outline

This study is composed of an introduction and five chapters. Chapter 1 discusses two theoretical directions in the literature on economic sanctions, particularly as regards their role in conflict resolution. From the beginning of the century until the mid-1960s there existed a general consensus that economic sanctions are highly useful as a foreign policy tool, and during World War II and the cold war era, the various actors in international politics often utilized them. For a complex variety of reasons, most of these applications seemed somewhat unproductive. Consequently, the 1960s and the 1970s produced numerous case studies and other research which took a second view, one that was highly skeptical about the efficacy of economic sanctions and judged that their performance in international affairs was unimpressive. These antithetical views provide a framework for the argument advanced here that sanctions possess a limited but real efficacy.

Historically, sanctions have been applied in three ways: (a) as international legal actions imposed by a world organization such as the League of Nations on a single state, such as Italy; (b) as multistate collective actions, as in the case of the Soviet Union and its satellites against Yugoslavia; and (c) as one-state punitive measures, as in the case of the United States and Cuba.

Sanctions, embargoes, and boycotts are but some of the coercive powers in international relations. They may be limited to one item, as was the case of the Arab oil embargo; or they may include a number of selected commodities, as was the case of the United States and its Western allies against the Soviet Union and the Communist bloc; or they may be comprehensive, as in the case of the Arab boycott of Israel. As Donald L. Losman explains, 'A general embargo proscribes any and all trade relations (with the possible exception of those directly related to humanitarian needs), while selective sanctions cover only a limited number of commodities.'[35] In putting them into effect, the sanctioner can either withhold sales for a specified period of time, as was the case with the Arab oil embargo or the United States grain embargo, or the sanctioner can remove the time limit and increase the impact of his sanctions by simultaneously withholding sales and purchases, as in the case of the Arab boycott of Israel or the United States boycott of Cuba.

Chapter 2 explores some historical antecedents of sanctions, with particular attention to the two most celebrated cases: the League sanctions against Italy in 1936 and the United Nations sanctions against Rhodesia in 1966. Previous studies have used these two cases to argue against the utility of sanctions in international policies. Chapters 3 and 4 focus more closely on the variables implicit in sanctions applied multilaterally and unilaterally and identify those that are most important in determining the sanctions' success or failure. Chapter 3 explores in detail the 1973/74 Arab oil embargo as a major case study, and Chapter 4 analyzes the 1980 US grain embargo against the Soviet Union. Chapter 5 outlines the conclusions of the authors regarding the political effectiveness of sanctions based on detailed analysis of the major cases studied.

Types of analysis

In the absence of a basic philosophy of cooperation in recent years, the traditional means of conflict resolution among nation-states, whether processes (such as negotiations, good offices, and mediation) or institutions (such as the United Nations arbitral panel or the International Court of Justice), seem to have become less and less effective in settling major conflicts. Nation-states are more likely to solve their major problems through unilateral actions than to wait for a consensus to emerge from the international community. Nations vary in the degree to which they depend on military power to solve conflicts. Short of exercising their military option, they may employ political and economic weapons in order to achieve their foreign policy objectives. Whenever the limits of compromise are stretched beyond the bounds deemed acceptable internally, the state concerned is more inclined to retaliate or pressure the unfriendly state or its allies into making more substantial compromises on the given issue.

The international relations literature on conflict resolution leads one to conclude that generally speaking, there are three main methods, depending on the degree of hostility among the parties:

(1) diplomacy and negotiations;
(2) economic sanctions and embargoes;
(3) military actions.

A good conceptual distinction among three types of international conflict, based on the channels in which conflict is articulated, can be found in Michael Haas's *International Conflict* (1974):

> First of all, conflict could be expressed within existing procedural channels, such as through conventional diplomacy or at the United Nations. A second type of international conflict could be outside of, but not antagonistic to, customary channels. A third kind would be conflict that destroys existing channels in order to replace them with new procedures and mechanisms.[36]

Haas's approach is useful in sorting out types of conflict, but it clearly explains neither the relationship between the various types nor the level of conflict at which each is likely to occur. A better approach for the purpose of this study is that of Rudolph Rummel and Raymond Tanter, who, using factor analysis of foreign conflict variables, were able to derive the following categories:

(a) Diplomatic conflict involves the use of formal methods by means of which states traditionally have dramatized differences of opinion nonviolently, such as by lodging protests, by declaring diplomatic officials to be *personae non gratae*, and by withdrawing ambassadors or officials of lower rank.

(b) Belligerent or noninstitutionalized conflict is nonviolent yet takes place outside polite channels from articulating demands and displeasure; examples of noninstitutionalized international conflict behavior include severances of diplomatic relations and impositions of sanctions.

(c) Military conflict is manifest in the decisions to embark upon wars or limited military actions short of war; military conflict includes all of the overt steps taken by decision-makers from the decision to go to war up to the actual outbreak of large-scale combat between armed forces.[37]

The type analyzed here is 'belligerent conflict,' and our focus will be on the imposition of sanctions or embargoes.

Tentative assumptions to be explored

The literature on economic sanctions raises a number of questions:

Are economic sanctions useful as a political weapon in international relations?

How effective are they?

What are the limits of economic sanctions, as a substitute for the use of military force, in achieving political goals or in pursuing urgent national objectives?

Why are some economic sanctions more effective than others?

What are the conditions which influence the effectiveness of sanctions as political levers?

The present exploratory study seeks answers to such questions. Towards that end, the following propositions are advanced as hypotheses:

Proposition One: Economic sanctions are useful and effective as political weapons in international politics. However,

political elites, fearing that a target nation may escalate its response, thus triggering war, use caution in
applying sanctions. This is particularly so if the target
is a powerful nation that is highly dependent on the
embargoed commodity.

Proposition Two: The effectiveness of an economic sanction varies
with its duration. The longer a sanction continues,
the more effective it is likely to become, provided
no other sources of supply become available for target nations. Nations imposing economic sanctions
should not expect immediate or short-term results.

Proposition Three: The success of sanctions is directly related to the
wealth of the nation imposing them. Primary pro-
ducers who depend on exports of a single commodity
are not likely to use sanctions effectively. The commodity embargoed will eventually 'leak' to international markets and subsequently become available
to the target nation. Sanctions have little impact
when they are selective.

Proposition Four: The success of an economic sanction varies with the
ability of the sanctioner to make the measure a collective effort. Failure of a nation to convince another
to join it strains the two nations' political relationship.

Proposition Five: When sanctions are imposed, the most severe sanctions will be imposed on small states. Little enthusiasm will be found for the application of stringent
measures against a powerful nation that violates international law.

Proposition Six: Sanctioners should not assume that their economic
sanctions will necessarily be more harmful to the
target nation than to themselves. A sanction imposed
against an affluent country with a high propensity
to import may in the long run prove more harmful
to the sanctioner than to the target.

Theoretical framework

This work builds upon the ideas of the major theorists in the field of
economic sanctions, and the theory of economic sanctions remains the

chief theoretical framework within which the subject matter of this book will be treated.[38] Nevertheless, this theory is not sufficiently sophisticated at present to explain the complex behavior of the nations that impose sanctions and those that are their targets. On the contrary a rigidly literal interpretation of the theory has misled a number of scholars to conclude that because declared initial optimum goals of the sanctions were not achieved, the sanctions policy was not successful and sanctions as a tool of foreign policy were dismissed as ineffective. Consequently, in this study, the Kuhnian notion of paradigm, rather than sanction theory, provides the major tool for understanding the effectiveness of sanctions.

1 Economic Sanctions in International Relations

Theoretical directions

The notion of paradigm

The term 'paradigm,' as introduced by Thomas Kuhn in his thoughtful work, *The Structure of Scientific Revolutions* (1962), means a universally recognized scientific achievement that for a time provides model problems and solutions to a community of practitioners.[1] Bill and Hardgrave, exploring the implications of 'the Greek term *paradeigma* meaning to set up as an example.'[2] have shown that

> the concept of paradigm refers to the fact that (1) the particular scientific community holds basic assumptions about what it is investigating; and (2) examples of recognized exemplary scientific research exist that are accounted for in terms of these assumptions.[3]

Kuhn suggests that a paradigm comes about because it is 'sufficiently unprecedented to attract an enduring group of adherents away from competing modes of scientific activity. Simultaneously, it is sufficiently open-ended to leave all sorts of problems for the redefined group of practitioners to resolve.'[4] In the beginning a paradigm is 'largely a promise of success discoverable in selected and still incomplete examples.'[5] As a result, it becomes 'an object for further articulation and specification under new or more stringent conditions.'[6]

Kuhn views scientific development schematically, as going through three stages: the preparadigmatic, the paradigmatic, and the postparadigmatic. In the preparadigmatic stage, several different conceptual schemes, long-standing views, or models compete with one another to answer scientists' questions. Past scientific achievements, as acknowledged for a time by a particular scientific community, supply the foundation and the background for this practice. Work in progress provides support for the present-day argument. Each model has its champions, i.e., scientists who are always ready to stand by it and search for ways to defend it. Kuhn describes this stage of the development of a science as one characterized by much 'random fact-gathering,' which 'in the absence of a reason for seeking some particular form of recondite information . . . is usually restricted to the wealth of data that lie readily at hand.'[7] Throughout this stage 'competition between segments of the scientific community' becomes 'the only historical process that ever actually results in the rejection of one previously accepted theory or in the adoption of another.'[8]

In *The Methodology of Comparative Research* (1970), Holt and Richardson raise the question: How does a science move from this period of confusion into a stage where a paradigm is accepted by common consent and most scientific activity becomes normal research? They respond: 'When the adherents of a particular competing paradigm can demonstrate that their approach is more successful in solving a few problems that a wider group of practitioners in the field recognize as significant, that paradigm should gain in status.'[9] Kuhn adds this proviso: 'To be more successful is not, however, to be either completely successful with a single problem or notably successful with any large number.'[10] It is only when experiment and theory are articulated that discovery can emerge. Once the paradigm is found, it guides research and experiment, and a whole school of thought amalgamates, with its own laws and rules of procedure. An established paradigm rules, and allegiance is transferred from the old regime to the new. Scientific work is focused on a range of problems where many puzzles are brilliantly solved.

The fascinating scientific strength of paradigms is the explanatory power they carry within them, which, by a process of self-destruction, gives birth to new ways of looking at things. In providing 'models from which spring particular coherent traditions of scientific research,'[11] and in guiding research 'even in the absence of rules,'[12] they train scientists to be more observant, more inquisitive, more analytical, more demanding, and more critical. Since the paradigm provides scientists with a somewhat directed approach, they begin to conduct their inquiries in a more scientifically rigid fashion. Research and experimentation, of course, will inevitably provide new information that does not fit the existing paradigm, and as more and more anomalies appear, an atmosphere of crisis fills the air. This crisis environment provides the incremental data that are necessary for a fundamental shift of paradigms, for from within the prevailing confusion a new paradigm emerges to solve the anomalies and provide answers to the old problems. Willis W.

Harman explains vividly the psychology of how scientific paradigms are replaced:

> A watershed point is reached where the accumulated weight of discrepancies and anomalies that cannot be fitted into the old paradigm tips the balance, and scientists find it more profitable (in emotional as well as rational terms) to seek a new paradigm than to patch up the old.[13]

Finally, a sociological component of the process has been identified by Dennis Pirages: 'Paradigms remain dominant within the social system of science for long periods because disciplinary reward structures encourage conformity to the established scientific norms.'[14] Kuhn describes this rational, emotional, and social transition as a 'scientific revolution,' defined as 'those noncumulative development episodes in which an older paradigm is replaced in whole or in part by an incompatible new one.'[15] An important aspect of this destructive-constructive conception of how paradigms change is that the decision to reject one paradigm is always simultaneously the decision to accept another: 'the judgment leading to that decision involves the comparison of both paradigms with nature and with one another.'[16]

The presence of unsolved puzzles or anomalies does not imply the failure of a paradigm; as Kuhn says, a revolution 'need not be a large change.' 'Micro-revolutions' occur regularly between major revolutions. Nor is there any absolute standard of validity by which the state of a discipline can be measured. Kuhn is relativistic in this respect: 'We may . . . have to relinquish the notion, explicit or implicit, that changes of paradigm carry scientists and those who learn from them closer and closer to the truth.'[17]

These ideas have caused continuing controversy among philosophers and social scientists. However, in spite of all the criticisms that have been directed at Kuhn or the book, the explanatory value of the notion of a paradigm should not be denied. Paradigms do guide scientific research and they do provide, in Holt and Richardson's words, 'an interesting and useful perspective from which one can look at theories in the social sciences.'[18] Larry Laudan describes them in his book, *Progress and its Problems* (1977), as 'broad quasi-metaphysical insights or hunches about how the phenomena in some domain should be explained.'[19] He asserts: 'Included under the umbrella of any well-developed paradigm will be a number of specific theories, each of which presupposes one or more elements of the paradigm.'[20]

The rise and fall of a paradigm: economic sanctions from Idealpolitik to Realpolitik

Willis Harman has suggested that Kuhn

> uses the term 'dominant paradigm' to signify the basic way of perceiving, thinking, and doing that is associated with a particular vision of reality. Applied to a whole society, the term connotes more than an ideology or world view and less than a total culture. It is largely embodied in the unquestioned, tacit understanding shared by people in that society and is transmitted not through overt 'teaching' but through the exemplars encountered in everyday life.[21]

From the turn of the century until the mid-1960s, the dominant paradigm that governed our understanding of economic sanctions could be summed up in the following equation:

$$\text{Rationality (Guarantee + Sanctions)} - \text{Neutrality} = \text{Security + Morality}$$

This paradigm had its roots in the period preceding World War I, but the ferocity of the war resulted in its spreading particularly among intellectuals, academicians, and statesmen. The chief advocates of this paradigm, the Genevan School of Thought (GST), followed this main line of argument:

Statement 1: The balance of power system is dead. It has failed to prevent wars and maintain the peace. What is the alternative?

Statement 2: The collective security system is the answer. It is far superior to the balance of power system in securing the peace. But how can this system be achieved?

Statement 3: By the establishment of an international organization. How will this system enforce the law without military conflicts?

Statement 4: By the establishment of international economic sanctions. This weapon is powerful, effective, relatively cheap, bloodless, and, moreover, easy to use to bring any aggressor to his knees.

Statement 5: Economic sanctions have a moral power. They enjoy universal public support.

Statement 6: States are innately rational. With the economic threat

> hanging over their heads, they will not find it worth-
> while to deliberately wage wars of aggression.

Statement 7: Neutrality is a precarious concept which the community of nations needs to abandon.

For more than four decades, climaxing in the 1930s and despite challenges, this paradigm served most analysts as the major theoretical framework by which to understand sanctions. With time and experience modifications and adjustments were made, but the basic premise that the economic sanction could function as a coercive weapon in international relations remained. These ideas were shaped by the atmosphere of the times, particularly by the memories of the horrors and cruelty of World War I.

The followers of the Genevan School of Thought succeeded in incorporating these ideas into the Covenant of the League of Nations. According to Philip Kerr, the League of Nations was founded upon three ideas, which clearly bear the imprint of the GST:

> The first was regular conference of all the nations of the earth
> for the consideration of their common affairs. The primary correc-
> tive to the exaggerated national egoism which inevitably ends in war
> was to be the constitutional unity and the regular assembly of the
> whole human family in a Parliament of man. The second idea was a
> solemn agreement among all nations that they would not go to war
> without submitting their disputes of whatever kind either to judicial
> or arbitral settlement, or to impartial investigation and report by the
> League during a reasonable period of time, though war itself was not
> outlawed as an ultimate resort. The third idea was agreement that if
> any nation broke this undertaking and went to war without permit-
> ting investigation and report, such a war was to be the concern of
> the whole world, which would enforce sanctions against the
> Covenant-breaker, that is, economically isolate it, and possibly take
> naval and military action against it also.[22]

Kerr also says that in approaching the problem of the prevention of war,

> the framers of the Covenant felt that they could not deny to nations
> the ultimate right to use war; they concentrated on inducing them to
> submit their disputes to impartial investigation and report before
> resorting to war, and to combine to take 'sanctions' against any state
> which went to war in defiance of this obligation.[23]

The GST was also successful in incorporating its views into other international treaties and agreements such as the Kellogg-Briand Pact, which, by condemning war, also condemned neutrality, and the Hague Agreement of 20 January 1930, whereby the governments of the creditor nations came to terms with Germany as to the final settlement of reparations. The Hague Agreement included a 'sanctions clause' in case some future German government might not execute the agreement faithfully.

The rise of a 'new' paradigm

In the post-World War I era, the assumption was that war arises out of the attack of a vicious 'aggressor' upon an innocent 'victim'; consequently, war between nations was renounced and outlawed and was no longer accepted as the source or subject of rights. Furthermore, change by force was declared illegal and immoral, and nations were urged to cooperate selflessly to preserve the peace. They would assemble in good faith to identify the aggressor, and by a united boycott, embargo or other economic sanction against the guilty nation, compel peace. This postulate, that peace could be preserved by identifying and punishing 'aggressors,' was invested with high value: joint action against any challenger of the system, it was thought, would preserve the peace. The theoretical foundation of this 'new paradigm' is thus that the threat of using force will in itself lead to the 'enforcement' of peace.

The League of Nations, initially forged as 'peace machinery,' epitomized this ideology. The predominant conception was that the system of international relations prior to 1914 constituted 'international anarchy,' because it lacked an excellent 'organization' for peace to enforce 'law and order.' As W. Arnold Forster put it,

> the striking fact is that what the world would not now concede to
> any private belligerent fighting for his own hand the world has,
> rightly or wrongly, conceded to the League of Nations, for defending the common peace.[24]

Given these assumptions about war and peace, the power that the world had conceded to the League was the power to impose sanctions. Since war had been declared illegitimate, fewer wars were expected. With sanctions available to be applied against aggressors and aid and assistance to be provided to the victims of aggression, fewer nations would contemplate breaking the law by waging aggressive wars. With fewer wars, frequent sanctions would therefore not be required, thus reducing the number of occasions when force was used. In this respect, the prevalent conception of peace was founded on the belief that, inasmuch as the majority of the powers would by the victory have become satisfied with their positions, they would have a vested interest in maintaining the peace. The disinherited would become reconciled to their fate because free trade, which proponents of these views foresaw, would reduce the importance of political boundaries. It was hoped that under this 'new system' long decades of peace and tranquillity would bless Europe and the world, and if war occurred, other nations would participate in the system, judge each case on its merits, and exert on the guilty party enough pressure to deter aggression. Under the 'new system' it was hoped that Europe and the world would advance in material and spiritual prosperity. 'War,' wrote Nicholas Politis in his book *Neutrality and Peace* (1935), 'can be made impossible only as the result of a sort of general insurance against war, by means of a system of collective security based upon the loyal acceptance of the consequences flowing from the outlawry of war.'

Invalidation of the 'old order' was necessary in order to lay the foundation of the 'new,' so the old international system and the law under which it grew came to be characterized as defective, leading to anarchy and chaos; under its rule, turmoil and hostility were said to be normal ways of life, resulting in the corrosion of liberalism, democracy, and the economics of *laissez-faire*. War and conflict were perceived as natural corollaries of the 'old order,' whose system of alliances and balance of power had been unsuccessful in preventing the greatest war in history, as Neville Chamberlain pointed out in a speech delivered in June 1936.[25] The system of alliances was perceived as questionable and hazardous, maximizing the friction which international competition necessarily arouses. That the 'old order' had developed as highly as possible the instruments of conciliation, mediation, and arbitration, and supported negotiation as a form of bridging differences, and that it produced long periods of tranquillity and was somewhat successful in limiting wars to narrow areas, and that commerce flourished and prosperity spread to ever-wider regions — all this was intentionally ignored by the proponents of the 'new order,' who saw only that the 'old order' had 'made no real effort . . . to suppress war.'

A 'new order' needed new assumptions on which to build. Towards this end, the theory of 'enforcing peace' by imposing economic sanctions, as represented in Articles X and XVI of the Covenant of the League, served the high purpose of preserving the *status quo*. Relentless campaigns for enforcement provisions, or 'teeth,' were launched, in the form of treaties of guaranty, boycotts, embargoes, and sanctions against aggressors. As David D. Mitrany has demonstrated in *The Problem of International Sanctions* (1925), the discussions on the Protocol show that the problem of international sanctions was considered 'the crux of the whole problem of the prevention of war.'

A review of contemporary theory reveals a strong conviction as to the political efficacy of economic sanctions throughout the period in which the Genevan School of Thought paradigm was dominant. The following quotations (along with those cited in Appendix I) illustrate this consensus.

J. C. Smuts (late 1918):
The breaker of the moratorium . . . should . . . become *ipso facto*
at war with all the other members of the League . . . which will
sever all relations of trade and finance with the law-breaker, and
prohibit all intercourse with its subjects, and also prevent as far as
possible all commercial and financial intercourse between the subjects of the law-breaker and those of any other state. . . . The effect
of such a complete automatic trade and financial boycott will necessarily be enormous.[26]

A. E. Zimmern (1918):
It is enough to emphasize the fact that the economic weapon is the
most powerful in the varied armoury of the Allies, and that, if the
Alliance holds together and consolidates its forces, no human power
can prevent it from ultimately — and indeed, as all the omens indicate, soon rather than late — bringing victory, final and decisive,
to the Allied cause.[27]

Signor Schanzer (September 1921):
Hence the great importance we attach to the correct interpretation of
article 16; . . . which constitutes the most powerful sanction at
the disposal of the League of Nations; and I would add the most
characteristic sanction and the sanction most in conformity with
the spirit of the Covenant and with the idea which inspired the
creation of the League of Nations, since it allows us, as far as possible, to avert wars and to settle international disputes by peaceful means.[28]

D. Mitrany (1925):
The cause of international arbitration alone justifies a country in shouldering the risk and burden of applying sanctions; it alone justifies a country in claiming the creation and support of sanctions.[29]

William E. Rappard (1925):
But arbitration alone, if it is sufficient to decide which of two litigants, if recalcitrant, is to be outlawed, is quite insufficient to outlaw war and still more to prevent war by enforcing peace. For that purpose the authors of the Covenant, in articles 10 and 16, provided for what is known as sanctions.[30]

Sir Austen Chamberlain (March 1925):
The 'economic sanction,' if simultaneously directed by all the world against a State which is not itself economically self-sufficing, would be a weapon of incalculable power. This . . . was the weapon originally devised by the authors of the covenant. . . . Some scheme of sanctions is certainly necessary. Without it a League of Nations would be as insecure as a civilised society without magistrates and police.[31]

W. Arnold Forster (24 November 1925):
The world has concluded, I think, that this blockade weapon is more indivisible and far more deadly than had formerly been supposed; and that an instrument so atrocious ought not to be left in the power of any private belligerent to use at his own discretion. Blockade, boycott, the general strike, noncooperation — all are alike in being detestable; all represent failures of human reason. But blockade involves so intolerable an interference with neutral commerce, and especially so intolerable an injury to the belligerents' civil life, that it stands on a different footing from the others.[32]

Philip Kerr (October 1929):
The peace of Europe today depends in a large measure upon the obligation undertaken by Great Britain under the Covenant and the Locarno Treaties to use economic sanctions against a treaty breaker, that is, to interrupt its trade with neutral powers.[33]

Committee on Economic Sanctions (1931):
General knowledge, in any country considering aggressive action, that world-wide economic sanctions might be invoked against it,

would certainly call into action the fears of all business and industrial interests in that country; and their influence, exercised
entirely directly and within the country, would in many cases suf-
fice to turn the scale against the contemplated aggression.

Influences of that sort become more and more powerful as a
country becomes more and more completely industrialized; and they
would weigh more heavily in the greater industrial States than in the
backward nations. And since it is clear that only these great industrial States can seriously contemplate embarking on a war of modern
type, the psychological effects of economic sanctions – when employed merely as threats – are strongest in just the areas where
deterrents are most needed.[34]

Raymond Leslie Buell (June 1932):
It is possible to attain real security, the reduction of armaments,
and an objective attitude toward treaty revision and other political
problems only with the establishment of an international organization, in which international sanctions play a fundamental part. If
the governments fail to establish a system of international sanctions
... then the world is doomed to a continuance of the war system.

A system of international sanctions is especially important as a
preventive of illegal war.[35]

Albert E. Hindmarsh (1933):
Self-help sanctions, such as wanton use of force by states acting on
their own behalf, are the ultimate means of enforcing international
obligations in the present stage of international society. The practical problem to be settled is the supplanting of state self-help, based
on arbitrary force alone, by positive international sanctions, founded
on the will and law of the world community.[36]

C. K. Webster (1933):
It is Article XVI that guarantees a state, not against all attack, for
that cannot be done, but that it shall receive assistance if it is
attacked, and that the attacker shall be subjected to retaliation,
economic and military, from all the other members of the League.[37]

Charles Cheney Hyde (27 April 1933):
Collective intervention manifested through a boycott is a powerful
weapon of self-help. It may sap the strength of the country against
which it is applied as effectively as a victorious hostile army or a
triumphant blockade. It marks the welding together of economic

power to crush or penalize a weaker adversary. It is nonamicable in conception and operation. It is the expression of conflict by forces that may be as relentless and effective as the sword or the submarine.[38]

C. F. Remer (1933):
It seems that coercion will continue to hold a place in international relations. If, as we hope, the accepted form of coercion is no longer to be war, the boycott in some form will, no doubt, find an important place. It is, undoubtedly, the world's oldest form of nonviolent coercion. With the renunciation of war it may become a powerful weapon.[39]

John I. Knudson (1938):
What effective measures, short of war, can be taken? Article XVI of the League Covenant provides for the application of economic sanctions against an aggressor, and by this means the preponderant majority of the nations may unite in denying a nation the necessary materials for the successful conduct of war.[40]

Norman Angell (1938):
the whole argument behind the suggestion that effective sanctions meant war, was completely fallacious; that had you been prepared to defend the law, the Covenant, those whom you have undertaken to defend under the Covenant, with the same energy with which, it is assumed as a matter of course, you would defend your property, there would never have been any question of having to fight at all.[41]

Sir Charles Webster (March 1956):
These developments, which have enabled the United States to assume effective leadership of the free world and to accept responsibilities in a manner few thought possible in 1944, could not have occurred unless a universal system of sanctions by combined forces had first been set up.[42]

Commission to Study the Organization of Peace (1957):
we recommend that urgent attention be given to the development of United Nations sanctions against internationally illegal behavior likely to disturb international peace and security, but not involving actual hostilities.[43]

Presidents Taft and Theodore Roosevelt, and Senator Henry Cabot Lodge, were representative of those in the United States who supported the idea of using sanctions to enforce international law. At the Paris Peace Conference, the American drafts of a League of Nations charter likewise made provision for sanctions.[44] Another major proponent of economic sanctions was President Woodrow Wilson, who said in the autumn of 1919:

> If any member of the League of Nations breaks or ignores these promises with regard to arbitration and discussion, what happens, war? No, not war but something more tremendous than war.
>
> Apply this economic, peaceful, silent deadly remedy and there will be no need for force. The boycott is what is substituted for war.[45]

Thirteen years later John Foster Dulles wrote:

> The great advantage of economic sanctions is that on the one hand they can be very potent, while on the other hand they do not involve that resort to force which is repugnant to our objective of peace.[46]

President Franklin D. Roosevelt shared a similar view. On 5 October 1937, he declared:

> It seems to be unfortunately true that the epidemic of world law-lessness is spreading. When an epidemic of physical disease starts to spread, the community approves and joins in a 'quarantine' of the patients in order to protect the health of the community against the spread of disease.[47]

But 'most Americans were against the idea,' and 'did not think that the epidemic could reach them,' so instead the thought itself 'was put in quarantine for three unhappy years.'[48]

The consensus among practitioners in the field to assign a high value to the political utility of economic sanctions arose from the convictions that:

1. Sanctions would prevent war by threatening to punish aggressors. This would lead states disposed to disturb international peace to take into serious consideration the possibility of incurring League penalties. By setting precedents, sanctions would act as a deterrent to other countries which might be tempted to launch aggressive wars in the future.
2. Sanctions have a punitive effect. They punish the aggressor for

having undertaken an illegal war imposing on him heavy sacrifices resulting from their prohibiting commercial and financial intercourse between target nation and sanctioners.

3. Sanctions would settle international disputes by peaceful means without resorting to force.
4. Sanctions give substance and meaning to international law, which will be above the will of individual nations and prevent them from taking the law into their own hands. They will also impress other nations that the League is not to be taken lightly.
5. Sanctions could make a significant segment of the target's population decide that its government is undesirable as they begin to perceive it as leading them in dangerous directions.
6. Sanctions would lead to a decrease in imports of luxury goods, thereby affecting consumption of these goods by the wealthy and upper middle class and creating incentive for them to find a basis for accommodation with the sanctioner.
7. Sanctions would restrict the extent of a target's aggressions by (1) imposing on aggressors high financial costs; (2) making it more difficult for them to import goods essential to the conduct of war; and (3) isolating them within the international community.
8. Sanctions are concrete means by which international public opinion may be mobilized against an aggressor.

An important book which reflects the mood and politics of the times is *Boycotts and Peace: A Report by the Committee on Economic Sanctions* (1932). The authors' consensus of opinion is that a new era in the world's attitude toward war has begun with the completion of the Pact of Paris, and that the conditions which gave rise to the doctrine of neutrality have undergone profound change, so that a plan for cooperation against aggressor nations is urgently needed. Article XVI of the Covenant of the League of Nations, which provides for complete economic isolation and possible military sanctions against any power which resorts to war in violation of its covenants, is not regarded by the committee as a satisfactory solution. With the United States, the Soviet Union, Germany, and Japan outside the League, no boycott of an aggressor by the member nations could be effective. Furthermore, the complete nonintercourse provided for in Article XVI was considered so drastic that League members would shrink from putting it into effect. Neither was the use of armed force favored by the committee. Consequently, the committee recommended a much more moderate and flexible system of sanctions. It called for drawing up of a protocol or agreement supplementary to the Pact of Paris binding the signatories to consult together in case of hostilities with a view to selecting appropriate measures of nonintercourse. As measures which could be applied, the committee suggested: (1) an embargo on the shipment of arms or munitions or other absolute contraband; and (2) such further economic sanctions and concerted measures short of the use of force as may be determined to be appropriate and practical under the circumstances. With great foresight, the members of the committee urged that in each case there may be some key material or product which the aggressor needs and which can be shut off with comparatively little cost to the boycotting nations. Radical factions among the GST were not happy with those 'mild' proposals, expressing skepticism whether, in the excitement of the moment, such 'moderate *ad hoc* measures' could deter an aggressor and describing them as neither 'revolutionary' nor 'adequate.'

The dissidents' camp

Of course consensus does not imply or require absence of dissent. A number of voices reflected skepticism regarding sanctions. J. M. Spaight in *Pseudo-Security* (1928) launched a bitter attack on the sanction clause in the Covenant:

> There lies the whole difficulty in the way of organizing an effective sanction in a community of independent states. The provision for penalties can never be made complete, the circle can never be closed. . . . To try to complete the cycle of sanctions is in the end to reach absurdity; not to complete it is to leave the door ajar to war. The difficulty is that in the international community your criminal and your policeman have a way of exchanging roles.[49]

John Dewey wrote in June 1932:

> The problem of the use of sanctions to achieve a peaceful international organization involves many questions. But two great principles run through the complexity of details and reduce them to clarity and order. The first of these principles is that the use of sanctions is impracticable, so much so that any attempt in that

direction is sure to make international relations worse
better. Even the attempt to push it to the front in disc
ill-advised, for it distracts attention from the measures li
of efficacy in improving the relations among nations. The
principle is that even if the use of coercive force by joint ɛ   ....nt
were possible it would be undesirable, since resort to force fastens
upon us the war system as the ultimate means of settling international controversies. 'Enforcement of peace' is a phrase which
combines two contradictory ideas.[50]

In *Sanctions Begone! A Plea and a Plan for the Reform of the League*
(1936), General H. Rowan-Robinson recommends the amendment of
the Covenant by eliminating the sanction of Article XVI and substitut-
ing for it action on the lines of the United States's neutrality legislation
— but otherwise to make no substantial change in the structure or constitution of the League. Hans Widmer in *Der Zwang Im Völkerrecht*
(1936) shares Rowan-Robinson's skepticism, but for different reasons.
In the words of C. John Colombos, Widmer

> is of the opinion that international sanctions are influenced by a
> conflict between legal and political considerations, and that in the
> result it is the principles of opportunism rather than the legal rules
> which are successful. The author is thus very skeptical about the
> value to be attached to sanctions under the League of Nations. Self-
> defence remains, in his view, the rightful and most necessary sanc-
> tion even for the States members of the League.[51]

Objections raised against the use of economic sanctions can be sum-
marized as follows:

1. Sanctions tend to generalize war rather than localize or isolate it;
2. It is impossible to define aggression, because it is most difficult
   to appraise the causes of war and to assess blame;
3. No nation can be singled out and condemned as a criminal in
   the same way that individuals are arrested and punished as law-
   breakers within a country;
4. Sanctions will tend to perpetuate the international *status quo*,
   together with its many injustices;
5. Sanctions are sure to make international relations worse instead
   of better;
6. Sanctions distract attention from the measures likely to be of
   efficacy in resolving a conflict;

 7. The imposition of sanctions involves the risk of war;
 8. The policy of sanctions will be applied selectively, since it may prove easier and more effective to direct them at small, weak nations rather than at big, powerful ones;
 9. The solution of problems between nations lies not in the development of a system of sanctions but rather in the removal of the underlying causes of dispute;
10. Sanctions are impractical;
11. Sanctions would harden resentment and bitterness in target nations against sanctioners, thus making an eventual settlement more difficult to reach;
12. Sanctions would jeopardize the sanctioner's trade position with other customers, since it may be labeled as an unreliable supplier.

Nevertheless, the idea of sanctions as an instrument with the ability and potential to suppress and terminate 'a particular form of undesirable behavior or to discourage such behavior in the future'[52] came to have great appeal. Conceived as a 'realistic alternative to military power and consequently to many consistent with the ideal of a peaceful world,'[53] international economic sanctions came to be considered a viable weapon in the armory of foreign policy, in particular because 'economic pressure was an important factor in the final defeat of the Central powers.'[54] The appeal of sanctions derived also from their being considered not only politically desirable but also morally legitimate. In a paper read on 24 November 1925, W. Arnold Forster reiterates this theme:

> Let me assume, to begin with, that a forcible international sanction can in certain circumstances be morally legitimate. . . . for my part I have not the faith to assert that absolute non-resistance is a practicable policy for the community. I see that national forces do exist and that world-wide pacifism does not; and I can only suppose that in politics what we have to consider is not what is the uttermost leap of the conscience 'as far as thought can reach,' so much as how we can make the longest practical step in the right direction. And we shall surely be moving in the right direction if we will accept, in place of the anarchic decisions of private force, the judgments of reason backed by an ultimate international sanction.[55]

Such strong convictions were buttressed by the

> belief in the innate rationality of states and the efficacy of public opinion, together with the expectation that states would not be

willing to endure again the hardships and expense of the First World War. . . . Surely no nation in the future would feel it worthwhile to wage war deliberately for territorial gain or to satisfy national prestige. . . . The League's machinery for regulating disputes was based on this optimistic assumption about the limits beyond which nations would not consider it worthwhile to go. There was also an element of fatalism in this belief.[56]

Testing the dominant paradigm

As we have seen, a general consensus prevailed regarding the efficacy of sanctions. The powerful nations saw sanctions as a way to minimize conflict with other powerful nations while simultaneously preventing others from getting too greedy and overstepping their boundaries. Ironically, small powers also had faith in the credo, thinking that 'sanctions would strengthen their security against the imperialistic tendencies of the greater powers.'[57] The great powers were for the idea of sanctions provided they were not invoked, particularly against themselves.

Until 1936, the sanctions provided by Article XVI of the League of Nations Covenant had neither actually been employed by the League to stop an actual war, nor proposed for wars which were threatened. One reason was that the sanctions of Article XVI were considered 'drastic' and 'irksome' by many of the states which, though not directly affected by the war in question, would be called upon to share the burden of applying them.

In the words of Sir Thomas Holland, in *The Mineral Sanction as an Aid to International Security* (1935), 'Article XVI of the League's Covenant has proved to be too comprehensive and too drastic to employ without danger of disastrous repercussions' (p. 9). Like the authors of the 1932 *Boycotts and Peace*, Holland searched for some other sanctions that would be effective in preventing war, but less difficult to apply than Article XVI. He states:

The proposition then before us is to formulate some restraining sanction which can be, and will be, put into force 'immediately' – a sanction that will be to the pact-breaker so obviously a practicable menace that it will seldom, if ever, be put into force at all. The object clearly is to prevent an initial act of war, and instead, to enforce judicial settlements of international disputes by reference to the

Council and Assembly of the League or to the Court of International
Justice according to the terms of the Treaty. (p. 16)

Holland proposes for this purpose an embargo by all other states
upon supply of minerals to an aggressor – presumably, to both warring
parties. His thesis is based on the assumption that 'The greater a nation's
scale of armaments, the greater is its dependence on the mineral resources of other countries (p. 31). This leads him to conclude, 'no
nation could possibly stand alone as an aggressor if subjected to the
Mineral Sanction (p. 25). The essence of Holland's argument is that
'Obviously no sane nation would go to war if it could not hope to
continue it indefinitely.' He minimizes the adverse effects of a mineral
embargo on the states imposing it by maintaining that the target country
will be compelled, 'when war-clouds pass away' to replenish its stock
by purchase from the country that has surplus supplies for sale; presumably from the same country that enforced the sanction.

Until the Ethiopian crisis of 1936 the League, dominated by major
power politics, particularly those of Britain and France, shied away
from invoking sanctions to resolve international crises, opting instead
for negotiations and conciliation. At times when the paradigm was put
to small tests it proved successful, as in the case of the Yugoslavian invasion of Albania in 1921, when the mere threat of sanctions forced the
Yugoslavians to retreat. In the Manchurian crisis of 1931 the League
adamantly refused to invoke the sanctions article against Japan, thus
encouraging Mussolini to believe that the League would take a similar
attitude if he invaded Ethiopia. Consequently, the record of sanctions
up to the Italian-Ethiopian conflict was without flaw, and the advocates
of sanctions could point to concrete examples of the system's utility.

Now Kuhn asserts that 'paradigm-testing occurs only after persistent
failure to solve a noteworthy puzzle has given rise to crisis. And even
then it occurs only after the sense of crisis has evoked an alternate candidate for paradigm.'[58] For sanctions theory such a situation arose
immediately following the 1931 Japanese invasion of Manchuria. The
'alternate candidate' was continued aggression by other major powers,
resulting ultimately in war. Testing, in Kuhn's words, was demanded
as part of the competition between the two rival paradigms for the
allegiance of the scientific community. In his address to the American
Society of International Law, held in Washington on 27 April 1933,
Charles Cheney Hyde observed, 'the weapon is there; and of late not
only has attention been focused on it, but also appeal has been made
to seize and brandish it.'[59]

With the Italian invasion of Ethiopia, the picture changed drastically. Public opinion, perceived to be the moral force behind the use of sanctions, demanded that the concept be put to the empirical test. By then, sanctions dissidents were gaining momentum, accusing the GST followers of being utopians and challenging them: 'If the idea of sanctions is capable of practicable application, how is the policy of the League of consistently refusing to invoke them to be accounted for?'[60] Under such pressure, the GST theorists had no other option but to put the paradigm to the empirical test by activating Article XVI of the Covenant against Italy. This proved fateful, for the paradigm failed to deliver the way it was expected.

The collision of theory with reality in 1936 resulted in disenchantment, but not to the extent of abandoning the faith. Rather, adjustments were made to try to accommodate the idea to the changing times. To save the major paradigm — high utility of economic sanctions — a secondary paradigm — collective security — had to be sacrificed. Consequently, the main casualty of the Italian victory in Abyssinia, intellectually speaking, was the concept of collective security. 'On the part of those who believe in the principle of collective security as applied to international relations,' wrote C. G. Fenwick, 'the confession of the failure of the League has been naturally a regretful one.'[61] Neville Chamberlain best reflects the mood felt by many when he said in June 1936:

> The policy of collective security seemed to us . . . an attractive alternative to the old system of alliances and balance of power which nevertheless was unsuccessful in preventing the greatest war in history.
>
> The circumstances in which the dispute between Italy and Abyssinia began appeared to offer an opportunity for the exercise of that policy which could hardly be more favourable for its success. The aggression was patent and flagrant, and there was hardly any country to which it appeared that a policy of sanctions could be exercised with a greater chance of success than upon Italy. There is no use for us to shut our eyes to realities. The fact remains that the policy of collective security based on sanctions has been tried out, as indeed we were bound to try it out unless we were prepared to repudiate our obligations and say, without having tried it, that the whole system of the League and the Covenant was a sham and a fraud. That policy has been tried out and it has failed to prevent war, failed to stop war, failed to save the victim of the aggression. I am not blaming anyone for the failure. I merely record it now

because I think it is time that we reviewed the history of these events and sought to draw what lessons and conclusions we can from those events.[62]

Similarly, Norman Angell in *Peace with the Dictators* (1938) asserts that the 'decisive factor in causing both Britain and America to retreat from the collective principle is the argument that any attempt to defend law would expose us to risk of attack from the law breakers. "Sanctions mean war." That slogan really meant "law means war".'[63]

The GST group responded with claims that though collective security might be dead, the concept of sanctions was still alive. They maintained that if members of the League had pursued the policy of sanctions and intensified it, it would have been possible to preserve the independence of Abyssinia. The cause of failure, they argued, was not to be found in the Covenant, but in the application of its articles by member states.

> Mr. Eden explained that the conditions in which the measures taken 'were expected to operate' had not been fulfilled. M. Blum gave the real reason for the failure of the League when he said: 'Doubtless the League has shown itself powerless to prevent aggression and to stop war, but the cause of failure is not to be found in the Covenant. It is to be found in the tardy, uncertain and equivocal application of the Covenant.'
>
> Both M. Litvinoff, Soviet Commissar for Foreign Affairs, and Mr. Te Water, of the Union of South Africa, spoke unhesitatingly of the failure, not of the League, but of its members to live up to their obligations under the Covenant. Article 16 was not only applied, said M. Litvinoff, but there was every attempt made to confine the action taken to the barest minimum.
>
> Both the French and the Soviet delegates made it quite clear that their governments would not consent to striking sanctions and Article 16 from the Covenant, although both favored the lifting of sanctions in this particular case. French views on reform of the League were further elaborated later in the week by French Foreign Minister Delbos, who demanded that Articles 11 and 15, as well as 16 should be strengthened.[64]

The GST embarked on another study of the problem of sanctions in the summer of 1936, in the light of the Italo-Abyssinian experiences. Their objective, as outlined in the introduction of their book entitled *International Sanctions* (1938), (Chatham Study Group), was 'to try to discover how far the constitution of a system of sanctions for the enforcement of international legal obligations, at any rate in appropriate cases, is a feasible proposition.' After a cursory examination of the purpose of sanctions, whether preventive or punitive, the authors explore such matters as the feasibility of various types of cooperative international force, but their major concern is the imposition of sanctions against Italy, appraising the difficulties of 'gaining steady and continuous public support for sanctions in the enforcing states,' and of the 'stimulus to patriotic action provided by sanctions in the state against which they are applied.' They conclude that sanctions have not really been tried. The final paragraph of the book reads:

> The reader may possibly conclude that it is the absence of this 'union of wills,' rather than any technical obstacles, or lack of efficacy in the measures available, which prevents the sanctions of the Covenant from being the safeguard of peace and deterrent of aggression which they were considered to be by their designers. The question still remains whether, if the world lacks the spirit of courageous and self-sacrificing cooperation on which sanctions depend, any alternative course is available whereby the calamity of war can be permanently averted.

While *International Sanctions* merely touched upon the fundamental issues and made no attempt to analyze the Italo-Ethiopian crisis exhaustively, Albert E. Highley's *The First Sanctions Experiment* (1938) does so, concluding that sanctions in the Ethiopian affair were weakened by their belated application, by the mixing of sanctions and conciliation, by too many exemptions, by political obstacles, especially the German occupation of the Rhineland, which upset the 'political equilibrium,' and by the failure of mutual economic assistance to sanctionist states.

The attempt to check Italy's conquest of Ethiopia by economic sanctions brought out the limitations of sanctions whose application was not generally backed by members and powerful nonmembers of the League. Consequently, the major powers took the greatest blame for failing to apply the sanctions effectively, and the paradigm, though somewhat damaged, was restored.

The decline and fall of the idea of neutrality

While promoting the concept of sanctions, the 'new order' found it necessary to break down the doctrine of neutrality, particularly American neutrality. Since wars were begun by malicious 'aggressors' against innocent 'victims,' the countries of the world were conceived as a sort of *posse comitatus*, from which it was immoral, if not illegal, to remain aloof. The sources and justifications of the doctrine of neutrality came under persistent attack, and the 'new order' called for its abandonment in the name of universal peace. This 'worn-out' doctrine had no place under the new regime, whose formula for peace called for collective economic and military intervention against aggressors, and which sought to engender peace by the threat of force. A typical expression of this view is that of Charles Cheney Hyde and Louis B. Wehle, written in January 1933:

> It should be clear that the employment of a boycott against a
> country engaged in war amounts to a direct participation in the
> conflict, which may in fact prove to be as decisive of the result as
> if the boycotters were themselves belligerents. It is defiant of the
> theory of neutrality and of the fundamental obligations that the law
> of nations still imposes upon nonbelligerent Powers. Concerted
> schemes for using the boycott rest, therefore, upon the theory that
> it is better, at least for the members of the boycotting group, to take
> sides, and to determine which is the good, and which the bad bel-
> ligerent, and then to enable the good one to crush its adversary, than
> to remain strictly nonparticipants, observing the full obligations
> that go with nonparticipation. It is an indictment of neutrality as a
> peace-producing or peace-maintaining agency in the life of the inter-
> national society.[65]

The GST disciples realized that there could be no hope of collective action unless the nations of the world were prepared to meet any danger of war, which the application of sanctions might provoke. Furthermore, they feared that their effort to organize the peace might bring them into direct conflict with nonmembers of the League, particularly the United States. In his book *The League of the Protocol and the Empire* (1925), Roth Williams raises this question: 'ask the United States whether they would promise, in case they were satisfied at the time that a State condemned as an aggressor were really an outlaw and a peace-breaker, not to raise any objections to the application of sanctions by the League against that State.' Quincy Wright's *The United States and Neutrality* (1935) argues against American isolationism, maintaining that American economic and diplomatic ties with the rest of the world were so many and so intimate that American security was inextricably connected with that of the other Powers. In such a situation, Wright argued, America's real interest lay in collaboration to attain general security.[66] If this collaboration was to be effective, it must be precise and genuine. To that end, Wright concluded, only full cooperation in a system of sanctions could insure the stability of the international system upon which, in the final analysis, American domestic security depended. Charles Warren expressed similar views. Writing in the January 1936 issue of *Foreign Affairs*, he urged that American neutrality policy be revised:

> And so we are brought once more to the inevitable conclusion that the only sure way to keep out of war is to help in preventing the occurrence of a war. Moreover, the problem before the United States is not quite so simple as it appeared to some two years ago. The question is now, not merely whether we shall join or whether we shall continue to keep out of the League of Nations. It is not merely whether we shall refuse to aid the League in its attempt to avert a war. Now we are confronted with the question whether we will actually oppose and injure the League's efforts, by refusing to the President power to help shorten a war. That is a very grave question, which, in the consideration of amendments to the neutrality law, each of us ought to ponder with deep concern. There are very many Americans who, while possibly not yet prepared to advocate our entry into the League, are nevertheless not desirous to see the United States actually obstruct any efforts of the League to maintain peace. Though we may not yet be ready to join in collective action to prevent a war, should we not now be ready at least to frame legislation so as to enable the President, without implicating this country, to aid in preventing the continuance or the spread of a war?
>
> Is it not possible that Americans who opposed the League as an ineffective body to promote peace, may, without inconsistency, be willing to assist the League in an actual, effective move to curb a war, if such assistance can be rendered by the adoption of an American policy which, while not discriminating between belligerents,

will tend to reduce the supply of sinews of war of both, and hence to shorten a war? World conditions have greatly changed since 1920, indeed since 1934. Events are often stronger than words. Events may convince where arguments have failed to persuade.[67]

The United States's persistence in its traditional neutrality became an insurmountable obstacle to the GST, as it paralyzed the League, causing other states to follow the US's lead rather than the League's on a number of occasions. But, in spite of the Neutrality Resolution of August 1936, there was some hope that America would adhere to the concept of international economic sanctions and the GST disciples intensified their efforts to reverse the United States's neutrality policy. Writing in the *American Journal of International Law* in 1936, L. H. Woolsey identified five fallacies associated with neutrality. These are:

1. It is a fallacy to believe that neutrality is an assurance against becoming involved in war. This is especially true in any major war in which sea power is an important factor. In every such war in the history of the United States it has become eventually involved.[68]

   Another important factor is that of sentiment. There is always sympathy for the underdog, particularly if he has been inoffensive. . . . There is also sympathy for the difficulties of peoples of the same race, customs and ideals, other things being equal.[69]

2. Another fallacy of neutrality is the thought that it operates impartially. The configuration of the continents and of the countries into which they are divided as well as the differences in their natural resources, will always prevent the equal operation of the rules of neutrality as well as the rules of warfare.[70]

3. A third fallacy in regard to neutrality is that a country may be neutral and at the same time exercise discretion in determining the moral issues of a war, that is, in determining the aggressor, applying sanctions, or discriminating in the application of neutrality laws. Such discretion is the antithesis of neutrality. The two ideas are as immiscible as oil and water.[71]

4. A fourth fallacy of neutrality is that while our attitude in the

present conflict may tend to minimize our involvement, yet in a future war it may not come back to plague us. It is important that the United States should not establish a boomerang neutrality. It is very easy to do this unless it is realized that conditions determine the development of law. It is clear even now that the submarine and the airplane, not to mention other inventions, are going to force a modification of the laws of neutrality in respect of blockade, visit and search, sinking of prizes, etc.[72]

5. A fifth fallacy of neutrality is that the United States is free to modify its laws on the subject *ad libitum*. Aside from being bound by the law and practice of nations in this regard, the United States at the present time is bound by several bilateral and multilateral conventions on the subject. Not to mention the Kellogg-Briand Pact of 1928, under which high authorities claim there is no longer any neutrality, there is the Convention of Maritime Neutrality of American States of 1928, which lays down definite rules to be followed by neutrals and belligerents, the Hague Convention of 1907 on Rights and Duties of Neutral Powers in Naval War, which have crystallized certain sections of international law on neutrality and which the United States is obligated to recognize and apply as the law of the land.[73]

The attack on neutrality was not unopposed. Many scholars in the United States stepped forward to defend it and to assail sanctions. One such writer was Edwin Borchard, whose views as expressed in the January 1936 issue of the *American Journal of International Law* so completely epitomize those of the GST opponents that they warrant quotation *in extenso*:

In spite of the fact that the recent contrivance for collective security has brought the world collective insecurity on a scale hitherto unknown, and, by reason of adopting force as the chief agency for peace, has been attended with an astronomic increase in armaments, there are many who still cherish the belief that a device for strangling a revolver against the *status quo* affords the ideal 'peace-machinery.' The present threat of sanctions against Italy is hailed as a demonstration of the validity of the theory, in spite of the fact that it not only has not prevented war but has created an atmosphere little conducive to peaceful deliberations or satisfactory solutions. In reality, by reason of its tending to incite and ignite war, it has so operated as to impair economic recovery, disturb international psychology which alone renders possible the preservation of peace. The mere possibility of sanctions will foster the quest for self-sufficiency and stimulate the demand for raw materials under sovereign control. Small countries in possession of important natural resources are thereby exposed to new dangers. . . .

Far better is it to cultivate a genuine philosophy of detachment from European quarrels, a strong motivating factor in American independence and once deemed a national tradition.

Borchard concludes:

The philosophy of minding your own business has not yet been improved upon as a way to peace, sanity and tolerable life.[74]

The advent of the United States

One main lesson learned from the 1936 episode was the need to have the support of major powers – members and nonmembers. A major strengthening of the concept of economic sanctions occurred when America gave its support to the idea. 'Up to this time,' wrote Professor Benjamin H. Williams in 1943, 'the record of the United States was rather consistently against economic sanctions.'[75] However, the war changed American attitudes towards joining the United Nations and applying collective economic sanctions. Williams heralded in 1943 America's entry into the fold:

The economic sanctions developed by the United States in the years immediately preceding Pearl Harbor have much significance. As the architects of a new world order now draw up plans for the defense of the international community against war, they can include economic sanctions with greater assurance of American approval than in 1919. For certain types of such sanctions have in the last few years taken their place among our precedents, and the United States may well be expected to view proposals for their use with a more friendly eye than at the close of the first World War.[76]

Williams concluded:

A nation is bound, to a certain extent, by its past. In 1919 and

1920, when the United States contemplated the change from the law of impartial neutrality, deeply imbedded in American practice, to the unneutral policy of aiding one set of belligerents as against another, the difficulties of making the transition were great. At the end of the present war the United States will be looking back upon a radically different set of precedents regarding neutrality than those which were remembered in 1919. When terms of world organization are considered, it would appear that economic sanctions should meet with much less American opposition than formerly, since they have already had an important place in our policy. And the prospect that the vast economic power of our country may not be used to support aggressor nations but rather to defeat them should make the task of providing an effective international organization appreciably lighter.[77]

Prelude to paradigm shift

The important role played by sanctions throughout World War II caused the GST group, now moved to New York, to reevaluate the paradigm and study ways and means to make it more effective. One major lesson learned from the 1936 episode had been that the chances of sanctions could be enhanced by a clarification of some vague points in Article XVI, and by making clear and definite the obligations of the League's members and the conditions for applying sanctions in the future. In view of this a modified version was incorporated in the Charter of the United Nations. Recalling the 1936 experience, however, the sanctions advocates compromised on one main point, namely, the idea that international sanctions must be applied through an international organization (the United Nations) to be effective. The moral right to employ sanctions was extended to regional organizations, state pacts, and, in a limited sense, to individual nations, mainly the United States in its crusade against communism and world anarchy.

The major experience which brought some of the dissidents back into the fold was the 1951-3 boycott of Iranian oil by multinational oil companies, supported by their home governments, in retaliation for the Iranians' nationalization of Iran's oil industry. As a result of the boycott, the Iranian government was punished economically, paving the way for the coup that ousted the Iranian Premier, Mossadeq, and restored the Shah to power. The major consequence of this second major test for the paradigm was that the idea of economic sanctions regained some of the credibility it had lost in the jungles of Ethiopia.

The lesson learned from the Iranian experience was that, in order to achieve maximum effectiveness within a shorter interval of time, sanctions need to be accompanied by other pressures. Sanctions are heavy bulldozers; they have the power to cut fresh inroads and cause deep internal cleavages in the target nation's political system; they prepare the way for other options, such as diplomatic conciliation (a political solution) or military action. In Iran, sanctions on their own neither moved the Iranian government to compliance, nor did they cause the overthrow of the Mossadeq regime. However, they did cause such economic deprivation and political instability that when the coup was finally executed, it was obvious that the road had been prepared in advance.

Nevertheless, anomalies persisted and an atmosphere of crisis soon prevailed. The old hard-line dissidents found grounds to question once more the credibility of the paradigm. The deterrent, coercive force of sanctions was to a certain extent discredited when they were imposed against Cuba in 1960, but a major test for the paradigm came in 1966 when the United Nations imposed sanctions on Rhodesia for its Unilateral Declaration of Independence. Many antisanctionists found in this an opportunity to claim that the concept had failed.

> League of Nations sanctions were ineffective against Mussolini's takeover of Ethiopia, and United Nations sanctions for years had little effect on the Ian Smith regime in Rhodesia. United States efforts to restrict trade with North Korea, Vietnam, and Cuba yielded negligible dividends.[78]

These episodes were followed by another major test in 1973 when the Organization of Arab Petroleum Exporting Countries (OAPEC) declared an oil embargo against Western nations that supported Israel, hoping that this would lead world public opinion to pressure Israel to withdraw to its 1967 borders. Both advocates and opponents of sanctions claimed victory on this highly controversial issue. The GST disciples, though opposed in principle to the application of the embargo, argued that the paradigm had passed the test, and though the declared objective of forcing Israel to withdraw was not achieved, the embargo did lead to a major power shift in favor of the Arab countries. Bard E. O'Neill wrote, 'Although in retrospect the embargo lasted for but a few months and, at most, merely inconvenienced the American public, its impact on policy was profound and its ramifications wide-ranging.'[79] Ibrahim F. I. Shihata, legal advisor to the Kuwait Fund for Arab Economic Development, shared such views as he concluded his analysis of the 1973 Arab oil embargo with a positive appraisal: 'In retrospect,' he wrote, 'the Arab oil measures have proved to be an effective instrument for reestablishing concern for the long-awaited peace in the Middle East.'[80] Nevertheless, the sanctions dissidents, who by now had gathered a large following, maintained that in its two most crucial tests the paradigm had failed, since the OAPEC embargo did not realize its stated goals, nor was there any evidence to suggest that sanctions against Rhodesia had been effective.

The contemporary paradigm

The consensus among practitioners in the field during the last decade has shifted towards discounting economic sanctions as an effective coercive tool in international relations, and presently a low value is assigned to their utility. A careful review of the literature illustrates this point and reflects a widespread skepticism about their efficacy, as the following quotations show. (See Appendix II for more quotations.)

Alexander Eckstein (1966):
the U.S. embargo is practically of no economic significance, for China has been and is currently able to obtain virtually all the goods she needs from other countries at no significant additional cost. Therefore, the embargo has only a symbolic meaning.[81]

Dennis Austin (March 1966):
sanctions also have an air of failure about them, which has persisted despite the present efforts of the United Kingdom Government to use economic weapons against the Rhodesia Front.[82]

Fredrik Hoffmann (1967):
the contention is formulated that, for political reasons, the probability of successful sanctions is fairly low.[83]

Johan Galtung (April 1967):
In this article the conclusion about the probable effectiveness of economic sanctions is, generally, negative.[84]

J. Wilezynski (July 1967):
The strategic embargo has not visibly weakened the military

potential of the socialist countries, nor has it deterred them from pursuing policies they had committed themselves to. Far from becoming intimidated, their attitude often hardened. The detente in East-West relations (however modest in scope) in recent years is not a product of the tightening up of trade controls in the West but rather of their relaxation.[85]

James Burnham (14 November 1967):

The economic sanctions have failed to bring the Ian Smith regime to heel. The sanctions have not ruined the Rhodesian economy and have not forced Rhodesia to renounce UDI. . . . The sanctions prove inconvenient but not deadly.

It is not only Rhodesia that teaches this lesson. The failure of economic sanctions against Italy, in connection with the Ethiopian war, is the classic between-wars case, and all examples since the end of World War II reconfirm.[86]

Muriel J. Grieve (October 1968):

the evidence suggests that sanctions have not been effective but for political reasons their continuance for another year seems advisable.[87]

Gunnar Adler-Karlsson (1968):

From looking at all the facts presented in this book it is hard to avoid the overall conclusion that the described embargo policy has been a failure.[88]

Robert McKinnell (1969):

A preliminary, and largely superficial, survey of the economy under sanctions might therefore offer justification for concluding that sanctions forced the economy to adapt, but did not cripple it. . . . Quite clearly, however, there is much to justify the widely held view that the policy of sanctions damaged the economy less than had been expected, and failed to achieve its avowed political purpose.[89]

Ota Sik (December 1970):

no hindrances to and limitations of East-West relations, such as embargoes and similar measures, can prevent the growth of Soviet military power. On the contrary, this embargo policy only contributed to Soviet efforts to render autonomous various militarily important sectors of production, quite apart from the fact that a large country rich in natural resources always finds means to prepare all important products and supplies from outside, even in the face of the strictest embargo policy.[90]

Peter Wallensteen (1968):
The general picture is that economic sanctions have been unsuccessful as a means of influence in the international system.[91]

Eshmael Mlambo (1972):
In their own way of measuring success, the Rhodesian Front could claim up to 1971 that victory had been on its side. . . . It has succeeded in making Britain defy world opinion by preferring to talk to the settlers at the expense of the African owners of the country. Economic sanctions have been discredited.[92]

Margaret Doxey (Summer 1972):
Summing up the analysis of the UN and southern Africa, one must concede that the deterrent and coercive force of sanctions is weak on almost every count.[93]

George W. Baer (Spring 1973):
Far from imposing on the Italian people a desire to reverse their government's policy, sanctions made the Ethiopian war popular.[94]

Larry W. Bowman (1973):
Rhodesia's unilateral declaration of independence was promulgated on November 11, 1965, and Britain, as threatened, implemented a policy of economic sanctions to force the Rhodesian Front to return to constitutional government. Britain's efforts were supported by the United Nations, which attempted to isolate Rhodesia economically and politically. Today in 1972, nearly seven years after UDI, not one nation has formally recognized Rhodesia; on the other hand, sanctions have failed to induce her to change political direction.[95]

Klaus E. Knorr (1973):
In principle, collective trade sanctions should be more effective than economic reprisals by one state or a few, since they would be based on an internationally cumulative degree of monopolist and monopsonist control over the world market. . . .

In practice, however, collective trade and other economic sanctions have proved abortive. . . .

In the light of recent history, the value of threatening economic reprisals cannot be considered high. What has made the threat value low is the sharpened sensitivity of poor and weak states to any attempt at coercion. For this reason, the value of economic threats seems, at present at least, subject to secular depreciation.[96]

F. D. Holzman (June 1973):
at present, in peacetime, even a very tight embargo may be a cause of passing inconvenience and delay, and perhaps a small cost, but no more than that. Small costs like these are especially easy for a centrally-planned economy to bear.[97]

Leonard T. Kapungu (1973):
   The application of economic sanctions against Rhodesia has provided some new insight for the enforcement process of the United Nations. One point that has been driven home by this experience is that economic sanctions alone are a blunt and ineffective instrument of peace enforcement.[98]

Rustum Ali (1976):
The 'oil weapon' cannot be effectively used in the future.[99]

Robert Blake (1977):
   For the next few years the force was not major enough. Harold Wilson . . . invited the United Nations to impose mandatory sanctions. These had no obvious effect on the Rhodesian economy.[100]

Samuel P. Huntington (Fall 1978):
Harnessing economic power to foreign policy goals presents formidable obstacles: bureaucratic pluralism and inertia, congressional and interest-group politics, the conflicting pulls of alliance diplomacy; and most important, in dramatic contrast to military power, a pervasive ideology that sanctifies the independence, rather than the subordination of economic power to government.[101]

Franklyn Holzman and Richard Portes (Fall 1978):
Might the possibility of withholding technology exports nevertheless increase the bargaining power of the West on noneconomic issues? This seems doubtful for several reasons.[102]

Robert E. Klitgaard (1978):
historical evidence suggests that trade embargoes have little effect on the transfer and advancement of technology.[103]

Harry R. Strack (1978):
   Until 1974, the Rhodesian economy prospered in the face of

United Kingdom and United Nations sanctions — sanctions which had failed to achieve their declared goal of causing enough internal political change to terminate the 'illegal rebellion' by the Smith regime. Not only did sanctions fail to achieve their major goal, but they may have been a contributory factor to the deterioration of a situation which they were designed to alleviate.[104]

Martin Meredith (1979):
   In theory, there were good reasons why the imposition of sanctions should have worked. . . . Wilson believed that Smith, in declaring UDI, had been 'under intolerable pressure from some of his colleagues and from unreasoning extremists of the RF,' and that when sanctions began to take their toll, he would be willing to come to terms.
   Far from weakening the resolve of white Rhodesians, however, sanctions helped close their ranks.[105]

Penelope Hartland-Thunberg (July 1979):
Either in terms of inducing a retreat from the unilateral declaration of independence (UDI) or in terms of isolating Rhodesia, sanctions must be judged a failure, both despite and because of the changes that accompanied the punitive measures.[106]

Donald L. Losman (1979):
Sanctions have thus far been unsuccessful in each of the cases studied, despite the target economies being relatively small and highly vulnerable.[107]

Richard H. Ullman (Summer 1979):
   In fact, the issue of sanctions is now more symbolic than real, for sanctions have been only partially effective. Although foreign trade and investment have diminished, the shrewd white Rhodesians have managed to market their country's chrome and tobacco, and to get the foreign goods they have needed — including, especially, oil and weapons. Lifting sanctions now would make foreign sales and purchases easier, but alone would have no major impact upon Rhodesia's economy. Although that economy has been badly hurt in the past few years, it is the escalating war and not sanctions that has done the damage.[108]

Milton Friedman (January 1980):
All in all, economic sanctions are not an effective weapon of political warfare. . . . The resort to economic sanctions is a confession of

impotence, crafted primarily for domestic consumption, to reassure the public. It will have little or no influence on the Russians.[109]

Robert L. Paarlberg (Fall 1980):
whenever food exports are manipulated in pursuit of noncommercial objectives, the odds are stacked heavily against success.[110]

Gerald F. Fitzgerald (July 1980):
    After a detailed examination of the practice of a great number of international organizations, the author [Charles Leben] considers sanctions to be of doubtful effectiveness. They are applied only exceptionally. However, even nonapplied sanctions are a positive element in that the mere threat of a sanction helps to reinforce the process of international accountability of a member state to a given organization and its other member states. Nevertheless, it must be concluded that at best the deterrent effect of sanctions is very weak.[111]

Judith Miller (Summer 1980):
while trade boycotts, embargoes, and other economic sanctions are legitimate alternatives to military action, they rarely work.[112]

Observations and analysis of historical cases in which the implementation of sanctions seemed not only to fail to achieve their objectives, but at times actually harmed the sanctioner, led scholars to conclude that economic sanctions are unlikely to produce the desired effects for the following reasons:

1. The difficulties involved in the adoption and implementation of collective sanctions;
2. The difficulties in gaining universal agreement as to which issues require actions and as to the means of achieving general support for the application of sanctions to such issues;
3. The willingness of other suppliers to provide the target nation with needed commodities because the economic and, at times, the political incentives to do so will be too tempting to turn down;
4. The difficulties involved in extending the sanctions beyond tolerable time limits. Paradoxically, the longer the sanctions are imposed, the more diverse become the opportunities to circumvent them. Long-term imposition of sanctions is seen to permit diversification of the economy, including substitution of products,

development of alternative sources of supply, and arrangement of barter deals for provision of necessities;

5. The difficulties of preventing supplies from being rerouted through third parties, particularly some international companies who specialize in sanctions-busting owing to the enormous profits involved;

6. The resilience and adaptability of target states. As sanctions will strike a serious blow against the foundation of the political regime of a target nation, those in power will resist the imposition of sanctions by making the necessary changes in the state's economy;

7. The difficulties of political-economic coordination between the sanctioning parties themselves and also between them and third parties, neutrals, and other major powers;

8. The fact that not all states are equally sensitive to economic pressure — an agricultural, self-contained community is obviously less vulnerable to such coercion than an industrial one;

9. The fact that not all states cooperating in the economic sanctions will bear an equal burden, and that sometimes the burden may prove intolerable, leading to the breakdown of the sanctioners' *esprit de corps*;

10. The threat that an effective sanction may cause a humanitarian problem, since financial pressures hit not only the political regime but also innocent civilians, who may suffer most from it;

11. The possibility that an embargo will not deter from aggression any country which is convinced it can bring a war to a successful conclusion within a short time, or has in advance accumulated large stocks of essential materials;

12. The fact that an aggressor, single-mindedly determined to achieve his ends by force, strikes swiftly and hard; while an international organization composed of more than 150 nations with diverse interests must at best move slowly;

13. The difficulties of imposing sanctions against powerful nations which might have perpetrated greater crimes against international peace than those against whom sanctions were actually imposed. With their veto power in the Security Council, the superpowers not only will not allow sanctions to be imposed on themselves, but will also veto any sanctions resolution directed against their allies or client states.

In addition to these difficulties, many analysts have maintained that sanctions have counter-productive, or 'backlash' effects. Some of these are:

1. That sanctions serve rather to unite than to fragment the society of the target country;
2. That sanctions stimulate the country's economic development by promoting greater self-reliance and self-sufficiency. They provide the target with a drive to produce the necessary commodities themselves and promote their efforts to develop alternative sources and substitutes;
3. That sanctions create a confused international market situation resulting in higher costs and expenditures for all — sanctioners, target, and third parties.

These conclusions and observations were reached in the Kuhnian tradition in which 'testing occurred as part of the competition between two rival paradigms for the allegiance of the scientific community.'[113] The failure of one paradigm to stand the test resulted in the emergence of another. Here, it is most significant to note that all those problems raised were not new. The literature on sanctions during the 1920s and 1930s reflects an awareness that such defects do exist. There were even hypotheses as to how to mitigate the negative effects. Nevertheless, the general tendency under the *ancien régime* was to underplay the negative aspects and overemphasize the positive ones; however, under the 'new' regime the general tendency was to focus on the negative aspects of economic sanctions and overlook or deemphasize the positive side. Thus, it became fashionable to think of sanctions as symbolic gestures which nations resort to when they want to record displeasure or to express strong disapproval of certain policies or actions taken by other nations.

GST disciples and the new paradigm

Within the 'scientific community,' the process of transfer of allegiance from the old paradigm to the new one is still under way. However, as Kuhn predicts, this conversion process cannot be forced, and 'those whose productive careers have committed them to an older tradition' will resist and claim that 'the older paradigm will ultimately solve all its problems.'[114] Accordingly, the mentors of the GST felt the need, if not to attack, at least to stem the tide and keep the followers in line. So far, most of the attacks on the concept of sanctions have come from writers on the celebrated case of Rhodesia. To clear the record, two GST disciples submitted a report to the Secretariat of the UN in 1972 in which they asserted:

After four and a half years of full-scale Mandatory Sanctions following resolution 253 in May 1968 two things are clear. First, that sanctions have not worked in the sense of forcing the illegal regime to abandon its illegality and return to the *status quo ante* the rebellion. The Smith regime is still very much in control in Salisbury and there is every indication that it will continue in control indefinitely if sanctions are only maintained at their present level. Second, it is also clear that sanctions have achieved certain important results. Apart from their effects upon the Rhodesian economy they can be said to have achieved a number of more limited aims as follows:

(a) They have denied outright victory to the Smith regime.
(b) They have kept Rhodesia in a state of complete diplomatic isolation.
(c) They have forced the regime to go on struggling for economic survival at ever rising costs to itself.
(d) They have encouraged and strengthened internal opposition to the regime by demonstrating continuing world interest in its cause.
(e) They have maintained international concern over the Rhodesian issue.
(f) They have sustained the world view of the unacceptability of the regime.

At their present level of functioning, therefore, sanctions may be said to have achieved a stalemate: the world at large can express its disapproval of the illegal regime in Rhodesia without either exerting itself too much or taking action that will seriously cost it anything; and the Smith regime can continue in uneasy control of Rhodesia, sitting on a racial powder keg, and having to spend more and more of its energies and resources in devising new ways to evade sanctions and, in consequence of them, standing still economically.

To break this deadlock much tougher action is required on a whole series of fronts by the United Nations.[115]

Similarly, Ronald St. John Macdonald still finds the value of sanctions in the present international system to be 'substantial.' He writes:

> There are situations, as in Rhodesia, where no consensus can be achieved on the use of military force, where diplomatic and ideological pressures have not been as effective as it was hoped that they would have been, and where the international community continues to feel that additional pressure is necessary. Economic sanctions, moreover, are a peaceful form of pressure and it is arguable that in this day and age the avoidance of military conflict is a good in itself. It is also important to remember that the economic weapon is merely one of a range of measures and that its impracticability in some situations should not deter from its usefulness in others, such as the Dominican Republic.[116]

Robert Blake's *A History of Rhodesia* (1977) points out that at least one aspect of Rhodesia's economy was hurt by sanctions:

> There can, however, be little doubt that sanctions have aggravated what has all along been the great problem for Africans — rural unemployment. . . . Growth of the rural economy presupposes a reopening of export markets and a massive capital investment in the form of dams, irrigation, new roads, etc. Neither of these things are going to happen until sanctions are lifted.[117]

In a similar vein, Elaine Windrich asserts:

> Certainly the United Nations sanctions programme has had the effect of at least eroding the basis of the Rhodesian economy in terms of withholding international investment for expansion and of making 'sanctions busting' an increasingly expensive and difficult task.[118]

Stephen Park, in a booklet published by the Carnegie Endowment for International Peace, called on the American government (on whose cooperation the effectiveness of any sanctions depends) to institute 'a better system for monitoring compliance' with UN sanctions, asserting:

> For whenever the American government does less than it can to meet its international legal obligation to observe the UN sanctions program, a final question is raised about American concern for international law as well as the laws of our own society.[119]

Others, such as Larry W. Bowman, warn that the literature on the Rhodesian sanctions case must be used with care. Within Rhodesia 'the government has censored economic data in order to conceal both successes and failures; yet these are the only statistics we have on the overall effect of sanctions.'[120] P. B. Harris is much more blunt. He writes:

> What is remarkable, however, is that even the analysis of the effects of sanctions policy has become a matter for debate, i.e., a political matter in fact. Statistics (the final category after 'damned lies') have become not a neutral element in the sanctions rationale, but a form of political debate in themselves. It has become a matter of importance, both in Whitehall and in Jameson Avenue, to make the figures show a trend of events which is the trend the one side would wish to have.[121]

To illustrate the impact of political orientation even on the reporting of sanctions' effects one need only compare the articles in the London *Economist*, which in the early stages of the sanctions debate reflected much unwarranted optimism, reporting on 4 March 1967 that 'Rhodesia has yet to feel the real bite of sanctions; but the bite is getting sharper,' with those published in the conservative American journal *National Review*, which asserted that the sanctions 'will neither make Smith retract,' nor will they 'change the political position in Rhodesia.' On the contrary, 'the Smith regime, rebellious and illegal, as ever, has dug in. . . .'[122] It is most instructive to compare articles in the *National Review* during the first few years of the sanctions, whose thrust was 'Lift sanctions because they will accomplish nothing,' with those written in the late 1970s, whose thrust was 'Lift sanctions because they have accomplished everything.'[123]

The problem of statistics and precise evaluations is brought up in other works on economic sanctions. For example, Dan S. Chill, in his book *The Arab Boycott of Israel* (1976), writes: 'The exact monetary effect of the Boycott on Israel's economy is uncertain. This is due to the impossibility of estimating the economic activity that would result were the boycott rendered inoperative.'[124]

Post-paradigmatic Era

In spite of the above more or less feeble efforts, the new paradigm is being born from the old. As the preceding schematic description has indicated, a revolution did occur. Kuhn has denied that there exists a 'precise answer to the question whether or how well an individual theory fits the facts.'[125] However, he adds: 'It makes a great deal of sense to ask which of two actual and competing theories fits the facts better.'[126] This hint gives us the guidance we need to settle questions of competition between paradigms, particularly when we recognize that 'competition between paradigms is not the sort of battle that can be resolved by proofs.'[127]

The mid-1960s marked the early stage of the paradigm shift. At the time the trend against sanctions was not easy to detect, as many were still satisfied that they worked. But mounting problems which the old paradigm could not solve or explain gave an impetus to practitioners in the field to look for new ways of viewing the world, and a new set of norms, values, ethics, and beliefs resulted.

Willis Harman[128] has suggested three types of conditions that indicate when a transformation in a paradigm is imperative. First, the complex of problems, dilemmas, and discontinuities appears to be unresolvable within the prevailing paradigm and so creates pressure for a shift in that paradigm. Discontinuities become so great that only a change in basic values can resolve them. Second, the presence of various 'lead indicators' becomes increasingly prominent. 'Studies . . . suggest certain typical occurrences tend to appear one to three decades ahead of the central change.' As Kuhn points out, a conscious challenge to an operative system in itself constitutes another lead indicator. Third, a competitor paradigm — a model that embodies the requisite kinds of value shifts — can be identified helping to make a transformation seem plausible.

The preceding observations describe conditions that have been met. A new dominant paradigm has emerged. To help explain and evaluate this paradigm shift, we need to engage in a detailed description and analysis of sanctions practiced on the international arena by three major actors: international organizations, state alliances, and individual states.

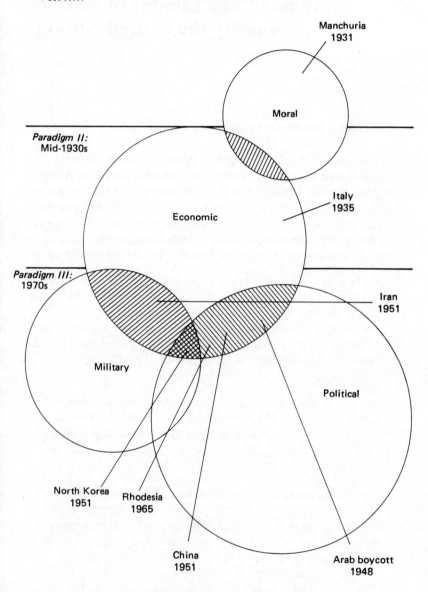

Figure 1 The sanctions paradigm shift

Universal Sanctions: Punitive ions by the League of Nations and by the United Nations

I Punitive actions by the League of Nations

The establishment of the League of Nations presented the world, for the first time in history, with an international system of guarantee and punishment. Embedded in the Covenant of the League of Nations adopted in April 1916 was the concept of collective security guaranteed by collective sanctions. Member nations, the strong as well as the weak, agreed on the need to incorporate in the Covenant a nonmilitary deterrent weapon to enforce the peace. Rita and Howard Taubenfeld write:

> Influenced by the slow but seemingly grinding effect of the comprehensive economic blockade employed against the Central Powers during the first World War, by the attractiveness of an essentially nonmilitary enforcement system, and perhaps most important, by the difficulty in obtaining agreement on more, the League of Nations made the 'economic weapon' in Article 16 of the Covenant the heart of the League's peace-enforcement powers.[1]

All preliminary schemes and earlier drafts of the Covenant, without exception, incorporated sanctions provisions.[2] The final draft Convention of the League proposes four kinds of sanctions: diplomatic, legal, economic, and military. The proposed text of the economic sanctions article was:

> Other sanctions of an economic nature can be employed by the League of Nations, by which it will be enabled to exercise an efficient control over the recalcitrant state, by various measures which may extend to placing it under an absolute commercial, industrial or financial ban.
>
> The principal measures in question are:
> (a) *Blockade*, consisting in the prevention by force of any commercial intercourse with the territory of the state in question.

(b) *Embargo*, i.e., the seizure and temporary sequestration, in the ports and territorial waters of the member states, of ships and cargoes belonging to the delinquent state and its nationals, as also the seizure of all goods destined for such state.

(c) Prohibition of the supply of raw materials and foodstuffs indispensable to its economic existence.

(d) Prohibition of the issue by such state of public loans in the territories of the member states; refusal to allow stock issued elsewhere to be quoted on the official Exchange, and even withdrawal of any previous permission for the quotation of the stock of such a state.

The sanctions thus provided will be all the more efficacious and their application will be all the more prompt, in that the member states will have previously arranged to protect themselves against any reprisals to their prejudice, by means of an economic organization adapted to facilitate their cooperation and mutual assistance.[3]

Article XVI of the final draft of the Covenant, without using the specific word 'sanction,' describes the action that members of the League were obliged to take against a member that went to war in violation of the Covenant:

Member states were to subject the law-breaking nation to the severance of all trade or financial relations, the prohibition of all intercourse between their nationals and the nationals of the Covenant-breaking state, and the prevention of all financial, commercial or personal intercourse of any other State, whether a Member of the League or not.[4]

In other words, this article provides for sanctions against any member state which resorts to war before attempting to resolve its claims through peaceful means. Against such states two kinds of measures are to be taken: (a) economic pressure, and (b) military action. Article XVII provides that those coercive measures should be applied also against a nonmember state which resorts to war against a member state. The military actions were envisaged only as a means of preventing the boycotted state from retaliating upon, and seeking to break through, the cordon of League states applying the boycott. In addition, paragraph 4 of

Article XVI provides a form of sanction which is hardly coercive in nature − expelling the violating member.

'The prevention of war was the chief object for which the League of Nations was created,' wrote John Spencer Bassett in his book *The League of Nations* (1930).[5] To achieve this end, the variety of sanctions included in the Covenant aimed at organizing 'the force of a group of states in accordance with the principle of cooperative defense to neutralize the illegal use of force by the aggressors.'[6] The most important of those sanctions was the economic sanction, whose objective was 'to bring about the economic isolation of a defaulting state by denying to it all commercial, financial, and trade facilities so far as these are within the control of members of the League.'[7] During his campaign to secure his country's entry into the League, President Wilson made lengthy explanations as to how he envisioned that economic sanctions would operate to keep the peace. 'Supposing,' he said, 'a state went to war in defiance of the Covenant, you know what happens then? You say, "We form an army and fight them." Not at all. We shut their doors and lock them in. They are absolutely boycotted by the rest of mankind. I do not think that after that remedy it will be necessary to do any fighting at all.'[8]

It is important to note that the 'Covenant was left by its authors, of set purpose, a rather vague and indeterminate instrument of peace. There are many ventholes or safety-valves in it.'[9] One of the Covenant framers, the French jurist F. Larnaude, refers in his book *La Société des Nations* (1920) to the absence from the Covenant of precise, clear, trenchant formulae.[10] The reason for such vagueness is explained by Max Huber in 1924. Huber attributes this discrepancy to the fact that the framing of the Covenant was dominated by conceptions derived by British statesmen from their experiences of imperial rule.[11] The original sanctions clause was much diluted by the Assembly resolution of 4 October 1921, which gave the right to each League member state to decide whether a given act of force constituted an act of war in violation of the Covenant.[12]

During the last years of the League, many members had second thoughts in regard to Article XVI. Some felt that it was a mistake to impose on other members of the League the duty of using economic and, if necessary, military power to put a stop to aggressive wars. Conversely, it was frequently suggested that the sanctions provided in the Covenant were not sufficiently forceful and ought to be strengthened.[13] In the absence of its own military forces, this article was the only enforcement provision the League had; in fact, it was meant to be the 'teeth' of the League. However, with the relationship between Article X and Article XVI left unclear, and the circumstances under which sanctions would be recommended left undefined, the League had little power, as was clear from the experiences in which it attempted to activate the sanctions article against recalcitrant members.

League sanction practices

The first challenge came in November 1921. The use of armed force by Yugoslavia against Albania constituted an occasion for the League to consider applying Article XVI. After the Yugoslavian troops advanced into Albanian territory, the British government requested the Secretary General to summon the council with a view to the application of economic sanctions against Yugoslavia. The Council met a few days later, but in the meantime the troops were withdrawn. Yugoslavia frankly admitted that the possibility of economic pressure left open no other recourse.[14] Its exchange fell and the loan the Yugoslav government was negotiating was refused.[15] As a result, the threat of invoking the sanction article against a small nation violating the League's Covenant was enough to force the termination of hostilities and secure the withdrawal of occupation troops.

However, the picture was drastically different when a big nation was involved. Such a situation materialized when Japan invaded Manchuria in September 1931. Apprehensive lest they anger Japan, France and Britain were reluctant to apply League sanctions, or even to consider the idea. The United States, though not a League member, felt equally strong regarding the League's policy of applying economic sanctions against Japan. American leaders were reluctant to take any stand or commitment that could lead to war. In the Manchurian episode, 'American statesmen were adamant that no sanctions should be employed against Japan apart from the force of international public opinion.'[16] The President of the United States, Herbert Hoover,

> did not intend to cooperate even in nonmilitary sanctions against the aggressor: 'sanctions are roads to war.' 'The American Government would be delighted if the League of Nations would impose sanctions, and would do nothing to interfere with such action, but it would not impose sanctions on its own.'[17]

The only move which the United States decided to take was to apply a 'moral sanction' which, according to Hoover, is a 'nonrecognition doctrine' that 'would mobilize opinion behind the principles of the Kellogg Pact.'[18] Consequently, the League 'both protested and investigated,' but took 'no action to thwart the aggressor,'[19] and the Assembly made no effort to treat the invasion 'as a resort to war under the Covenant.'[20] It did, however, recommend to members that they withhold recognition of the fruits of Japan's military action. This constituted a mild form of sanction, which had, however, no observable practical effect.[21] When in October 1932 a League of Nations commission of inquiry found Japan guilty of aggression, Japan announced its withdrawal from the League. That the League took no action to thwart the Japanese aggressors proved most unfortunate. It gave the Italian government grounds to believe 'that Ethiopia might be seized with equal impunity.'[22]

'There is a direct and significant interconnection between the actions of the Japanese militarists and those others, in Ethiopia, the Rhineland, Spain, China, Austria, Czechoslovakia, and Albania, which culminated in general war in Europe,' wrote A. L. Stimson in his book (co-authored with M. Bundy) *On Active Service in Peace and War* (1947).[23] Gaetano Salvemini maintained that the Manchurian crisis of 1931–2

> was the dress rehearsal for what in 1935–36 was to be the East Africa crisis. In this later crisis Mussolini was to take a position identical with that of Japan towards China in 1931–32. The American and the British Governments were to follow approximately the same line as in the Far Eastern crisis of 1931–32. The French Government was to go one worse, and range itself openly on the side of Mussolini.[24]

Case study: the Italian episode

Ever since the League was formed, it had been dominated by major-power politics, particularly those of Britain and France. An insightful description of this power struggle is offered by Vera Micheles Dean, who wrote on 6 November 1935:

> Since the World War France has steadfastly furthered the idea of a strong and efficient League, on the assumption that League sanctions would be applied only to one possible aggressor – Germany. Britain, pursuing its traditional policy of balance of power on the Continent, has time and again checked France's attempts to

transform the League into an instrument of French hegemony. . . . At the same time, Britain's reluctance to apply League sanctions against Japan in Manchuria and to undertake clearcut commitments in central and eastern Europe have served to weaken the League and diminish its prestige.[25]

This was the atmosphere when Ethiopia, fearing an Italian invasion, had appealed to the League of Nations for support. The Council of the League, led by Britain and France, 'tried to hedge, to negotiate, to compromise.'[26] In September 1935, the Italian-Ethiopian issue was brought before the Assembly for debate. The small states were deeply affected, for, as Alfred Nemours of Haiti declared, 'Great or small, strong or weak, near or far, white or colored, let us never forget that one day we may be somebody's Ethiopia.'[27] But as the events of the next few months showed, eloquent rhetoric is not enough to prevent aggression or to end it once started.[28] On 3 October 1935 Italian troops marched into Ethiopia with the aim of resurrecting the past glories of Rome.

'In many respects,' wrote Ruth B. Henig, 'The Italian invasion of Abyssinia was the most clear-cut case of aggression which the League of Nations had to face in the interwar period.'[29] The invasion was considered as 'an illegal resort to war'[30] and the indictment of Italy by the League automatically brought Article XVI into force.

On 11 October 1935, acting in accordance with Article XVI of the Covenant, the League, in the first example of such action,

recommended a wide variety of measures of nonintercourse aimed at Italy, including a prohibition of arms shipments to Italy, of the floating abroad of Italian public and private loans, of an extension of credit to Italian agencies or corporations, a prohibition on the importation of goods from territory under Italian control, and an embargo on the exports of specified goods, mostly in the category of war materials.[31]

The purpose of imposing sanctions against Italy was twofold:

One was to uphold the Covenant and encourage collective security. The other was to end the war by putting pressure on the Italian government so as to make it amenable to a negotiated settlement. It was expected that economic and financial measures (as opposed to military means) would be sufficient, over a period of time, to achieve this.[32]

On 2 November 1935, the League members decided that economic and financial sanctions against Italy must go into operation on 18 November. This decision marked 'a milestone in the world's struggle to devise an effective system of collective security.'[33] As John I. Knudson wrote:

> This was the first instance in League history where such measures had been undertaken. The League machinery, which so often proved cumbersome, was able to function with unusual swiftness. The members of the League, excepting three, undertook to apply economic and financial pressure against Italy. This new test of League power was adopted not as a penalty, but as a means of rendering Italy's military efforts ineffective.[34]

Lord Davies observed at the time that it was a marvel so much work was done so quickly and so well.[35] However, the French, as well as the British, feared that 'sanctions against Italy might unleash a European war which would serve Germany as a pretext for satisfying its territorial ambitions.'[36] In their view 'Germany was the enemy, and it was all-important to keep Italy on their side rather than drive her into the arms of Nazi Germany.'[37] To achieve this end and at the same time absorb the pressures coming from other member states and from public opinion, the British and French delegates held a secret conference on the eve of the Assembly, at which they agreed not to allow sanctions to go too far. The occasion was thus described some months later by Laval:

> I had some conversations at Geneva with Sir Samuel Hoare and Mr. Eden. We found ourselves instantaneously in agreement upon ruling out military sanctions, never contemplating the closure of the Suez Canal; in a word, we agreed to rule out everything that might lead to war.[38]

The reluctance of the big powers to impose measures against other big powers when such measures were perceived as precipitating war made the League reject all sanctions

> which undoubtedly could have stopped the military actions. . . . Embargoes were excluded on food, coal, steel, and oil. The sanctions committee refused to cut off Italian access to the Suez Canal or to blockade the Italian mainland. Diplomatic relations were continued with Italy.[39]

Both Italy's vulnerability to sanctions on a number of commodities, and the policy of appeasement pursued by the British government are illustrated by Sir Thomas Holland's *The Mineral Sanctions* (July 1935), which mentioned a number of commodities, such as rubber, coal, nickel, oil, and tin, which Italy lacked and which might be cut off, thus paralyzing her war effort.[40] But Holland's suggestions fell on deaf ears among British officials, because the British government had no desire to see economic sanctions produce any results. An English journalist reports that 'a prominent member of the British delegation' told him at Geneva in September 1935: 'It is of no use to blink the fact that, if sanctions succeed this time, we shall be morally bound to resort to them in future similar cases.'[41]

The League's recommendations went into force on 18 November 1935. Four kinds of sanctions were imposed:

> an embargo on the shipments of arms, the prohibition of loans and of extension of credit, an interdict on imports from the offending country and of exports to it of many manufactured goods and raw materials needed to carry on war. They did not ban the export of food to Italy; and . . . they never prohibited the export of coal, steel, and especially oil — all indispensable to Italy for winning the war.[42]

The one sanction that could have been most effective, had it been implemented properly, was the oil sanction. Oil was an absolute necessity to the Italian war machine; deprived of their oil supplies, the Italian army would have had no choice but to retreat.[43] 'If the League put an embargo on oil and if the United States did likewise, Mussolini was doomed.'[44]

The Italian oil supply had come mainly from countries leading the embargo against Italy; nearly all of those chiefly concerned had made up their minds to take part in the embargo if the others did so. It is true that the United States, which did not join the League, could have supplied Italy with oil. Italian purchases of oil had already risen steeply. But the United States Congress, in late August of 1935, passed the first Neutrality Act. 'This legislation instructed the President to apply an embargo on the export of arms to nations at war and permitted him, at his discretion, to warn American citizens against traveling on belligerent ships.'[45] President Roosevelt, who initially criticized the law's failure to distinguish between aggressor nations and their victims, used the act to align the United States with the League of Nations in applying sanctions on the sale of critical raw materials to Italy.[46] However, to make it clear that the United States 'was acting on its own, independently of the League Council,'[47] President Roosevelt on 11 October instructed Secretary of State Cordell Hull to inform the League 'that the United States cannot and will not join other nation or nations in sanctions but will go as far as laws allow to avoid giving material assistance to belligerents.'[48] Hull, himself 'a dedicated Wilsonian,'[49] was 'deeply concerned that if the League of Nations imposed sanctions on the export of oil to Italy, American business would step in to supply the petroleum that Italy needed to continue waging war.'[50] Consequently, on 30 October he issued a public statement

> urging Americans not to engage in trade with the belligerents, warning that the government was keeping a close watch on such commerce. Finally, on November 15, he issued a much more specific warning in which he stated that the sale of oil, copper, trucks, tractors, scrap iron, and scrap steel to the belligerents had increased considerably in the past few weeks. 'This class of trade,' Hull declared, 'is directly contrary to the policy of this Government as announced in official statements of the President and Secretary of State, as it is also contrary to the general spirit of the recent Neutrality Act.'[51]

Brice Harris in his book *The United States and the Italo-Ethiopian Crisis* (1964) concludes that such public statements were clear indications that the American government felt committed to cooperate with the League of Nations in an embargo on oil to Italy.[52] However, the Roosevelt administration, without a specific legislative mandate from Congress, had no legal power to prevent the 'particularly sharp rise in oil shipments'[53] to Italy. According to the *Christian Science Monitor*, exports to Italian Africa jumped from a monthly average of $25,403 during 1934 to $367,785 in October 1935 and $583,735 in November — an increase of 3,148 per cent over November 1934. In particular, crude oil exports rose from 61,708 to 417,474 barrels, or almost 600 per cent during the same period;[54] petroleum exports to Italian Africa showed an increase of 1,186,304 per cent.[55]

Many experts contend that a fully enforced oil sanction could have exhausted Italy into 'total withdrawal from Ethiopia.'[56] Nearly all of the League nations concerned were resolved to take part in the embargo, but each was nervous about the possibility of war with Italy. Britain, for one, 'was a strong advocate of sanctions while remaining highly concerned lest the enforcement of these bring her into open clash with Italy.'[57] H. R. Wilson stated in *Diplomat between Wars* (1941):

> I believe that some members of the British Cabinet were impressed with the continued reports from Italy that Mussolini and the Italian people were in a frame of mind to assault Great Britain if the League adopted the petroleum embargo which was then under discussion. Even those members of the Cabinet who did not so believe were unable to guarantee that this was not the fact.[58]

Anthony Eden later wrote in his memoirs: 'There was failure to see in advance that any effective sanctions, even economic ones, must carry with them the risk of war.'[59] Consequently Britain and France, in an effort to appease Mussolini, informed the Duce that 'there was no intention of enforcing sanctions that were "military," to which his uncomforting reply was that he would take an oil sanction as an act of war.'[60] So when the vital question of oil sanctions arose in the deliberations of the League, the British, having 'inquired of Mussolini whether he would object to his oil being cut off; when he told them that he would, they successfully resisted oil sanctions at Geneva.'[61]

Furthermore, in a speech to the last League Assembly, on 10 April 1946, the French delegate M. Paul-Boncour admitted:

> In that case [Italian invasion of Ethiopia] sanctions — or at any rate economic sanctions — were decided on, but . . . they were slow-motion sanctions, imposed by driblets. We recoiled before the only two sanctions which would have been effective — the cutting-off of oil supplies and the closing of the Suez Canal.[62]

Consequently, all League members, notably Britain, Venezuela, the Soviet Union, and Rumania, continued to sell oil to Italy. Switzerland, Austria, and Hungary never even agreed to apply any kind of sanctions. Germany, 'while it did not join with the League powers in imposing sanctions on Italy, declared its neutrality and placed an embargo on the sale of arms, oil, textiles, iron, steel, and other items to both belligerents.'[63]

Internally, the League's attempts to apply sanctions against Italy resulted in a struggle between Britain and France, who 'wanted to try to come to terms with Mussolini,' and the smaller powers, who 'were eager to enforce rigidly the coercive provisions of the Covenant.'[64] In the United States, the League of Nations 'was still unpopular . . . and Britain and France were not prepared to go beyond the feeble efforts they exerted'[65] at a time when the 'United States was unprepared to render any tangible assistance to the League of Nations in a showdown.'[66] Consequently, while economic sanctions were put into operation, the French and British governments were intensifying their search for a settlement of the dispute which would placate Mussolini. Such efforts were spurred by the 'spectre of oil sanctions'[67] which a number of member nations were persistently demanding. To avoid such a decision, in early December 1935, five days before the question of the oil embargo was to come up at Geneva, the French Prime Minister, M. Laval, and the British Foreign Secretary, Sir Samuel Hoare, offered Mussolini the secretly prepared Hoare-Laval proposal giving Italy control of most of Ethiopia. The details of the plan were leaked to the French press, which published them.[68] This raised such indignant public outcries that Hoare was forced to resign and the plan was disavowed, but not without unfortunate effects. The signing of the Hoare-Laval agreement 'aroused mistrust among the League members,'[69] causing delay in applying further sanctions. Gordon A. Graig wrote:

> It compromised the Western cause, at least in the eyes of the
> United States, whose cooperation in economic sanctions was vital
> if Italy were to be stopped; and it caused a period of mutual recrimi-
> nation between London and Paris that necessarily postponed effec-
> tive action.[70]

According to Arnold Toynbee, 'American isolationism exchanged its mood of repudiating the profits to be made out of other people's war for a mood of refusing any cooperation with the League.'[71] In addition, the Hoare-Laval diplomacy 'exposed the unwillingness of France and Britain to intensify economic sanctions and risk a serious clash with Italy.'[72] The League showed more signs of weakness when, in violation of a clause of Article XVI, it refused Ethiopia's appeal for financial aid.

Standing alone, the poorly armed Ethiopians had no hope of repulsing the onslaught of the huge Italian army, which had at its disposal the most sophisticated machinery of modern warfare. Nevertheless, the fighting throughout the winter season between the Abyssinians and Italy

> heartened those in the West who continued to work for the im-
> position of more stringent economic limitations on Italy; and
> Anthony Eden carried on extensive negotiations with other League
> members with the objective of winning assent for oil sanctions

against the aggressors — but at the crucial moment this hope was dashed.[73]

It is most ironic that the *coup de grâce* to the whole sanctions ordeal was delivered from two contrasting sides — Britain and Germany. In a complete about-face the British Chancellor of the Exchequer, Neville Chamberlain, made a speech in which he declared that the continuation of sanctions would be 'the very midsummer of madness'[74] and called for 'a reduction in the functions of the League to accord with its real power.'[75] On the other side of the English Channel, German troops on 7 March 1936 occupied the Rhineland, simultaneously repudiating the Locarno Treaties and those clauses of the Versailles Treaty which stipulated that this area must be kept free of military garrisons or installations.[76]

The failure of the French and British governments to act against Hitler's breach of treaty law 'increased general insecurity and led the smaller states to revise their commitments.'[77] Distrust among nations increased, each looking to protect its interest on its own as best it could. Germany's occupation of the Rhineland

> greatly perturbed France, and caused her to favor a policy of lifting sanctions against Italy, and applying them against Germany. Great Britain adhered to her former sanctionist policy, which caused a threatened rift between herself and France. As a member state of the League, the support of Italy to check Germany as a violator of treaty obligations was not forthcoming so long as sanctions were still in force against her. A paradoxical condition existed where Italian assistance was needed against Germany at the time economic and financial pressure was directed against Italy herself.[78]

Meanwhile, sanctions against Italy, while striking a severe blow to the Italian economy, were insufficient to prevent the conquest of Ethiopia.[79] That they had been felt is evident in the report drawn up by the Committee of Eighteen and issued in April 1936. Trade figures for February, covering thirty countries, show that Italian exports declined 59 per cent from the total during the corresponding month of the previous year, following a drop of 53 per cent in January. The report indicated that another nine months or so would be required before sanctions became fully effective.[80] However, time ran out, and the 'Rhineland coup' put an end to any serious attempt to apply oil sanctions against Italy. Mussolini was able to finish his military operations without interference, and by May 1936, the conquest was complete.[81] The fall of Ethiopia was a

> surprise to the member states of the League, as it was expected that a prolonged struggle would occur in the conquest of such a vast country, during which time the economic sanctions would prove effective.[82]

Early in July 1936, the Assembly met to take steps to end sanctions. In his speech to the Assembly, the Emperor of Abyssinia scored the assembled nations

> for deserting one of its members in need, and warned the other small states that they need not expect assistance from the League. . . . He accused League members of paying lip service to the Covenant and castigated them for failing to offer any real assistance to Ethiopia or to adopt any measures seriously impeding Italy.[83]

In his concluding remark, the Emperor appealed to the assembled delegates:

> God and history will remember your judgement. Representatives of the world, I have come to Geneva to discharge in your midst the most painful of the duties of the head of a state. What reply shall I have to take back to my people?[84]

Speaking in the Assembly the following day, 'Mr. Eden, British Foreign Secretary, and M. Leon Blum, French Prime Minister, answered the Negus' last question: "Sanctions would be lifted." '[85]

On 4 July 1936, a resolution was adopted bringing to an end the economic sanctions against Italy. The Assembly resolution was passed with but one opposing vote — that of Ethiopia. The system of collective security had been sacrificed, and the balance of power system was back in full effect.[86] As one authoritative journal explained it at the time:

> The issue that confronted members of the League in this Assembly seems to have been whether to lift sanctions for the purpose of bringing Mussolini back into the concert of Europe, at the same time sacrificing the principles of the Covenant, or whether to continue sanctions with the probable result of heightening tension in the Mediterranean and possibly bringing Italy and Germany together. That this danger was not entirely unreal became evident last week in

the conclusion of an Italo-German air pact and the announcement on July 12 of an Austro-German agreement, openly approved by Italy. In their decision to put the Abyssinian disaster aside, League members hoped that they would be preparing to resist any future aggression or *faits accomplis*.[87]

In her book *The League of Nations* (1973), Ruth B. Henig gives a perceptive analysis of why the impact of the League's Italian sanctions was so limited:

> At the prompting of the British Government, the League adopted a policy of mild economic sanctions against Italy with the intention of making them progressively more stringent. There were difficulties from the start, however, stemming from the ambiguity of the Rules of Guidance adopted by the League Assembly in 1921 to serve as an interpretive guide to Article 16 in the light of the nonuniversality of the League. . . . With the United States, Japan and Germany out of the League, the British and French Governments were aware that the effectiveness of economic sanctions was likely to be limited, unless their cooperation could be assured. Only from the United States was this assurance likely to be forthcoming. Furthermore, Austria and Hungary declared their inability to participate even at this level of activity. As to stringent economic sanctions on such vital war commodities as oil, or progression towards military sanctions, neither the British nor the French Governments were prepared to risk the implications which might arise from the imposition of such measures.[88]

There is no doubt concerning the power and impact of an oil sanction even though it was not put to the test. Had it been applied, Mussolini's army in Ethiopia would have been paralyzed. The proposition to apply it had put to the test the political will and determination of the big powers to oppose Mussolini's fascism. In his book, *Peace with the Dictators* (1930), Norman Angell makes a forceful argument in favor of this proposition:

> in fact there was not any doubt as to whether oil was an instrument of war which caused the oil sanction to be lifted. . . . Your people (British) were frightened out of the position they had taken by threat of war.
>
> Italy said: 'If you refuse to let me have oil, I will go to war with you; I will do to your cities what I propose to do to the Ethiopian villages and which I cannot do unless you supply the oil.'

Whereupon the British public began to say: 'This changes the situation. Evidently the oil sanction means war and we must at all costs avoid war. So Italy had better have the oil, without which she cannot make war.'

And there entered into British public discussion a slogan fathered mainly, it is true, by the government and government supporters, but adopted in large part also by Pacifists, in these terms: 'Sanctions mean war.' On that ground sanctions were abandoned.[89]

While partial economic sanctions had not been able to prevent the Italian conquest of Ethiopia, they had imposed a rather severe strain on the chronically weak Italian economy.[90] That such measures and the threat of more stringent economic sanctions had been effective is evident in the fact that Italy, in a secret agreement with Spain on 28 November 1936, found it necessary to insert a whole section dealing with economic sanctions:

> The fourth section called for joint Italo-Spanish action aimed at abolishing or radically modifying Article 16 of the Covenant of the League of Nations . . . and stipulated that should one of the contracting parties find itself at war or the victim of collective punitive action the other would adopt an attitude of 'benevolent neutrality,' making available supplies and facilities to the first-mentioned party.
>
> It is apparent from this Italo-Spanish agreement that the experience of even moderate economic sanctions during the Italo-Ethiopian War had proved traumatic in Rome. At that time the Spanish government had faithfully supported the League in its action against Italy. Now Rome sought to assure itself of Spain's 'benevolent neutrality' in a similar contingency. More than this, Rome sought to gain access to Spanish sources of raw materials and to bind Spain to Italy in a particularly close relationship.[91]

By contrast, in none of the treaties that Italy signed with other nations prior to the 1936 sanction episode was such a specific demand included. The Rome Protocols which Italy signed on 17 March 1934 with Austria and Hungary make no mention of sanctions, Article XVI, or 'benevolent neutrality.'[92]

The Ethiopian case 'brought home to the lesser states that the totalitarian powers are far readier to attack a small nation that displeases them, than League states are to defend their fellow members.'[93]

Alex Millward's comment on the League's use of sanctions against

Italy reflects the sentiments and views of many experts in the field: 'Far better not to attempt sanctions at all than adopt merely half-hearted and ineffectual methods.'[94]

As Winston Churchill put it in a debate in the House of Commons on 6 April 1936 over the use of League sanctions against Italy:

> We cannot undo the past, but we are bound to pass it in review in order to draw from it such lessons as may be applicable to the future, and surely the conclusion from this story is that we should not intervene in these matters unless we are in earnest and prepared to carry our intervention to all necessary lengths.[95]

Before concluding this discussion, it is instructive to go back and have a second look at the objectives of economic sanctions as they were initially formulated by the League. M. Motta, head of the Swiss delegation, stated, 'By their nature and purpose, such sanctions are not designed to be and, in our eyes, do not constitute hostile acts. They aim at exercising moral and particularly material pressure on one of the parties in order to induce it to restore peace.'[96] Other League delegations shared the same views. M. de Porto Seguro of Chile pointed out, 'The measures to be taken will be only provisional and designed simply to bring about the restoration of peace'[97], while M. Zaldumbicle of Ecuador asserted, 'The sanctions envisaged under the Covenant involve no punitive intention, no element capable of wounding the pride of any nation which, under the influence of impulsive but transitory feelings, may embark upon a war. They are simply a form of pressure intended to bring back as soon as possible to the path of peace the party which has left it.'[98] Dr Ivan Soubbotitch, member of the League of Nations Committee of Eighteen responsible for implementing the sanctions, expressed a similar opinion:

> The sanctions were a legal obligation analogous to the penalties of criminal law. They were not just a matter of policy. There had been a violation of international law and Italy, whose army had started to invade Abyssinia, had been declared an aggressor and made subject to sanctions.[99]

This shows that from the outset there were no illusions as to the limits of the economic sanctions against Italy, and no delegate entertained any false hopes that such measures would force Italy out of Ethiopia.

The Italian-Ethiopian crisis thus provided some essential lessons regarding the use of economic sanctions by a world organization to keep the peace. The next important question which poses itself is: Did the United Nations learn those lessons?

II Punitive actions by the United Nations

In the preface to his classic work *The Law of the United Nations* (1950) the late Hans Kelsen observed that the separation of law from politics is possible insofar as law is not an end in itself but a specific social technique for the achievement of ends determined by politics. This Kelsenian view of the relationship of law to politics is relevant in our study of the Charter of the United Nations, particularly as applied to measures not involving the use of armed force as outlined in Article 41.

The philosophical foundations of the United Nations, like those of the League of Nations, were the doctrines of the Geneva School. In *The League of Nations and the Rule of Law* (1936) Alfred Zimmern disentangles the ideas which underlay the League Covenant and traces them to their origins in the earlier history of international organizations.[100] One major influence which Zimmern discusses is the concept of the Concert of the Great Powers, whose essence is to be found 'in the regular conferences of the powers whose strength both permitted and obliged them to accept special responsibility for the organization of international order.'[101] The harmonization of the great powers' policies had been essential for winning World War I, and it seemed only logical that this approach would be vital for the maintenance of peace after the war. Consequently, 'the idea of the Concert is to be found at the heart of the Charter.'[102]

In addition, the League's Covenant was based on the concept of collective security, which was a modern extension of the old-fashioned bilateral treaty guarantees. Nevertheless, the UN Charter, like the League's Covenant, was basically big-power politics, which ostensibly organized joint and mutual guarantees for all members, but realistically did so only for the powerful few. This was at the heart of the failure of sanctions under the League. The UN was founded on the assumption that there was a Five-Power Community with world-wide strength; consequently, the powers of the Charter were tailored to suit their interests. The Security Council 'was empowered to decide on behalf of the whole UN whether peace is threatened and whether sanctions should be applied, and such decisions, when taken, were to be binding on all members.'[103] However, the system of collective security of the United Nations was 'only a system for enforcing peace, but not for the enforcement of international law in general.'[104]

The same circumstance which gave birth to the League influenced the creation of the United Nations:

> The apocalyptic experiences of the second World War, the 'total' character of war, the tremendous power of new weapons of mass destruction, the coming of the atomic age, soon followed by the space age, have created worldwide fear of a third World War; they have tremendously strengthened the conviction, existing since the first World War, that war nowadays has become too dangerous; the competence to go to war must, therefore, be taken away from the individual states, the international community itself must control the use of military force in international relations.[105]

Although the Charter does not use the term 'sanction,' it contains provisions that clearly stipulate sanctions. It refers to them as enforcement 'measures' with the evident character of sanctions. Under Chapter VII of the United Nations Charter, the Security Council was empowered to impose mandatory economic sanctions on recalcitrant members. The Council may opt for such measures when it concludes that under Article 39 of the Charter a threat to the peace or a breach of the peace exists. Article 39 stipulates:

> The Security Council shall determine the existence of any threat to the peace, breach of the peace, or act of aggression and shall make recommendations, or decide what measures shall be taken in accordance with Articles 41 and 42, to maintain or restore international peace and security.[106]

Article 41 of the Charter states:

> The Security Council may decide what measures not involving the use of armed force are to be employed to give effect to its decisions, and it may call upon the Members of the United Nations to apply such measures. These may include complete or partial interruption of economic relations and of rail, sea, air, postal, telegraphic, radio and other means of communication, and the severance of diplomatic relations.[107]

Under Article 25 of the Charter, members agreed to accept and carry out the decisions of the Security Council in accordance with the

Charter.[108] However, Article 39 uses the term 'recommendations,' which caused considerable confusion and a heated legal debate on whether member nations are bound legally to obey the Council's decisions. The Council could make two types of recommendations: voluntary and mandatory.

In direct contrast to the League, the United Nations' approach to the application of sanctions 'is contingent upon the formulation of a number of principles, findings, and determinations by organs of the United Nations which provide the legitimate basis for UN action.'[109] Agreement among the five permanent members of the Security Council is required prior to the implementation of sanctions by 'a pains-taking and deliberate escalation from selective optional sanctions through an intermediate stage of selective mandatory sanctions reaching "comprehensive" mandatory sanctions.'[110] The process requires a long time after the initial action is taken by the violating member.

Voluntary or nonmandatory economic sanctions place no enforcement obligations upon member states. They are merely recommendations by the Security Council, and member states that disregard those recommendations are not in violation of the UN Charter. John Halderman suggests that such decisions are not to be considered as collective measures.[111]

It is generally admitted that these recommendations lack sanction in the juridical sense.[112] Their value and strength is political and moral,[113] aiming to reform the member's conduct and return it to the conduct that is considered desirable and is recommended by the international organization. As rightly observed by A. J. P. Tammes, mandatory decisions as well as recommendations frequently carry their own sanction in the mere strength of the language they use.[114] As Jorge Castaneda has said:

> The objective sought by the United Nations in adopting certain language, in reiterating previous resolutions, or in exercising political pressure on a member, is fundamentally the same as when it uses sanctions to mobilize public opinion with the objective of eliciting a certain conduct.[115]

However, based on the authority of the Charter resolutions, measures recommended by the Council to maintain or restore international peace and security, under Article 39, have a binding nature and have the force of law. Castenada concludes:

> It is difficult to establish whether a Security Council recommendation

is binding. . . . In addition, a complete study of the practice of the Security Council does not demonstrate convincingly that this organ considered any of its recommendations as binding.[116]

Based on this conception of law as a coercive order, Hans Kelsen maintains:

> In order to establish a legal obligation, a sanction must be attached to the contrary behavior. And if a sanction is attached to a certain behavior, the contrary behavior is the content of an obligation. . . . Under Article 39, the Security Council may consider noncompliance with its recommendation . . . to be a threat to the peace and take enforcement action. If such enforcement action is interpreted to be a sanction, then it must be assumed that the members are under the obligation to comply with a 'recommendation' (of the Council).[117]

In his examination of whether enforcement measures taken by the Security Council under Article 39 constitute sanctions in the legal sense or purely political measures, Kelsen notes the possibility that both theses may be correct and discusses in detail the arguments in favor of each. But his conclusions lean towards considering the enforcement measures taken by the Council as discretionary political measures, and not as sanctions. Goodrich and Hambro make the following assessment:

> The basic principle of the security provisions of the Charter, as distinguished from that of the Covenant of the League of Nations, would be nullified if, after the Security Council had reached a decision regarding the application of measures not involving the use of armed force, discretion were left to members of the organization as to whether they should carry out those measures or not.[118]

Alf Ross in *The Constitution of the United Nations* (1950) takes a similar view, arguing that

> Security Council recommendations have the same binding force as decisions, on the basis of the representative nature of the Council, that is, on the basis of the fact that the members recognized, in conformity with Article 24, that the Security Council 'acts on their behalf'. . . . Single members are bound by the decisions of the Council, having thus waived the right, for instance, to resist, politically, a recommendation by the Council for the settlement of a dispute or the like.[119]

However, not all scholars of international law accept the premise upon which Ross bases his argument — the affirmation that all members renounced the right to oppose, politically, the Council's recommendations when they ratified the charter including Article 24.

However, in spite of all the controversy, there is general agreement: in drafting the Charter of the United Nations, the general tendency that prevailed was 'the predominance of the political over the legal approach.'[120]

One major problem which plagued the League's application of sanctions and returned to haunt the United Nations's efforts to apply Article 41 is the enforcement of sanctions by nonmember states. In the case of League sanctions against Italy it was very clear that to be effective the sanctions needed to be collective. As a nonmember of the League, the United States felt no obligation other than a moral one to adhere to the League's sanction resolutions. Moral considerations did not stop America's business community from going about business as usual in their trade with Italy. Consequently, the drafters of the Charter attempted to close this loophole. Article 2(6) stipulated:

> The Organization shall ensure that states which are not members of the United Nations act in accordance with these principles so far as may be necessary for the maintenance of international peace and security.[121]

Similar to the experience of the League, there are a number of states outside the United Nations whose participation in sanction measures is vital to ensure effectiveness. Switzerland, West Germany, East Germany, North Korea, and South Korea are not members of the United Nations. The United Nations had to ensure not only that its members would abide by sanction resolutions (which many of them do not), but also that nonmembers too would comply — a task made harder in the light of the members' not setting good examples themselves. However, sovereign nonmember states had challenged the validity of this Article, asserting that they could not be bound by decisions in which they had not taken part. A number of international lawyers, among them the West German D. von Schenck and the Swiss Rudolf Bindschedler, argued that states not members of the United Nations have no obligation to abide by sanction resolutions.[122] Others such as Hans Kelsen have argued that an obligation for nonmembers to participate in United Nations measures does exist.[123]

The Charter of the United Nations differs from the Covenant of the League of Nations in its view of the use of economic sanctions as an instrument of peace enforcement. In Article XVI of the Covenant provision was made for the immediate application by members of certain specified economic and financial sanctions, should any member resort to war in disregard of its covenants under Articles XII, XIII, or XV.[124] The Charter takes quite a different approach. It provides no such 'automatic sanctions,' and, furthermore, UN members 'are under no obligation to apply diplomatic, economic, financial or military sanctions against the state which has violated the peace or threatened to do so until the Security Council has determined the measures that are to be taken.'[125] Under Article 41, the Security Council is given the discretionary power to decide what nonmilitary measures are to be used under the provisions of Article 39. While Article XVI of the Covenant placed upon all members of the League the definite obligation to apply the enumerated sanctions immediately, Article 41 gives the Council the freedom to decide whether such measures shall be used, and if so, what specifically these measures are to be.[126]

Economic sanctions by the United Nations were enforced, though ineffectively, against a number of states considered to have violated its Charter, such as the People's Republic of China and North Korea in 1951,[127] South Africa in 1963,[128] and Portugal in 1969.[129] But the UN sanctions against Rhodesia in 1965[130] have proved to be the most celebrated case in discussions of the effectiveness of economic sanctions.

Case study: the Rhodesian episode

No sanctions experience illustrates the intertwining of the political and economic spheres more graphically than the case of the United Nations's sanctions against Rhodesia.[131]

In the early 1960s, after most African nations had gained their independence, they began to voice more adamantly their concern over governments that practiced racism on the African continent. To many of those nations, 'Communism became a secondary peril, and apartheid was viewed as a greater danger than the dictatorship of the proletariat.'[132] Consequently, independent African nations, particularly members of the United Nations, began to demand that sanctions be imposed against racist governments in Africa.

A particular target of African opprobrium was the colony of

Rhodesia, to which the British government wished to grant independence, but only after elections that would result in black majority rule. To thwart such British designs, the regime of prime minister Ian Smith acted on 11 November 1965 to preserve white domination by unilaterally declaring Rhodesia's independence from the British Empire. This act was held to be illegal by the international community, and consequently the UN Security Council decided 'to call upon all states not to recognize this illegal racist minority regime in Southern Rhodesia and to refrain from rendering any assistance to this illegal regime.'[133] A later Council resolution stated that the declaration of independence had 'no legal validity,' and referred to the Smith government as 'an illegal authority.'[134]

Britain, in an effort to assert its colonial rights, in the beginning took full responsibility for implementing economic sanctions against Rhodesia. The British government had consistently warned that the penalties for a unilateral declaration of independence (UDI) would be severe; that Rhodesia

> would become a target for trade boycotts and air transport bans
> and be isolated from the rest of the world; commonwealth prefer-
> ences and membership of the sterling area would be withdrawn. The
> warnings were repeated by the Labour Prime Minister, Harold Wilson,
> soon after he took office in October 1964: UDI, he said, 'would in-
> flict disastrous economic drainage and would leave Rhodesia isolated
> and virtually friendless in a largely hostile continent.'[135]

In response to the UDI, prime minister Wilson 'applied piecemeal economic sanctions; when one set of sanctions failed to make the right impact, he resorted to more extensive measures.'[136] The sanctions consisted of a number of economic measures in the hope that 'by showing Rhodesia that it was serious about sanctions, Rhodesian white leaders would quickly forego their rebellion.'[137] Immediately following the UDI, on 11 November 1965, Britain announced the cessation of all British aid, the removal of Rhodesia from the sterling area, a ban on a number of imported goods from Rhodesia, and the suspension of capital export to Rhodesia.[138] These steps were later followed by more stringent economic and financial measures. When all these efforts failed, Britain sought assistance from the United Nations.

In response, the United Nations Security Council on 20 November 1965 adopted Resolution 217, which imposed 'voluntary' sanctions against trade with Rhodesia. These sanctions involved eleven Rhodesian export commodities: tobacco, asbestos, sugar, hides and skins, leather, chrome, iron ore, copper, pig iron, live animals, and meat products.[139] The Council called upon the British government to take all appropriate measures which would prove effective in eliminating the authority of the Smith regime, and all member states were called upon to do their utmost to break all economic relations with Rhodesia.

Rhodesian prime minister Ian Smith minimized the possible economic repercussions of sanctions,

> suggesting that UDI would be no more than a 'three day wonder.' He obscured the controversy by arguing that Britain was unlikely to impose full sanctions and, even if it did, Rhodesia would be prepared for the consequences. A government assessment emphasized the way in which Rhodesia could retaliate: thousands of foreign African workers would be repatriated; Zambia would feel the effects of sanctions far more than Rhodesia; Britain would lose just as much trade as Rhodesia.[140]

On 17 December 1965 the British government 'delivered what was expected to be the *coup de grâce*: oil imports into Rhodesia were banned.'[141] In a statement to Parliament on 20 December, prime minister Wilson declared that the oil embargo was aimed at getting Rhodesia to return to constitutional rule.[142] But as Robert Blake's *A History of Rhodesia* (1977) has shown,

> Oil sanctions against Rhodesia broke the hitherto uneasy truce between Labour and Conservatives in Britain. . . . After UDI the Conservative line in Britain was at first one of guarded support for the British Government. The oil question showed up the concealed fissures in the Party's front. Some argued that the sanctions were too harsh, some that they were justifiable and might be effective, some maintained — rightly as it turned out — that whatever their justice they would not work, since they presupposed a blockade of the whole of southern Africa. This proved to be the case.[143]

In January 1966, prime minister Wilson told the Commonwealth ministers, assembled at Lagos, Nigeria for the purpose of deciding on action against Rhodesia, that Britain's economic sanctions would be enough to bring about Ian Smith's fall 'within a matter of weeks.'[144] This promise caused the African Commonwealth members, who were 'unanimous in the belief that economic sanctions alone would not end the minority regime,'[145] to adopt a wait-and-see policy. However, as the assurances offered by Wilson failed to materialize, the African members of the UN stepped up their pressure and demanded that the Security Council escalate to more stringent economic sanctions against Rhodesia. Britain, which had indicated that 'the time was not ripe for Security Council action,'[146] attempted to 'deflect the Security Council from considering across-the-board mandatory sanctions. This engendered considerable bitterness in the Security Council between African states and the white member countries led by the UK and the U.S.'[147] US ambassador Arthur Goldberg gave a spirited defense of the British position favoring limited mandatory sanctions. Speaking against the across-the-board sanctions, Goldberg stated:

> All of us are realistic. We hope that these additional measures will be effective but we recognize — and must recognize — the absolute necessity for moving in concert, step by step, as far as we can unitedly to meet this problem. And this council, as before, remains seized of the problem so that the additional measures which become necessary, if they do become necessary, can be ventilated here, debated here, and decided upon here.[148]

In favor of this position were pro-Western nations such as the Netherlands, New Zealand, Argentina, Japan, Uruguay, and China (Formosa). The Soviet Union supported the African position and demanded a wide range of sanctions.[149] In the middle there were nations such as France, which held that the Rhodesian problem 'was solely the concern of the United Kingdom, whose colony it is,'[150] and that the crisis had nothing to do with the United Nations. In the voting, the American-British position was approved by a vote of ten in favor to none against, with five abstentions. Nevertheless, 'even the request for imposition of sanctions, however limited, represents a much stronger UK position than any adopted before.'[151]

The adoption of mandatory limited sanctions by the Security Council on 16 December 1966 was seen by many observers as marking an important step in international affairs. A. G. Mezerik commented:

> The mandatory sanctions are unprecedented, never having been used before. Great powers . . . have, for the first time, not only agreed to accept sanctions but have pushed to get them adopted. The implications, however weak this first step, are momentous.[152]

These sanctions were mandatory but selective, and all member states were called upon to 'do their utmost' to break all economic relations with the white minority government. This was the first time the Council made use of collective enforcement measures under Article 41 of the Charter. In May 1968, it extended these sanctions by unanimously imposing a total trade boycott. This was a landmark decision, as it was the first time in UN history that full mandatory sanctions against a lawbreaking state were voted by the Security Council. Furthermore, a special committee was established to report on the sanctions' results. In March 1970, acting again under Article 41, the Security Council, following the abortive attempts of Britain to reach a settlement with the Rhodesian government, decided that all member states would sever all diplomatic, consumer, trade, military, and other relations with Rhodesia. Later Council decisions reiterated these demands and called upon all members to abide by them.

Although there was no consensus at the United Nations as to the precise objectives of economic sanctions against Rhodesia,[153] it was felt at the time that under the pressure of the sanctions Rhodesia's active trading relationships would deteriorate to the extent that the Rhodesian government would yield and renounce its unilateral declaration of independence. It was expected that member nations dependent on their commerce with Rhodesia would cease their trade, thus putting that country under great economic stress. However, few of these expectations materialized, and economic sanctions against Rhodesia 'were not as debilitating as expected, for trade continued with South Africa, the Portuguese Colonies and various sanction-breaking countries including France and Japan.'[154]

In his book *The Past is Another Country* (1979), Martin Meredith summarizes the reasons why sanctions seemed likely to work:

> In theory, there were good reasons why the imposition of sanctions should have worked. Rhodesia was a small, landlocked country, dependent on foreign oil supplies and foreign trade. About thirty-five per cent of its gross domestic product was earned from exports and a large proportion of these exports was bought by Britain. The tobacco crop alone accounted for about one-third of Rhodesian exports, of which more than forty per cent went to Britain. The bulk of exports, like tobacco, chrome and asbestos, were readily identifiable and thus less likely to slip onto outside markets unnoticed.
>
> Wilson confidently expected that the sudden decline in exports would have a multiplier effect throughout the Rhodesian economy causing unemployment, a drop in living standards, shortages and eventually enough internal opposition to UDI or a split within the RF to force Smith to sue for peace.[155]

Richard Arens and Harold Lasswell observed in 1964 that 'sanction policy calls for the mobilization of vigorous initatives on behalf of appropriate prescriptions.'[156] However, as applied to the Rhodesian case, the sanction program was neither carefully drawn up nor appropriately applied.

Piecemeal sanctions applied gradually dissipate much of their force and effect. The gradual approach 'enabled the Rhodesians to solve their difficulties at an easier pace, and each success they had bolstered their confidence and determination to win.'[157] On the other hand, Britain, whose 'rate of deficit in 1964 was one of the largest in British history,'[158] was in no position economically to assume effective leadership of the enforcement contingent. According to Robert Sutcliffe, the damage caused to the British balance of payments by the loss of the British export market in Rhodesia was not so 'spectacular' as to undermine the desire of the British government to enforce the sanctions.[159] However, the British government was more worried about the effect of such steps on other trading partners, particularly South Africa, with whom it had a favorable balance of trade. It seemed logical that if sanctions were to be made effective they ought to be extended to Portugal and South Africa, who would not abide by the UN measures and upon whom the Smith regime would be virtually dependent.

Portugal had only limited trade with Rhodesia, but Rhodesia, a landlocked territory, depended wholly on Portugal for its rail connection to the seaports of the Portuguese colony of Mozambique, which handled most of its foreign trade. Through its geographical position between Rhodesia and the Indian Ocean, Mozambique 'played a major role in sanction-breaking.'[160] South Africa, the third most important trade market for Rhodesia after Britain and Zambia,[161] announced that it would not participate in any boycott movement and that it would maintain normal friendly relations with both the United Kingdom and Rhodesia.[162] Soon after the oil embargo against Rhodesia was imposed, South African 'petrol for Rhodesia' movements helped supply Rhodesia with its oil.[163]

Rhodesia's growing economic dependence on South Africa led to the accusation that South Africa was the country solely responsible for its continued economic survival. South Africa, one of the most controversial members of the United Nations, had no interest in seeing the sanctions imposed by the UN in December 1966 and May 1968 succeed.

South Africa's Prime Minister, Dr Hendrik Verwoerd,

> could not afford to let sanctions against Rhodesia succeed in case
> the international community decided to try again with South Africa.
> Neither did he wish to be seen to be the direct cause of their failure,
> which might have ended in the same result. South Africa, he de-
> clared, would not interfere in the dispute between Rhodesia and
> Britain; nor would it participate in any boycott. Both intervention
> and boycotts were wrong, and all that South Africa wished to do
> was maintain 'normal and friendly' relations with both sides. There
> would be no special help for Rhodesia, just routine trade. Discreetly,
> however, he authorized South African organizations to facilitate
> Rhodesia's trade, finance and sanctions-busting operations, including
> the supply of oil that Rhodesia desperately needed to survive.[164]

John Barratt, former Director of the South African Insitute of International Affairs, analyzed the South African position:

> In spite of its growing concern, the South African government could
> not, and cannot, participate in sanctions, for two general reasons.
> First, sanctions have been recommended by the U.N. General As-
> sembly against South Africa itself, and the government has always
> considered it against its interests that sanctions should be seen to
> succeed anywhere. Second, it is highly doubtful that the government
> could maintain the support of its own white electorate if it took
> strong measures, such as closing its borders with Rhodesia, to impose
> pressures on Mr. Smith's government.[165]

Two other important trading partners, Zambia and Malawi, 'owing to
difficulties in finding alternative suppliers and the geopolitics of Central
and Southern Africa'[166] continued to trade with Rhodesia in essential
goods.

However, those were not the only countries that kept the Smith
regime afloat. Many countries, particularly Belgium, Switzerland, West
Germany, France, the Netherlands, Italy, Brazil and Japan 'turned a
blind eye to the surreptitious trade with Rhodesia,'[167] making no effort
to hinder clandestine traffic. France even gave official support to
Rhodesia, supplying her with vitally needed embargoed oil.[168] Most
European firms cooperated with sanction-breaking companies without
serious restraints from their governments. In Western Europe only
Denmark prosecuted and fined companies that violated the UN sanctions.[169]

In the United States, the newly appointed National Security Adviser, Henry Kissinger, ordered in April 1969 a general review of American foreign policy. After this review was completed a few months later, Kissinger recommended to President Nixon a relaxation of US measures against white Southern Africa. On Rhodesia he suggested that 'sanctions should be gradually relaxed.'[170]

The result was that the American government 'authorized sanctions violations, notably the Byrd Amendment, signed by Nixon in November, 1971, which allowed the importation of chrome, ferrochrome and nickel from Rhodesia.'[171] This amendment, contained in Section 503 of the Armed Forces Appropriation Authorization Act of 1972,[172] approved 17 November 1971, required the President to permit the importation of strategic and critical materials from non-Communist countries such as Southern Rhodesia, so long as such commodities are not embargoed from Communist countries.[173] This decision by the US Congress to import Rhodesian chrome in defiance of UN sanctions gave an unexpected

> psychological boost to the Smith regime just at a point when Rhodesian morale was at low ebb. From an American standpoint, such an initiative was hardly justifiable in economic or strategic terms. The United States had some 5.3 million tons of chromium ore in its stockpile, and additional sources of this previous metal . . . were available from the Soviet Union.[174]

On 25 September 1975, an effort to repeal the Byrd amendment was defeated when the House of Representatives, by a vote of 187 yeas to 209 nays, failed to pass H.R. 1287, to amend the United Nations Participation Act of 1945 to halt the importation of Rhodesian chrome. The Carter administration strongly supported the repeal of the Byrd amendment. Ambassador William B. Buffum, Assistant Secretary of State for International Organization Affairs, appearing before the Subcommittee on Africa of the Senate Committee on Foreign Relations on 10 July 1975, pointed out that, according to reports submitted to the Sanctions Committee of the United Nations Security Council, there had been to date 237 cases of alleged violations by various states of the UN sanctions against the Rhodesian regime, and that thirty-three of those cases involved US importation of Rhodesian chrome.[175]

Eventually, however, the Carter administration managed to obtain congressional repeal of the Byrd Amendment.[176] Underlying this position on economic sanctions were the concerns of black Africa, the security interests of the United States, and the competing foreign policy goals of American blacks and political conservatives.

Kissinger, described earlier by Ian Smith as an 'uninformed meddler.'[177] had been able to 'maneuver Smith into an agreement to transfer power to a multiracial government.'[178] which led, in the course of the next two years, to a transitional four-man executive council.[179] This was the bedrock on which the US Congress in 1978 set legal requirements for the lifting of sanctions against Rhodesia. Those requirements were that Rhodesia conduct free and fair elections open to all racial and political groups and that good-faith efforts be made to negotiate a peace settlement with the political and military opposition represented by the Patriotic Front for the Liberation of Zimbabwe (PFLZ). A campaign in the Senate to remove the sanctions gained momentum in April 1979, when Zimbabwe-Rhodesia held elections resulting in the installation of Methodist Bishop Abel Muzorewa as the country's first black prime minister. On 15 August 1979 Congress approved the following provision regarding sanctions against Zimbabwe-Rhodesia:

Sec. 408(a) The Congress finds that —

(1) It is in the interest of the United States to encourage the development of a multiracial democracy in Zimbabwe-Rhodesia based on both majority rule and minority rights;

(2) the elections held in April 1979, in which Zimbabwe-Rhodesians approved through elections the transfer of power to a black majority government, constituted a significant step toward multiracial democracy in Zimbabwe-Rhodesia;

(3) the Government of Zimbabwe-Rhodesia has expressed its willingness to negotiate in good faith at an all-parties conference, held under international auspices, on all relevant issues;

(4) it is in the foreign policy interest of the United States to further continuing progress toward genuine majority rule in Zimbabwe-Rhodesia and to encourage a peaceful resolution of the conflict; and

(5) the Government of Great Britain, which retains responsibility for Zimbabwe-Rhodesia under international law, has not yet taken steps to recognize the legality of the new government.

(b) In view of these considerations, the President shall —

(1) continue United States efforts to promote a speedy end to the Rhodesian conflict; and

(2) terminate sanctions against Zimbabwe-Rhodesia by November 15, 1979, unless the President determines it would not be in our national interest to do so and so reports to the Congress.

If the President so reports to the Congress, then sanctions shall be terminated if the Congress, within 30 calendar days after receiving the report under paragraph (2), adopts a concurrent resolution stating in substance that it rejects the determination of the President. A concurrent resolution under the preceding sentence shall be considered in the Senate in accordance with the provisions of section 601(b) of the International Security Assistance and Arms Export Control Act of 1976 and in the House of Representatives in accordance with the procedures applicable to the consideration of resolutions of disapproval under section 36(b) of the Arms Export Control Act.[180]

Members of the congressional black caucus and most US civil-rights groups insisted that the new multiracial regime in Salisbury was merely a front behind which the 4 per cent of Rhodesians who are white could effectively pull the strings of power. The constitution adopted by Zimbabwe-Rhodesia gave the 4 per cent white minority effective control of the police, military and judiciary for a decade, and the power to block constitutional change. As a result, the Carter administration, believing that the national interest would not be served by lifting the sanctions, opposed the Senate move on the grounds that the constitutional structure under which the elections were held was fatally flawed.[181] On 14 November 1979, in a memorandum to the Secretary of State, President Carter determined that it was in the national interest of the United States to continue sanctions against Zimbabwe-Rhodesia and requested a report from the Secretary immediately upon the conclusion of the constitutional conference on Zimbabwe-Rhodesia then in progress in London (the Lancaster House conference), which would describe its outcome and make recommendations for action by the United States with respect to termination of sanctions.[182] Elsewhere, the President let it be known that '[we] would ... be prepared to lift sanctions when a British Governor assumes authority in Salisbury and a process leading to impartial elections has begun. Our policy will continue to be that no party should have a veto over fair settlement proposals.'[183]

The drafting of a new constitution acceptable to Zimbabwe-Rhodesia's black majority government and the black nationalist guerrillas fighting the government was followed by the signing of a peace pact in London. Britain and the United States immediately moved to remove all economic sanctions against Rhodesia. On 1 December 1979, President Carter issued Executive Order 12183, 'Revoking Rhodesian Sanctions,' which read:

By the authority vested in me as President by the Constitution and statutes of the United States of America, including Section 5 of the United Nations Participation Act of 1945, as amended (22 U.S.C. 287c), and in order to terminate current limitations relating to trade and other transactions involving Zimbabwe-Rhodesia, it is hereby ordered as follows:

1-101. (a) Subject to the provisions of this order, the following are hereby revoked with respect to transactions occurring after the effective date of this order:

(1) Executive Order 11322 of January 5, 1967 (32 F.R. 119);
(2) Executive Order 11419 of July 29, 1968 (33 F.R. 10837); and
(3) Executive Order 11978 of March 18, 1977 (42 F.R. 15403).

(b) To the extent consistent with this order, all determinations, authorizations, regulations, rulings, certificates, orders, directives, licenses, contracts, agreements, and other actions made, issued, taken, or entered into under the provisions of such Executive orders and not previously revoked, superseded, or otherwise made inapplicable, shall continue in full force and effect until amended, modified, or terminated by appropriate authority.

1-102. (a) The Secretaries of State, the Treasury, Commerce, and Transportation, and the heads of other government agencies, shall retain the authority and responsibility for the enforcement of Executive Orders 11322, 11419, and 11978 with respect to transactions occurring prior to the effective date of this order.

(b) The revocation, in Section 1-101 of this order, of such prior Executive orders shall not affect:

(1) any act done or omitted to be done or any suit or proceeding finished or started in civil or criminal cases prior to the revocation, but all such liabilities, penalties, and forfeitures under the Executive orders shall continue and may be enforced in the same manner as if the revocation had not been made; or

(2) any violation of any rules, regulations, orders, licenses, or

other forms of administrative action under those revoked orders during the periods those orders were in effect.

1-103. (a) the Secretaries of State, the Treasury, Commerce, and Transportation, and the heads of other government agencies, shall take the appropriate measures to implement this order.

(b) In carrying out their respective functions and responsibilities under this order, the Secretaries of the Treasury, Commerce, and Transportation, and the heads of other government agencies, shall, as appropriate, consult with the Secretary of State. Each such Secretary and agency head and the Secretary of State shall also consult with other government agencies and private persons, as appropriate.[184]

The United Kingdom assumed legal and constitutional authority in Rhodesia with the arrival in Salisbury on 12 December 1979 of a British governor, Lord Soames, and a process leading to impartial elections within a British constitutional framework began. On the same day, the Parliament of Zimbabwe-Rhodesia repealed the unilateral declaration of independence, enacted on 11 November 1965, and voted to dissolve the government led by Bishop Abel Muzorewa.

The United Nations responded to these developments on 21 December 1979. The Security Council called on all UN members to terminate the measures taken against 'Southern Rhodesia,' ending all UN sanctions voluntary, mandatory, and comprehensive.

In letters to Congressmen Clement J. Zablocki and Stephen J. Solarz (chairman of the House Committee on Foreign Affairs, and of its Subcommittee on African Affairs, respectively), dated 31 December 1979 and 2 January 1980, and to Senators Frank Church and George S. McGovern (chairman of the Senate Committee on Foreign Relations, and of its Subcommittee on African Affairs, respectively), dated 2 January 1980 and 3 January 1980, Richard M. Moose, Assistant Secretary of State for African Affairs, wrote:

During the recent hearings in the House and Senate on Rhodesian sanctions, questions were raised concerning the relationship between action by the United States and action by the United Nations Security Council in the termination of sanctions.

President Carter terminated the application of sanctions by the United States against Rhodesia on December 16 because the objectives of the sanctions had been achieved. On December 21, the United Nations Security Council adopted Resolution 460 which calls upon all members of the United Nations to terminate the measures previously taken against Rhodesia under Chapter VII of the Charter. This action by the Security Council represents an authoritative confirmation that the objectives of the sanctions have been achieved and that there is no longer any basis for their continued application. It eliminates any doubt that the position of the United States in this matter is fully consistent with our international legal obligations.[185]

Before ending this discussion, it is instructive to take a second look at the objectives of the United Nations's sanctions against Rhodesia. Having determined that the UDI 'constitutes a threat to international peace and security,' the Security Council adopted on 20 November 1965 Resolution No. 217, which called upon

> all states to refrain from any action which would assist and encourage the illegal regime and, in particular, to desist from providing it with arms, equipment and military material, and to do their utmost in order to break off economic relations with Southern Rhodesia, including an embargo on oil and petroleum products.[186]

It was hoped that this step, along with all other appropriate measures, 'would prove effective in eliminating the authority of the usurpers and in bringing the minority regime in Southern Rhodesia to an immediate end.'[187] On 17 November 1966, the UN General Assembly in Resolution 2151 (XXI) announced that it

> 8. Calls once again upon the Government of the United Kingdom to take all necessary measures, including in particular the use of force, in the exercise of its power as the administering power, to put an end to the illegal racist minority regime in Southern Rhodesia and to ensure the immediate application of General Assembly Resolution 1514 (XV) and other relevant resolutions.[188]

This call for the use of force indicates that the feeling among the Assembly delegates was that sanctions would not be enough to terminate 'the illegal racist minority regime in Southern Rhodesia' and bring the rebellion to an end.

In a statement before the Subcommittee on Africa of the Senate

Committee on Foreign Relations made on 7 July 1971, David D. Newsom, Assistant Secretary of State for African Affairs, testified:

> Our policy . . . jointly with the British and other United Nations member states, has been to support measures other than the use of force designed to hasten an acceptable solution to the Rhodesian problem. We have actively supported the various U.N. measures to that end. We supported the Security Council resolution of November 12, 1965, condemning the Smith regime. We supported the December 1966 Security Council resolution imposing selective mandatory sanctions and equally strongly supported the resolution of 1968 making the sanctions comprehensive.
>
> The sanctions do not have a punitive intent. They are intended not to cause hardship for actions already taken but it is the hope that the sanctions, combined with other efforts, will influence the regime to change its policies and adopt as a basis for international acceptance the fundamental principle of eventual majority rule for the over 95 percent of the population which is African.
>
> Under the United Nations Participation Act of 1945, which provides authority for domestic enforcement of U.N. sanctions, President Johnson gave effect to these measures with Executive orders in 1967 and 1968. Barring a significant change in the Rhodesian situation, it remains our policy to endorse and support the economic sanctions now in force. The President and the Secretary of State reaffirmed this policy earlier this year.[189]

Robert B. Sutcliffe is one of the few experts who takes as his starting point for an analysis of the Rhodesian case 'what exactly the political purpose of economic sanctions has been.'[190] This leads him to affirm that

> the purpose of sanctions was not, as is often supposed, to produce a significant improvement in the political status of Africans in Rhodesia, let alone to produce majority rule or to bring Mr. Smith 'to his knees.' The purpose of sanctions was in fact merely to produce a return to 'legality,' in other words to end UDI.[191]

He concludes:

> So, in the context of what they were designed to achieve, sanctions have almost worked. If this seems a strange conclusion it is only because of the widespread delusions about what the working of sanctions would entail.[192]

3 Multilateral Sanctions: Multiple-State Collective Actions

Economic boycotts, suspensions of commercial intercourse, impositions of discriminatory tariff duties, and limitations on exports or imports have been resorted to increasingly by states as hostile, coercive measures in interstate relations short of declaring war. In his book *International Politics* (1958), Frederick L. Schuman maintains that such methods, which he calls 'acts of retortion,' are 'not in violation of legal rights.'[1] Schuman asserts that 'such measures are always within the bounds of customary international law and are performed entirely within the jurisdiction of the state taking such action.'[2] Schuman cites two examples: first, when in '1808–09 the Jefferson administration enforced an embargo on American trade with Britain and France in hope of bringing their governments to terms in the controversies over neutral rights,' and second, China's anti-Japanese boycott of 1931-2 in retaliation for the occupation of Manchuria.[3]

The Allied blockade during World War I used a system in which exports that normally went to the Axis powers were purchased by the Allies, in order to deprive their enemies of these goods and at the same time avoid adversely affecting industries in the countries imposing the boycott.[4] During World War II, economic warfare played a major role. Frequently belligerents bought or 'preempted' massive supplies of raw materials from neutral countries in order to deprive the enemy of them. The Allies tried to deny the Germans raw materials which Germany imported from abroad in order to keep its war machine going, and the Germans, for their part, tried through their submarine warfare to prevent American war supplies from reaching Britain.

The postwar strategic embargo

In the postwar era, as fear of Soviet designs spread in the West, Western governments started to impose upon themselves — collectively and individually — rigid restrictions on exports to the Eastern bloc. These restrictions were not necessarily confined to military, electrical, and power-generating equipment or petroleum products, but also included certain strategic metals and minerals and their byproducts. As the cold war between the Western and Eastern blocs intensified, Western countries decided on a policy of further extensive restrictions on trade with the Communist countries. Samuel P. Huntington explains that 'this denial approach assumed that war was highly probable, and that consequently Western nations should engage in no economic relations with the Soviet Union that might strengthen its economic, technological, and military war-making capacity.'[5]

Two contrasting philosophies on these trade restrictions prevailed in the Western camp. The first, promoted by the United States, opposed any Western exports to countries of the Eastern bloc on the grounds that these exports must inevitably assist in the buildup of economies which are essentially 'in the enemy camp.'[6] The other, more liberal view — favored by Britain — held a 'skeptical view about the restrictions the West imposes on its exports to the Eastern-bloc countries.'[7] The British argued that

> the cost of economic warfare (for example, when an economic belligerent buys up or 'preempts' massive supplies of raw materials in neutral countries in order to deprive the enemy of them) may be difficult to justify in terms of its effects. Similarly, in the present case, they argue that Britain may well hurt herself more than she hurts the Eastern bloc countries when she deprives them of British exports and so deprives herself of the money or goods which they would send in return.[8]

The British wanted a two-way trade, subject to certain minimal and essential safeguards, that could increase contacts and communication between the two blocs. At the same time, Britain agreed that there should be no sale to an Eastern-bloc purchaser of any material, such as newly developed potential military equipment, which could decisively tilt the balance of power between the two camps.

The compromise worked out between the American and British points of view amounted to compiling an agreed-upon 'strategic embargo list' consisting of all items considered to be of any strategic significance or judged to contribute directly to the bloc's strategic potential. The embargoes could not be applied under the aegis of NATO, because the group of embargoing countries was extended to include non-NATO countries such as Japan and West Germany. Therefore a body known as the Coordinating Committee on Export Controls (Co-Com) was created.[9] It reviewed the lists annually, adding new items or deleting old ones, and seeing to it that all countries of the alliance abided by that policy. However, there was 'no practical sanction against a Co-Com member country violating, by commission or omission, a strategic embargo rule.'[10] Most West European governments never openly admitted to their parliaments, or to the general public, that they cooperated in Co-Com, 'to such a point that spokesmen of the British Foreign Office have sometimes declined to acknowledge the existence of Co-Com.'[11]

Indeed, this sharp curtailment of trade with the Communist bloc for the purpose of impeding their industrial growth was not welcomed by some US allies, such as Japan and the nations of Western Europe, whose domestic prosperity depended on world trade. As a result, those nations succeeded in progressively narrowing the definition of goods deemed 'strategic' for purposes of the embargo. As Sheldon Appleton maintains in *United States Foreign Policy* (1968):

> In support of their policy of engaging in nonstrategic trade with Eastern Europe, America's allies argued that a tighter embargo would detract from their own economic strength and prosperity at least as much as it would from that of the Communist nations. They pointed out further that whatever fulcrum for political pressure might be provided by threatening to discontinue this East-West trade was bound to work both ways. Finally, they noted the possible political gains from the establishment of areas of shared East-West economic advantage, which might help in a limited way to relax international tensions.[12]

The Kennedy and Johnson administrations saw some merit in this argument, and American policies began to move more towards liberalizing commercial relations with the Communist nations, particularly when such liberalization could be viewed as a means to enable some of those countries to break away from Moscow or to maintain their independence.

When the Nixon administration took office in 1969 it pursued a foreign policy based on détente. This concept is defined as 'a relatively sudden shift in the relations of major powers, not actually at war with one another, from a state of tension and conflict to a state of negotiation and cooperation.'[13] Détente resulted in joint efforts to step up trade between the two superpowers, 'which actually entailed greatly increased exports by the United States to the Soviet Union (since Soviet goods are in relatively little demand in the United States).'[14] The aim of this policy was to give the Soviet Union enough of a stake in expanded trade, investment, and political consultation to entice it away from pursuing a policy of confrontation. In keeping with this policy of accommodation with the Soviet Union and continuing his preoccupation with maintaining the *status quo*, Secretary of State Kissinger resorted less to an open policy of economic sanctions and more to a tacit policy of negotiation and persuasion ('arm-twisting'). Consequently, the use of trade as a nonmilitary means of influencing Soviet policy seemed gradually to be diminishing. However, the use of trade as a political weapon depended very much on the ebb and flow of relations between the United States and the Soviet Union and on the changes in the international arena. When Kissinger left office in 1976 and Jimmy Carter became President, efforts to direct economic diplomacy against the Soviet Union were injected again into foreign policy. How effective was the strategic embargo? A report by a group of American experts concluded:

> In military and industrial terms, both sides are slightly hurt by the controls and the Soviet Bloc is probably hurt more than the free world. However, the cost of maintaining these controls in the free world must also be measured in other terms as well. The controls clearly strain somewhat the political ties among free-world countries and contribute slightly to balance of payments and employment difficulties on our side.[15]

The Soviet response: Comecon

In the Communist bloc, similar joint efforts were made to use trade and economic sanctions as instruments of Soviet foreign policy. Responding to the establishment in 1948 of the Organization for European Economic Cooperation (OEEC) for the purpose of distributing Marshall Plan aid among Western European countries, the Soviet Union, Bulgaria, Czechoslovakia, Hungary, Poland, and Romania in 1949 created the Council for Mutual Economic Assistance (Comecon).[16] It was later joined by East Germany and Albania, but the latter was expelled in 1961 for supporting China in the Sino-Soviet dispute. Mongolia became a member in 1962; in 1972 Cuba became the first Western nation to join. Lacking the technical superiority of the Western bloc, and consequently, in contrast to the Western strategic embargo alliance, Comecon was primarily a manifestation of the subservience of the Communist allies to Moscow, and an abrogation of the client states' independence of action in foreign relations. In spite of Soviet claims that the socialist bloc is a unified unit, the recent behavior of the members of Comecon demonstrates that no such homogeneous bloc exists, either in terms of internal relations, or in terms of their hostility toward capitalist countries. U. Stehr has suggested that Comecon in fact promotes intra-bloc relations of dependence and inequality. It accommodates desires of Soviet leaders for continuing economic influence and of Eastern European leaders for assistance in economic development.[17]

In the first postwar decade, the Soviet Union reoriented the trade of Comecon members and signed bilateral trade agreements with its satellite countries that were very favorable to the Kremlin. Furthermore, the Soviet Union had access to the planning processes of the Comecon members. Therefore, it had the power to shape the economic plans of Eastern Europe in the direction it preferred, and to direct their external trade policies to serve the interests of the Soviet Union. Comecon members were compelled to produce and export those products desired by the Soviet Union, and to limit their world trade to countries favored by the Soviet Union, in accordance with Soviet foreign-policy objectives.

Western boycott of Iranian oil, 1951–3

The boycott of Iranian oil by Western importing countries following the nationalization of Iran's oil industry by the government of Mohamed Mossadeq in mid-1951 illustrates an important case of joint efforts by governments and private concerns to utilize economic leverage, supported by military power, to coerce a nation into yielding to political and economic demands. Imposed by Britain and the international oil companies with the support of the other Western oil-importing nations, the boycott was highly effective in undermining the Mossadeq regime and led to its eventual collapse in 1954.

Iranian grievances against the Anglo-Iranian Company (later British Petroleum), which owned the Iranian oil industry and was the sole operator in Iran, were accumulating due to Iran's low share of the oil profits. Between 1913 and 1951, the Anglo-Iranian Company had gross profits of $3 billion, of which only $624 million went to the Iranian government. The remaining   2.4 billion was transferred abroad as profits for the rest of the shareholders, of which the British government constituted the majority interest.[18] According to Harvey O'Connor in his book *World Crisis in Oil* (1962), Iran received in 1950 ' 45 million and the British Treasury   140 million. In that year Iran realized more revenue from the state tobacco monopoly than from petroleum.'[19] The refusal of the Anglo-Iranian Company to agree to a fifty-fifty profit-sharing formula similar to those obtained by Venezuela and Saudi Arabia in 1949 led the Iranian government headed by Premier Mohamed Mossadeq to pass a nationalization bill in the Iranian parliament. Unable to resort to traditional gunboat diplomacy, for fear of Soviet intervention, the British government rejected Iran's offers of compensation, insisting on terms that would cover the company not only for its investments, but also for the profits on the oil reserves estimated underground — terms so excessive that they were certain to be rejected. Consequently, the British government took its case to the International Court, which held it had no jurisdiction on the matter, and to the Security Council, which proved unable to resolve the conflict. Simultaneously it launched a campaign of economic warfare against Iran, instituting a boycott on exports that effectively prevented Iran from transporting and marketing its own oil for nearly forty months. The last unfettered oil cargo left Abadan in the hold of the British ship *Sailor* on 21 June 1951, less than two months after Mossadeq had nationalized Anglo-Iranian's concessions. The boycott caused Iranian oil production to drop from 243 million barrels in 1950 to only 8–9 million barrels in 1952 and 1953.

In mid-1951 when the facilities of the Anglo-Iranian Oil Company were seized Iran was producing around 700,000 barrels of oil a day.[20] In an effort to weaken the Mossadeq government, the company halted work on most of the oil installations. It withdrew all its foreign technicians and virtually shut down the wells and the Abadan refinery,[21] then the largest in the world with a capacity of around 500,000 barrels daily. By 1954, stocks of refined products at the Abadan refinery that needed marketing were estimated at 10 million barrels.[22] Occasionally oil cargoes were picked up by tankers of independent Japanese and Italian companies, lured by Mossadeq's half-price offer, but they sailed under the threat of legal attack in their ports of destination. To offset its Iranian oil loss, Anglo-Iranian shifted its operations to its Kuwaiti and Iraqi concessions,[23] where production was increased to make up for the shortfall in world supplies caused by the boycott.

Although the Iranian nationalization removed the British from their exclusive position in Iran and offered American companies an opportunity to negotiate new, high profit deals, the Americans had severe reservations about a policy that would leave the Iranian nationalization intact. Mossadeq's act, to the Western governments and their home-based oil companies, represented a threat to their cheap and easy access to the natural resources of the Third World. If Mossadeq could nationalize oil with impunity, then nothing would stop other countries from following his example. The Iranian action had evoked dormant forces of emotional nationalism and xenophobia which the United States felt that it had to contain lest they prove contagious. The issue became the right of a country to nationalize and control its resources, and the oil companies' home governments, especially the United States, did not want to set any precedents.

According to Arthur Krock of the *New York Times*, President Truman believed that the Soviets would not go to war with the US because 'they did not know how to create the industrial machine they would require for World War Three.' One of these requirements was oil. Truman believed that 'the Russians were hundreds of thousands of barrels short of the daily million they would need.' Consequently to let the Soviets get oil from Iran was out of the question and to support a national regime which might at any point turn to the Soviet Union contradicted both American strategic interests and its policy in the area. Furthermore, the Americans feared the implications of the Iranian act on other Third World nations.[24] 'If the Iranians carry out their plans as stated, Venezuela and other countries on whose supplies we depend will follow suit. That is the great danger in the Iranian controversy with the British,' President Harry Truman confided to Krock on 24 May 1951.[25]

Failing to evaluate precisely the impact of his act on the Western powers, Mossadeq ignored Soviet enticements and put his faith in the United States, which had given him reason to believe that they would provide some measure of support in the face of British intransigence. The Iranian army and police, which had been under the tutelage of the American military since World War II,[26] and which then executed in August 1953 the CIA coup that restored Shah Mohamed Reza Pahlevi to power and placed Mossadeq under house arrest.[27] Under an agreement signed in Tehran by the Shah in October 1954, the Iranian oil industry was denationalized and full management and commercial rights were vested in a consortium of eight major companies; Anglo-Iranian (which changed its name to British Petroleum at the time) held only 40 per cent;

Shell got 14 per cent and CFP (France) 6 per cent. The major newcomers were the five giant American companies, getting 8 per cent each for a total of 40 per cent. Eight smaller American companies were brought in later at 1 per cent each.[28] For the new members, large or small, any stake in this immensely profitable and virtually riskless venture was, in the words of a British oil expert, 'like getting a license to print money.'[29] Under the new agreement the Iranian government received some additional revenues, though it exercised no decisive influence on the assets of the industry it now 'owned' and which was used freely by the companies. As Issawi and Yeganeh say in *The Economics of Middle East Oil* (1962): 'This fact makes the Iranian agreement . . . one of the most attractive contracts to the oil industry in the Middle East, as far as terms of payment are concerned.'[30]

The new Iranian contract with the companies was expected to restore Iran's output by 1957 to the level of 1950, when Iran ranked fourth as a world producer. Once the agreement was signed, ten consortium tankers under British, Dutch, French and US registry loaded within three days nearly 135,000 tons of crude oil and refined oil — more oil than Iran had been able to sell for more than two years after nationalization. The consortium also guaranteed to produce and purchase 68 million tons of crude in the first three years of operations. In addition, it hoped to refine 6,500,000 tons of oil in the first year and reach a refinery output of 30 million tons in three years. Iran's half-share of the profits over this period was expected to be $420 million, i.e., $140 million a year, compared with direct oil revenues of $45 million in 1950, the last full year of Anglo-Iranian operations, when the refinery processed 24 million tons of Iran's total production of 32 million tons.[31] In his inaugural address Dr Ali Amini, Finance Minister and head of the Iranian team that had negotiated the agreement, told the company's Iranian employees that the agreement 'offered Iran a greater opportunity to prove her native ability and efficiency.' He asked them to cooperate with the consortium staff so that it would be possible to 'fully Iranize' the industry at the end of the forty-year agreement.[32]

The Western powers' withdrawal of the offer to finance the Aswan Dam, 1956

In the midst of the cold war between the two superpowers, the United States and the Soviet Union, many nations of the Third World opted to adhere to policies which would keep them out of this bipolar conflict. Egypt's young nationalist leader Jamal Abdel Nasser, for example, was trying to pursue policies which could secure for his country political, as well as economic, independence. Nasser felt that 'ties of trade and investment in the past had meant exploitation and domination by the West,'[33] and he joined Tito of Yugoslavia and Nehru of India in championing the cause of nonalignment, or 'positive neutrality,' as it came to be called. US Secretary of State Dulles took the position that 'neutralism' was 'immoral,' and he sought to use economic aid as a means of inducing the uncommitted people to align themselves closely with the West.[34] Dulles applauded Tito's efforts to pursue 'positive neutrality,' highly publicizing it, because Tito, as the head of a large communist country lying in the midst of the Eastern bloc, was in a position to influence other communist countries. Nasser's move, however, was made in the heart of Dulles's own camp, among pro-Western countries with whom America was trying to build a southern bulwark against the communist threat. To Dulles that was treason, which should not go unpunished.

From the day he assumed the leadership of Egypt, Nasser realized that he could not muster support within Egypt or prestige outside it unless he could solve Egypt's chronic economic problems. Since his country's population was growing very rapidly and its limited fertile strips of land were swiftly shrinking, Nasser conceived the idea of building the High Dam at Aswan to irrigate a much larger area, thus providing extra strips of land where people could live and farm, away from the few highly populated urban centers. The Aswan High Dam was 'a huge project which Nasser hoped would harness the vast power of the lower Nile and serve as a symbol of how his regime was triumphantly taking Egypt into the twentieth century.'[35] The Aswan project, however, was far beyond Egypt's financial and technical capabilities. Its cost was estimated 'at over $1.3 billion and the time required to build it about 15 years.'[36] Nasser sought help from Western governments for the enterprise. Initially he obtained promises of $55 million from the United States, $15 million from Britain, and then $200 million from the World Bank after the other offers were forthcoming.[37] In his analysis of the situation, Walter LaFeber wrote:

> Dulles concluded that if he suddenly withdrew the offer, Nasser would suffer a disastrous political blow. The Secretary also assumed that Khrushchev would not, in fact could not, replace American aid,

an assumption with which Eugene Black concurred because of his belief that Nasser could not afford to become further involved with the communist bloc. Black nevertheless warned Dulles to go through with the deal or 'hell might break loose.' Both of Dulles' assumptions were tragically wrong. He compounded the mistake by announcing the American decision in a formal, direct announcement on July 19, 1956, at the moment the Egyptian Foreign Minister was arriving to discuss the project, and as Nasser himself sat in a widely publicized meeting with Tito and Nehru.[38]

When the Western powers rescinded their offer to aid Egypt in building the dam, Nasser, hoping to finance the dam project and related works from the revenues of the Suez Canal, issued a decree nationalizing the Suez Canal Company and taking over 'all its property and rights pertaining thereto.' In the nationalization speech, delivered to a mass meeting in Alexandria on 23 July 1956, Nasser explained that the initial American-British loan for the dam had been for $70 million over five years, while the canal earned the equivalent of $100 million yearly, of which Egypt had been getting only 1 million pounds sterling (nearly $2.3 million at the time) out of the company's 35 million pounds (nearly $100 million) in earnings.[39]

No doubt, the brisk withdrawal of the Western offer to finance the construction of the Aswan High Dam was a drastic blunder, a landmark in charting the decline of Western power and the rise of Soviet power in the Middle East. What was perceived to be a lesson for other nationalist leaders in the Third World who might in the future entertain similar ideas turned out to be the cornerstone upon which Nasser built his respect and prestige not only in Egypt and the Arab world, but among Third World nations generally.

It is obvious that US foreign policy-makers had acted on the assumption that the target nation (receiver of aid) would not be able to find a provider (in terms of aid called 'provider,' and in terms of commodities called 'producer') ready, willing, and able to provide the goods (in this context, financial and technical aid). They failed to appreciate the deep implication that such a huge venture would have for the other super-power, which was trying hard to open some channels of communication with the Arabs, who hitherto had not responded because the Soviets were mistrusted and feared. The significance of involvement with Egypt on the Aswan Dam, a project costing over $1.3 billion and lasting for at least fifteen years, did not escape the Kremlin leaders. It would mean economic and technical dependency on the Soviet Union of a leading Arab country in the center of a most strategic area in the world, at a time when the USSR was struggling against isolation and hatred.

Hindsight shows that Dulles and his advisors did not take seriously the substitute sources of supply that Nasser might resort to in order to obtain the financial aid and technical assistance denied him. Nasser made it very clear in his Alexandria speech that he had resorted to the nationalization of the Suez Canal to compensate for the lost Western financial aid. His assumption was that revenues from the canal would help finance the dam, with the Soviet Union providing the technical assistance.

The nationalization of the Suez Canal was Nasser's main counter-leverage. But he resorted to other counter-leverages as well, such as inciting the Arabs and the Third World against the Western powers and the Western multinational corporations operating in the Third World. For quite some time, the Suez Affair left Britain without diplomatic posts in three major Arab capitals — Cairo, Damascus, and Riyadh — in a sensitive region where it still had vital interests.

The Western powers underestimated the backlash that the withdrawal of their offer provoked. Even Eugene Black in his warning about the future implications of the use of aid as a political weapon, to squeeze Egypt and bring down Nasser, had said that 'hell might break loose.' The use of 'might' is significant here, because of the implication that it also 'might not.' Within the provider cartel camp, groups started blaming each other in an effort to pinpoint responsibility for the loss. The British blamed US Middle Eastern policies for the Suez Crisis. The Americans accused the French and British of pursuing an immoral and outmoded gunboat diplomacy on the Suez Canal. The trust and confidence among those powers were shaken, and each looked to its own interest as an individual state rather than as a member of a joint community. This attitude was much more pronounced during the 1973 Arab oil embargo when individual Western nations adopted self-centered approaches to ensure their oil supplies. This remains a classical case in which a target nation was able to defuse the economic weapon because it succeeded in finding alternative sources of supply. In addition, it was in a position to impose strong countermeasures.

The Arab states boycott of Israel since 1948

Multilateral sanctions have not been the exclusive prerogative of the two great alliances; they have been utilized also by Third World nations. The Arab states (excluding Egypt) still enforce a total ban on commercial and financial transactions with the state of Israel.[40] As one dimension of the war effort against Israel, this 'boycott is intended to prevent Arab states and discourage non-Arabs from directly or indirectly contributing to Israel's economic and military strength.'[41] According to Nancy Turck, the Arab boycott of Israel assumes three basic forms:

(a) The *Primary Boycott* in which the Arabs and their nationals refuse to trade with Israel or its nations.[42]

(b) The *Secondary Boycott* which involves the refusal by Arab states to trade with third parties, i.e., non-Israeli nationals or companies, which in the opinion of the boycott committee of the Arab League significantly contribute to Israel's economic and military strength.

(c) The *Tertiary Boycott* in which the Arabs forbid utilization of materials, equipment or services of a blacklisted firm by a non-blacklisted firm in its exports to or projects in an Arab country.[43]

In 1965, the United States passed antiboycott legislation which required all US exporters to report to the Commerce Department the receipt and nature of any request having the effect of furthering or supporting the Arab boycott. On 30 June 1965, Congress amended the Export Control Act of 1949 to include a statement that the policy of the United States is '(a) to oppose restrictive trade practices or boycotts fostered or imposed by foreign countries friendly to the United States; and (b) to encourage and request U.S. domestic concerns engaged in export to refuse to take any action or sign any agreement that would further such practices.' In phrasing the amendment the Congress used the words 'encouraged' and 'requested' rather than the stronger word 'prohibited,' which would place the force of law behind the act, making it illegal for those firms to take any action or supply any information that would support the boycott.

The issue of the Arab boycott drew considerable attention in 1975. On 26 February Senator Frank Church, Chairman of the Senate Foreign Relations Subcommittee on Multinational Corporations, made public a Saudi Arabian edition of an Arab boycott list of more than 1,500 American companies.[44] Along with the list were the regulations of the boycott office of the Arab League in Damascus, under which Arab countries were not to trade with companies on the boycott list if they had significant investments in Israel, if they helped Israel militarily, if they sold to Israel and not to Arab countries, or if they distributed pro-Israeli publications or films.

In hearings before the subcommittee on the same day, Harold H. Saunders, Deputy Assistant Secretary of State for Near Eastern and South Asian Affairs, testified that the lifting of the boycott was linked to resolution of the Arab-Israeli territorial dispute and expressed the view that the boycott could best be dealt with through quiet diplomacy and persuasion.

On 13 March 1975, in his testimony before the Subcommittee on International Trade and Commerce of the House Foreign Affairs Committee, Sidney Sober, Acting Assistant Secretary of State for Near Eastern and South Asian Affairs, described United States policy toward the boycott as follows:

> As stated on numerous occasions our position is clear and it can be summarized as follows: the United States opposes the boycott. We do not support or condone it in any way. The Department has emphasized our opposition to the boycott to the Arab governments on many occasions as it adversely affects United States firms, vessels and individuals. Where the commercial interests of American firms or individuals have been injured or threatened with injury, we have made representations to appropriate Arab officials.
>
> Consistent with our policy of opposition to the boycott, as reflected in the Export Administration Act of 1969, the Department of State has refused hundreds of requests from U.S. companies for authentication of documents relating to the boycott, as being contrary to public policy.
>
> A number of American firms with boycott problems have consulted with Department officials. These firms have been (a) reminded of their reporting responsibilities under the Export Administration Act and (b) encouraged and requested to refuse to take any action in support of restrictive trade practices or boycotts.
>
> A fundamental factor which has to be faced is that Arab governments regard the boycott as an important element in their position toward Israel, and one of the basic issues of the Arab-Israeli

conflict to be dealt with as progress is made toward resolving that conflict. Indeed, this is one of the issues which we have very much in mind as we continue our diplomatic efforts to help the parties achieve a just and lasting peace. The problem has been how to change effectively the underlying conditions which led to imposition of the boycott. We believe we can best serve this objective not through confrontation but by continuing to promote with the parties directly concerned a peaceful settlement of basic Middle East issues. We believe that our present diplomatic approach is the most effective way to proceed.[45]

Gerald L. Parsky, Assistant Secretary of the Treasury, referred to US efforts in discouraging the boycott by demonstrating the potential contribution of US firms to Arab economies. He described the policy of the Department of the Treasury as opposing any increased confrontation or alteration in the traditional US policy of a free and open market for trade and investment, 'in which capital flows are responsive to market forces unencumbered by governmental influence.' Charles W. Hostler, Deputy Assistant Secretary for International Commerce, expressed the opposition of the Commerce Department to legislative proposals to prohibit US firms from responding to boycott requests. Hostler stated that the Department of Commerce believed that 'American firms should not be restricted in their freedom to make economic decisions based on their own business interests, where no element of ethnic or religious discrimination in violation of U.S. law is involved.' He urged that there be no change in the 'antiboycott' provisions of the Export Administration Act.[46] On 20 November 1975, President Ford issued an executive order designed to tighten the antiboycott enforcement. This was followed in later years by a series of antiboycott pieces of legislation in Congress. As to the impact of such laws Nancy Turck remarks: 'There have been no published reports on the economic consequences of federal or state antiboycott legislation and it is difficult to estimate accurately their effect.'[47]

The Arab oil embargo, 1973–4

The practice of injecting politics into commercial transactions by a concerted effort of multiple states in the Third World is more vividly illustrated by the 1973–4 Arab oil embargo, in which the Arab oil-producing countries imposed production cuts and export limitations on industrial nations to coerce them into exerting pressure on Israel to withdraw from territories captured during the 1967 war. On 17 October 1973 the Arab oil ministers, following their meeting in Kuwait, made two public announcements. The first included the resolution to impose the oil embargo; the second elaborated upon the political background and motivations behind that decision. An analysis of those two statements leads one to identify the objectives of the oil embargo as the following:

First, to express solidarity with the other Arab states presently engaged in military engagements with Israel, and to play an active role in the achievement of the military and political objective of the October War, namely, to compel Israel by military force to withdraw from all the territories it occupied during the 1967 June War.

Second, to put pressure on the international community to oblige Israel to (a) 'relinquish our occupied territories,' and (b) restore 'the legitimate rights of the Palestinian people in accordance with the United Nations resolution.'

Third, to reward 'the countries that support the Arabs actively and effectively or that take important measures against Israel to compel its withdrawal.' The political communiqué issued along with the resolutions of the conference asserted:

> The conferees are eager that this production cut should not affect any friendly state which has helped or will help the Arabs in a fruitful and effective manner. They will continue to be supplied with the same quantities of oil they used to obtain before the reduction.
>
> The same special treatment will be given to every state which adopts an important measure against Israel to persuade it to end its occupation of the usurped Arab territories.

These measures were aimed to convince 'the great industrial states that consume Arab oil to adopt a measure or an action which indicates awareness of its general international commitment.' and also to neutralize some of them who 'have acted in a manner which supports and strengthens aggression.'

Fourth, to punish the various consuming countries who support and cooperate 'with the Israeli enemy.' Here, the United States was singled out, as it was considered to be 'the principal and foremost source of the Israeli power which has resulted in the present Israeli arrogance and enabled the Israelis to continue to occupy our territories.'

Fifth, to put pressure on the world community and prompt it to exercise its moral power to influence American policies in the Middle East, which reflected unequivocal support for Israel. The objective was to make 'the United States aware of the exorbitant price the great industrial states are paying as a result of its blind and unlimited support for Israel.'

The concluding sentence of the communiqué, overlooked by many observers, put forth the bottom-line conditions that needed to be met for the embargo to be lifted. It specified that oil production would resume 'when the world shows sympathy toward us and condemns the aggression against us.' For the long term, the explicit objectives of the embargo had been to force Israel to withdraw from Arab territories occupied in the 1967 war and restore the legitimate rights of the Palestinian people. However, the implicit short-term goal was to muster international support for the cause of the Palestinians, in itself believed to be a huge step towards achieving the longer-term goal of securing a total Israeli withdrawal from the occupied Arab territories. This objective was made more explicit in the 8 December 1973 meeting of the Arab oil ministers, during which it was made clear that the relaxation of the oil cutback measures was predicated on 'an agreement on a timetable for a withdrawal.' A statement issued at the time asserted that 'if agreement is reached on withdrawal from all the territories occupied since 1967, foremost amongst them Jerusalem, in accordance with a timetable which Israel agrees to and whose implementation is guaranteed by the United States, the embargo on exports to the United States will be lifted as soon as the withdrawal program begins . . . .'

Here it is important to note a shift in the use of the embargo. At this stage, the Arab producers were enjoying the benefits of higher prices and lower production output, and so their decision to continue the employment of the oil weapon was primarily for economic purposes – though they were reaping political affluence simultaneously as a fringe benefit.

When the embargo ran its course and was finally lifted on 18 March 1974, the official statement issued was short, mild, and general, providing only the minimum description of the reasons behind the rescission and what specifically the cutbacks had achieved. A statement explaining the political reasons for ending the embargo said:

> The ministers reevaluated the results of the Arab oil measures in
> light of its main objective, namely to draw the attention of the
> world to the Arab cause in order to create the suitable climate for

the implementation of Security Council Resolution 242. . . . The
ministers took cognizance of . . . the signs which began to appear in
various American circles calling (in various degrees) for the need of
an evenhanded policy. . . . American official policy . . . assumed a
new dimension vis-à-vis the Arab-Israeli conflict. Such a dimension
will lead America to assume a position which is more compatible
with the principle of what is right and just toward the Arab occupied
territories and the legitimate rights of the Palestinian people.

In the background was the conclusion and partial implementation of
agreements dealing with the disengagement of forces on the Egyptian
and Syrian fronts. At a time of intense secret diplomacy conducted by
Secretary of State Henry Kissinger, one cannot but support the conjec-
ture of many analysts that an agreement was being reached behind
closed doors. The editors of the *Middle East Economic Survey* note
that 'it is very possible that certain guarantees or "best endeavour" pro-
mises were confidentially communicated by the US to the Arab states
concerned regarding the implementation of UN Resolution 242.'[48] In
support of this, it is significant to note that Egyptian president Anwar
Sadat, who was establishing a close rapport with Kissinger, was one of
those adamantly insisting that the oil embargo be terminated to give the
United States an opportunity to prove the sincerity of its new evenhanded posture in the Middle East. With the exception of Libya and
Syria, the Arab oil producers 'felt that the United States had shown
enough good will in influencing Israel to carry out military disengagement with Egypt' to warrant the lifting of the embargo.[49]

Most analysts of the Arab oil embargo have assessed the success of
the oil weapon by evaluating its performance in terms of the ambitious
political objectives of (1) compelling the Israelis to withdraw to the
1967 borders, and (2) restoring Palestinian rights. Here, it is important
to note that these two objectives were the ultimate political goals of
the Arab military initiative of 6 October 1973. The oil weapon was un-
sheathed to complement the Arab war efforts, not to replace it. The
Arab oil producers meeting in Kuwait were well aware of the real
strength of the embargo, and no public statement was made to the effect that employing the oil weapon would by itself force Israel to withdraw from all the territories it occupied in 1967. On the contrary,
official Saudi pronouncements throughout the embargo were vaguely
worded to provide the Saudi government with flexibility to negotiate.

In retrospect, it is important to note that scholars who conclude that the oil weapon failed in 1973 measure the policy's accomplishments by the scale of its publicly declared objectives, i.e., to have Israel withdraw to its 1967 borders and to restore the legitimate rights of the Palestinians. They overlook the major role played by the oil weapon in restoring Arab self-confidence, in influencing the shifts of power that occurred in its aftermath, in accelerating the process of disengagement between the Arab and Israeli troops, in forcing the United States, Western Europe, and Japan to readjust their hard-line pro-Israel policy, and in pressuring Israel to withdraw its forces from the west side of the Suez Canal and parts of the Golan Heights, and to facilitate the exchange of prisoners of war. The Arab oil embargo has had strong economic repercussions in the countries which were either intentionally or unintentionally affected. At the same time it had weak economic repercussions for the countries that introduced it. Furthermore, the partial termination of oil exports and the decrease in oil production by the countries imposing the oil embargo had caused a big shift in oil prices in consumer nations while leaving oil prices in producing countries relatively unaffected. Thus the damage done to the countries imposing the embargo is minimal, but greater in the target countries.

Sanctions against Iran, 1980–1

Following the seizure of the US embassy in Tehran on 4 November 1979, and the holding of American personnel as hostages, the Carter administration brought the matter before the United Nations for action. On 31 December 1979 the Security Council, by a vote of 11–0 with the Soviet Union abstaining, adopted Resolution 461 which called on Iran to free the hostages. The resolution threatened that should the hostages not be released by 7 January the Security Council would 'adopt effective measures.' However, a Soviet veto on 13 January 1980 nullified a 12-2 vote in favor of invoking sanctions against Iran under Chapter 7 of the UN Charter.[50] The sanctions proposal made no reference to petroleum or to the freezing of Iran's financial assets abroad. In a statement after the vote, US ambassador Donald McHenry described the Soviet veto on the sanctions resolution as 'an act of political expediency designed to buy Iranian silence on Afghanistan and Soviet advantage in the area.'

After the failures of the UN sanctions the United States attempted to enlist the support of its European allies in the form of collective sanctions against Iran, to be imposed outside the framework of the United Nations. The Europeans, however, were reluctant to do so, for (1) political reasons — their conviction that economic reprisals would prove ineffective; (2) economic reasons — since sanctions would hurt the EEC, whose total exports to Iran amounted to 'more than \$1 billion per month';[51] and (3) legal reasons — because a number of European nations had no legal power to break their old contracts with Iran. The failed Security Council resolution would have conferred this authority through the provision of the charter overriding national legislative restrictions. One French official commented: 'The problem is that an embargo costs Europe a lot and does not have much impact on Iran.'[52]

The continued holding of the American hostages then prompted the United States to adopt economic sanctions unilaterally. On 7 April 1980, President Carter signed Executive Order 12205, 'Prohibiting Certain Transactions With Iran.'[53] This order embodied in large measure the operative paragraphs of the draft resolution that the United States had proposed in the UN Security Council on 10 January 1980. In a statement outlining US actions against Iran, the President stated:

> The events of the last few days have revealed a new and significant dimension in this matter of the 50 American hostages. The militants controlling the embassy have stated they are willing to turn the hostages over to the government of Iran, but the government has refused to take custody of the American hostages.
>
> This lays bare the full responsibility of the Ayatollah Khomeini and the Revolutionary Council for the continued illegal and outrageous holding of the innocent hostages. The Iranian government can no longer escape full responsibility by hiding behind the militants at the embassy. It must be made clear that the failure to release the hostages will involve increasingly heavy costs to Iran and to its interests.
>
> I have today ordered the following steps:
>
> First, the United States of America is breaking diplomatic relations with the government of Iran. The Secretary of State has informed the government of Iran that its embassy and consulate in the United States are to be closed immediately. All Iranian diplomatic and consular officials have been declared *persona non grata* and must leave this country by midnight tomorrow.
>
> Second, the Secretary of the Treasury will put into effect official sanctions prohibiting exports from the United States to Iran,

in accordance with the sanctions approved by 10 members of the United Nations Security Council on January 13 in the resolution that was vetoed by the Soviet Union. Although shipments of food and medicine were not included in the UN Security Council vote, it is expected that exports even of these items to Iran will be minimal or nonexistent.

Third, the Secretary of Treasury will make a formal inventory of the assets of the Iranian government, which were frozen by my previous order, and also will make a census or an inventory of the outstanding claims of American citizens and corporations against the government of Iran. This accounting of claims will aid in designing a program against Iran for the hostages, for the hostages' families and other U.S. claimants. We are now preparing legislation, which will be introduced in the Congress, to facilitate processing and paying of these claims.

Fourth, the Secretary of State and the Attorney General will invalidate all visas issued to Iranian citizens for future entry into the United States, effective today. We will not reissue visas, nor will we issue new visas, except for compelling and proven humanitarian reasons or where the national interest of our own country requires. This directive will be interpreted very strictly. . . .

I am committed to resolving this crisis. I am committed to the safe return of the American hostages and to the preservation of our national honor. The hostages and their families — indeed, all of us in America — have lived with the reality and the anguish of their captivity for five months.

The steps I have ordered today are those that are necessary now. Other actions may become necessary if these steps do not produce the prompt release of the hostages.[54]

But since Iranian-US trade had declined precipitously since the deposition of the Shah and the access to power of Khomeini, American economic sanctions were viewed as 'primarily symbolic.'[55] Left out of these measures was an embargo on food and medicine, which some Cabinet members, in particular Secretary of State Cyrus Vance, argued would violate the administration's own humanitarian policies. Food was where Iran was most vulnerable. Iranian agriculture had been hit hard by the revolution and the central government was not yet in full control of some of the most important food-producing regions.

On 17 April President Carter announced a ban on travel to Iran by

Americans, except for newsmen and those with special reasons, along with a ban on all imports from Iran. Also banned were all financial transfers between the US and Iran, except those involving news or the hostages' families.

Among the steps against Iran considered seriously at the time was a naval blockade to enforce the US economic sanctions. However, this idea was later abandoned since the consequences were unpredictable. It was feared that a blockade might (1) provoke the Iranian militants holding the hostages into harming them; (2) push the oil sheikdoms of the Gulf to curtail oil supplies to the West and Japan or raise oil prices; (3) propel the Soviet Union and the United States into a direct confrontation in the region; (4) spark anti-American sentiments in the Third World; (5) throw Iran into the Soviets' arms, since the USSR was willing to provide outlets and aid; (6) offer the Soviet Union an unprecedented opportunity to gain legitimate entry into Iran; and (7) be undercut anyway by Iran-Soviet rail and water links, and by routes via Turkey in the West and Pakistan in the East, thus providing alternative routes for Iran's import needs. In addition, there was no reasonable hope that a US naval blockade would persuade Iran to free the hostages.

Lukewarm European backing for the US economic measure threatened both to undermine the North Atlantic alliance and to jeopardize the emerging political cohesiveness in international affairs among EEC members. To defuse these threats, the European foreign ministers reluctantly agreed on 22 April 1980 to impose mild economic penalties on Iran. In adopting such measures, the European governments hoped that they would help to restrain the United States from taking any military action against Iran. Thus it took them by surprise when the US on 24 April undertook its abortive raid on Iran. The US rescue mission gave new urgency to the pressures on the European Community to join the American efforts against Iran. On 29 April the European heads of state confirmed the sanctions decision, in hopes that this would make the US avoid riskier military options. Though they were better than nothing, the United States was not satisfied with the European economic measures. The Americans kept pressing for more. In mid-May, US Secretary of State Edmund Muskie made a strong plea to several European foreign ministers in meetings in Brussels and Vienna for more meaningful sanctions to be imposed. In response to the US pleas for allied solidarity in efforts to free the captives, the European foreign ministers meeting in Naples on 17 and 18 May decided to impose an export embargo against Iran, but softened the measures in two significant ways: (1) by excluding from the embargo all contracts with Iran that had been concluded prior to the taking of the hostages, and (2) by declaring that the embargo would be suspended if efforts to secure the release of the hostages made 'decisive progress.' But a split among the Common Market nations emerged when Britain decided on 19 May to ban only future contracts for trade with Iran, which meant that sanctions would have virtually no immediate effect on rapidly growing British-Iranian trade. Japan followed the European lead, announcing that it would impose sanctions on Iran but exempting from the ban all transactions related to the　3.3 billion petrochemical complex which Japan was then constructing.

On the 444th day of the hostage crisis, 19 January 1981, an agreement was reached between the United States and Iran resolving the situation.[56] In accordance with this settlement, the United States revoked 'all trade sanctions which were directed against Iran in the period November 4, 1979, to date' (section 10 of the agreement). Lifting the embargo against Iran was the last order Jimmy Carter signed before he left office. On 21 January 1981, members of the EEC lifted the trade embargo and were followed shortly by Japan.

Case study: sanctions against Argentina – the Falklands episode

On 2 April 1982 Argentine military forces seized control of the British-held Falkland islands, about 250 miles (400 kilometers) off the Argentine coast in the South Atlantic. Sovereignty over the islands had long been contested between the two countries, Argentina maintaining that the islands belonged to it by proximity, and Britain asserting its rights on the basis that the inhabitants – nearly 2,000 – wished to remain a part of the UK and were by culture and descent British.[57]

The seizure of the Falklands by Argentina produced a political crisis in Britain. On 3 April the prime minister Margaret Thatcher told Parliament that the Falklands 'remain British territory' and that the government was determined to take action 'to see the islands are free from occupation.' Britain's immediate response was to sever diplomatic relations with Argentina, invoke economic sanctions, and dispatch a large naval task force to the South Atlantic. Defense Secretary John Nott vowed on 4 April that the government would 'restore British administration to the Falklands even if we have to fight.'

Efforts at a diplomatic resolution of the crisis began immediately.

Hoping that the issue would be resolved peacefully, the United Nations Security Council, on 3 April 1982, approved a resolution calling for an end to hostilities and the withdrawal of Argentine forces.

The Falklands invasion posed the most serious threat to prime minister Margaret Thatcher's Conservative government that had arisen since it took power three years before, and she responded by taking a firm line. While threatening militarily to recapture the islands, the prime minister attempted to exert pressure on Argentina by invoking economic sanctions. Those measures included: (1) freezing Argentine financial assets in Britain; (2) the suspension of new export credits; (3) halting all military sales; (4) banning imports of goods.

In retaliation, the Galtieri government declared a freeze on British assets in Argentina, which amounted to $4 billion as compared to $1 billion of Argentine assets in Britain. In addition, Argentina announced that it would suspend all payments to British banks – including the interest and principal due on the $5.8 billion it had borrowed from London financial institutions.[58] Though the British banks could have called Argentina into default, they were not eager to do so for fear of the effect on the banking system. To reduce the danger of being called into default, Argentina maintained that it was channelling payments as and when due into an escrow account in New York.[59]

In addition to its unilateral measures, Britain looked to its allies for support. On 6 April the British government formally requested that the European Economic Community (EEC) join in the economic sanctions; on 14 April the EEC agreed to impose a month-long ban on imports from Argentina. These sanctions were to be reviewed at the end of the month. EEC support for Britain was a response to Argentina's act of aggression rather than an indication of agreement with British claims of sovereignty over the islands. In retaliation against the EEC sanctions, Argentina banned all imports from the European member nations. The EEC boycott was subsequently joined on 17 April 1982 by Australia, Canada, New Zealand, and Hong Kong.

The United States, while criticizing the Argentine invasion, took an uncommitted attitude and exerted continuous diplomatic efforts to defuse the crisis. In a news conference held on 5 April 1982 President Reagan stated that the dispute presented a 'very difficult situation for the United States, because we're friends with both of the countries engaged in this dispute.' However, US mediation efforts met with little visible success. For both sides, the key to the dispute remained the thorny issue of sovereignty over the islands. Argentina was adamant that its ultimate claim to ownership of the islands be upheld, while Britain continued to insist on a withdrawal of Argentine troops and restoration of British control as a prelude to any further negotiations on sovereignty. Furthermore, Britain wished to allow the Falklands inhabitants to determine for themselves whether they wished to remain under the British flag.

After initiatives to achieve a diplomatic solution failed, the US abandoned its mediation efforts on 30 April 1982, and declared its support for Britain, ascribing its failure to Argentine intransigence. In addition to offering to provide military supplies to Britain, the US government invoked limited economic sanctions against Argentina and suspended all military exports. In a press conference held on 30 April 1982 President Reagan stated that the US had for the moment 'gone as far as we can go' in trying to find a compromise solution. He added:

> We must remember that the aggression was on the part of
> Argentina in this dispute over the sovereignty of that little ice-cold
> bunch of land down there, and they finally just resorted to armed
> aggression. I think the principle that all of us must abide by is,
> armed aggression of that kind must not be allowed to succeed.

On the same day, US Secretary of State Alexander Haig asserted that 'in light of Argentina's failure to accept a compromise, we must take concrete steps to underscore that the United States cannot and will not condone the use of unlawful force to resolve disputes.'

In Argentina, meanwhile, a crisis of liquidity was mounting in the country's financial system, as depositors withdrew nearly $1 billion from domestic banks in anticipation of worsening economic conditions. To offset these withdrawals, on 16 April 1982 the Galtieri government injected, through the central bank, millions of dollars into the banking system.

Shortly after the US abandoned its mediation efforts, on 1 May 1982, the conflict entered a new phase of active military engagement. This commencement of military operations, together with the economic sanctions, put severe stress on the fragile Argentine economy, obliging the government on 5 May to declare a collection of measures intended to help finance the war and shore up the economy during the crisis. Among those economic measures were:

(a) devaluation of the peso by 14.3 per cent against the US dollar,
     and the imposition of a special war tax of 1,000 pesos for each

dollar exchanged, imposed on top of the existing 10 per cent tax on dollar transactions;

(b) increasing the tax rebate for manufacturers who exported goods;

(c) reducing from 90 per cent to 80 per cent the amount of government guarantees for bank deposits;

(d) increasing gasoline prices by 30 per cent and imposing additional taxes on cigarettes and liquor.

On 17 May, just before the 30-day EEC ban was set to expire, Britain succeeded in persuading the European Community to extend its economic sanctions for another seven days. The British argued that negotiations at the United Nations to bring about a peaceful solution were at an extremely critical stage and that lifting the sanctions might prejudice them. Convinced that continuing the sanctions was essential to bring about a peaceful solution, the Common Market nations, with the exception of Italy* and Ireland,** agreed to extend the trade ban under Article 113 of the EEC treaty, which called for unified external trade rules. Italy and Ireland maintained that they would observe Article 225, which provided for cooperation so as to avoid market distortions. Both Italy and Ireland agreed not to undermine the effect of sanctions by other EEC countries and agreed to ensure that Argentine imports would not be directed elsewhere in the European markets.

As the one-week extension ended, the eight other member countries of the EEC agreed, on 24 May 1982, to extend the trade sanctions against Argentina indefinitely. The EEC support was aimed specifically at driving Argentina back to the negotiating table. British Foreign Secretary Francis Pym welcomed the accord on the sanctions, saying that it showed 'a degree of support which we're very appreciative of at this stage of the conflict.' Argentina continued to block imports from the EEC in retaliation.

The military struggle, meanwhile, went heavily in favor of Britain. On 14 June 1982 Argentina was forced to surrender, and a *de facto* ceasefire prevailed. The Falklands military debacle led quickly to the

---

*There are an estimated 2 million Italians in Argentina, and the country is Italy's second largest trading partner in Latin America. Public opinion in Italy had been largely critical of the British handling of the Falklands crisis.

**The Irish government was reluctant to back sanctions for fear of compromising its neutral status. Furthermore, there was concern that Ireland might appear to be giving tacit approval to Britain's use of force. The Irish official view was that suspension of sanctions would be more helpful in finding a diplomatic solution.

forced resignation of Argentine president Leopoldo Galtieri. In a message delivered to the United Nations on 18 June 1982, Argentina stated that 'there exists in fact, given the present circumstances, a cessation of hostilities, which Argentina observes, but this cessation will be precarious so long as the British attitude as evidenced by the military occupation, the blockade, and the economic aggression subsists.' The Argentine note said that 'the total cessation of hostilities' would be achieved only when Britain withdrew its military forces from the region and ended its economic sanctions and blockade. Britain, in a letter to the UN Security Council on 25 June, eased its demand for a formal declaration from Argentina that all hostilities in the South Atlantic be declared at an end. The letter stated that the British government was now simply hoping to receive 'positive indications which will allow it to conclude' that there would be no renewal of hostilities on Argentina's part. Such 'indications' might amount merely to a continuation of the informal ceasefire currently in effect.

As a result of the ceasefire, the foreign ministers of the European Community nations agreed on 20 June 1982 to suspend their economic sanctions against Argentina on the condition that there would be no further act of force in the South Atlantic. Britain opposed the end of the sanctions, arguing that they should be maintained until Argentina formally committed itself not to renew hostilities. This plea was rejected, but the EEC ministers agreed to reimpose the sanctions if Argentina violated the ceasefire. Military sanctions were maintained.

The US lifted its economic sanctions on 12 July 1982. President Reagan announced that the decision had been reached after a 'thorough review of the situation in the South Atlantic following the cessation of hostilities.' Reagan asserted that it was 'important now for all parties involved in the recent conflict to put the past behind us, and to work for friendship and cooperation.'[60] A ban on sales of military equipment was left in effect.

The ending of the US sanctions permitted Argentina to obtain new credits and guarantees from the Export-Import Bank and new guarantees from the Commodity Credit Corporation. The US hoped that removing the sanctions would help to restore good ties with Argentina and its Latin American supporters.

It was not until 14 September 1982 that Argentina and Britain ended their mutual financial sanctions. The agreement between the two countries did not affect sanctions on trade and commerce. While Britain favored the lifting of the trade embargo, Argentina would agree only on the financial sanctions, because Britain had made no concessions on the future of the Falklands. As part of the agreement the freeze on financial transactions was lifted, and Argentina consented to restore its relationship with British banks to that which had existed prior to the beginning of the conflict.

Assessment of sanctions against Argentina

The unanimity, rapidity, and sweeping nature of the sanctions imposed by the EEC, as well as the persistent efforts to make them as leakproof as possible, presented a striking contrast to the slow, incoherent EEC responses to the hostage crisis in Iran and to the Soviet Union over Poland, which were poorly drawn up and badly administered.*

In assessing the impact of the sanctions, the following main points emerge:

1. *The time element* The imposition of sanctions provided precious time for the different parties to pursue a diplomatic solution. At the same time, it allowed the British government time to prepare its military invasion. With the Falklands nearly 8,000 miles (13,000 kilometers) distant from Britain, the naval task force needed more than two weeks to arrive at their destination.

2. *Economic impact* There is no doubt that the multilateral sanctions imposed by Britain, the EEC, and the US had a considerable collective effect on the strained Argentine economy. On 5 July 1982 the Argentine government announced an emergency program to deal with an economy that was described by Argentine Economy Minister Juan Maria Dagnino Pastore as 'in a state of destruction without precedents.' In a speech televised nationally, Pastore stated that Argentina's financial system had deteriorated into an 'explosive situation' and warned that it would have to be restructured 'from its foundation.' Some of the measures announced were:

(a) devaluation of the peso, which currently traded at a rate of 15,600 to the US dollar, and its exchange at two different rates: a lower rate for export trade and a higher one for financial transactions such as international loans. The higher exchange

---

*A report from the European Parliament published in early April 1982 pointed out that during the hostage crisis, in spite of the sanctions imposed by the EEC against Iran, trade between the two sides actually rose by 50 per cent.

rate for financial transactions was intended to discourage the flight of dollars by undercutting the black market in dollars.*

(b) strict government controls on interest rates, imports, and currency.

According to Dagnino Pastore, the basic purpose of the emergency economic program was to stimulate an 'export offensive' that would increase Argentina's foreign exchange to help pay off its $32 billion foreign debt, one of the world's highest per capita foreign debts.

Argentina's economy, under pressure from the war and the sanctions, received another shock in May 1982, when the Soviet Union, Argentina's biggest single grain customer, buyer of nearly 70 per cent of the country's grain exports, suspended grain imports from Argentina, forcing the Argentinians to sell grain below market prices in order to earn much-needed foreign exchange.

There is no doubt that Britain's financial sanctions, especially the freeze of assets, presented substantial problems because of Argentina's huge debt. According to a *New York Times* report published on 9 April 1982, Argentina's international debt at the time stood at $32 billion, a figure more than four times higher than Iran's debt when the US declared a similar freeze on assets following the takeover of the US embassy in Tehran. Assessing the situation, a Swiss banker was quoted in the *Wall Street Journal* of 8 April 1982 as having remarked, 'The situation for Argentina is very grim because they live on credit.' A considerable amount of Argentina's debt was in the form of short-term loans that would require refinancing in the near future. In particular, Argentina needed to reschedule part of its foreign debt for the current year, which, without the British banks' cooperation, did not seem possible.

On the other hand, the impact of Argentina's suspension of all payments to British banks was somewhat mitigated. The bulk of the loans outstanding to Argentina by British banks were from international banking syndicates, which included American, European, and Japanese banks. Those banks were obliged to share repayments received from Argentina on a *pro rata* basis with the British. In this way, the British banks received about 75 per cent of the money due to them from Argentina during the freeze.[61]

*In late May 1982, and before the seizure of the Falklands, the Argentine peso traded at 12,000 to the dollar. By July, the trade rate was 22,000 pesos to the dollar and the financial rate at between 24,000 and 28,000 to the dollar.

Collectively, the sanctions imposed by the EEC quickly made Argentina's already desperate economic situation worse. The EEC took a third of all Argentine exports during the period 1975–80.[62] At the time, Argentina exported about 2 billion dollars' worth of goods annually to the Common Market. Consequently, EEC sanctions seriously impaired Argentina's earning power and weakened its ability to meet its international financial obligations. Furthermore, Argentina depended on the EEC, along with the US, for almost half of its imports. The impact of the sanctions on trade with Argentina was somewhat mitigated by the fact that the EEC countries, with the exception of Britain, had carefully exempted all trade subject to long-term contracts. This meant that normal trade in grain, beef, leather, and other goods continued through the war. Nevertheless, the London journal *The Economist* reported that the Argentine government interpreted the EEC sanctions 'as the single most harmful nonmilitary blow yet directed against Argentina.'[63]

As for the US sanctions, these came at a time when Argentine banks owed the United States over $9 billion − $5 billion of which was due for payment in the current year. (US exports amounted to nearly $2 billion each year, as compared with about $700 million of imports from Argentina, and the US Export-Import Bank provided loans of over $1 billion to Argentina, guaranteeing American exports.) Consequently, the sanctions compromised Argentina's position with US as well as international bankers, who are reluctant to lend to countries caught in grave international crises, particularly if they lack the support of the Western powers.

3. *The political dimension* On the political level, the impact of sanctions was at least threefold.

a. In terms of international economics, Britain's freeze of Argentina's assets, coming shortly after the US freeze of Iranian assets and the US threat to push Poland into default, heightened the growing politicization of the world financial markets. The move was another signal that foreign financial assets lie hostage in the hands of host governments and that those governments are ready and willing to use the weapon of the freeze to achieve political objectives. Such an atmosphere is likely to make other governments apprehensive about depositing their funds and investments in banks where political risks are perceived. They are likely to shift their operations from financial centers such as New York, London, Frankfurt, and Paris, to more neutral, secure centers such as Switzerland or Luxemburg. This could have serious implications for the economies of industrial nations which so far have been havens for international investors, particularly for the rich oil-exporting countries.

b. Central to the EEC decision to join the British sanctions against Argentina was the desire to express solidarity with a member state whose territory (albeit colonial territory) had been invaded. In this context, the EEC wanted to demonstrate its ability to act as a single entity in international affairs, and to show that European political cooperation could produce results. Although EEC unity came close to the breaking point when Italy and Ireland opted out of the embargo after thirty days, in general, EEC solidarity was effectively asserted.

c. While the US shift from neutrality to a position backing Britain had only a limited economic effect, as the bulk of Argentine–US trade was not affected by the shift, its political significance was considerable. Having failed to enlist US support, the Galtieri government counted on US neutrality to act as an impartial mediator in the conflict and was dismayed when the US sided with Britain.

4. *Psychological effect* Firm support from the European community reinforced Britain's diplomatic leverage and, at the same time, intensified the psychological pressure on Argentina. In sharp contrast to the strong support Britain received from its partners in the EEC, the Galtieri government enlisted only token public support from its partners in the Organization of American States (OAS). No Latin American country banned or restricted trade with Britain, the EEC, or the US. Nor was Argentina able to invoke the Inter-American Security Treaty, known as the Rio Pact, against Britain. This failure increased the Argentinians' sense of isolation and deepened the feelings of bitterness and frustration that stemmed originally from their military setbacks.

5. *Symbolic value* On 17 May a State Department official described the effect of the US sanctions as chiefly 'symbolic and psychological.'[64] But this symbolic effect had substantive aspects. The sanctions seemed to be a verdict of guilty handed down against Argentina by the American and Western European judges; consequently, they hampered Argentina's efforts to enlist support from pro-Western governments, and cast doubt in the international community on the morality of Galtieri's policies in the Falklands.

6. *Extraterritoriality issue* The British freeze was extended to include Argentinian assets in foreign-owned banks in Britain. However, in contrast to the US freeze of Iranian assets, the British government made no effort to extend the measure extraterritorially; overseas branches

and subsidiaries of British banks were not affected. Those banks were permitted to transfer Argentine funds to non-British third parties. This policy limited the impact of the financial sanctions.

7. *Rebound effect on sanctioners* The application of sanctions was not cost-free to the sanctioners, though they did not suffer as much as those against whom the sanctions were directed. In West Germany, Argentina's largest European trading partner, the loss of trade was economically felt,[65] while in Italy, the souring of relations with Argentina was experienced politically. For Ireland, the sanctions posed a political problem because of Ireland's neutral status. The socialist governments of France and Greece found it embarrassing to be called to defend the vestiges of Britain's colonial past, particularly since Latin America was a privileged recipient of their sympathies. The embarrassment was more severe for Greece which, in contrast to France, had no colonial Achilles' heel of its own to worry about. Furthermore, by imposing the sanctions, the EEC, as much as the United States, had allowed immediate political considerations to jeopardize long-term economic interests, thus risking the loss of lucrative markets — a possibility which, luckily enough for them, failed to materialize.

Conclusion to case study

From the beginning, Britain made it clear that its aims were limited to getting Argentina off the Falklands and restoring the British administration. Consequently, the main aim of the sanctions in the initial stage was to gain time and increase nonmilitary pressure on Argentina in hopes of forestalling hostilities in the South Atlantic. Following the commencement of armed hostilities, sanctions were maintained to intensify pressure on the weak Argentinian economy. However, at no time was there any illusion on the sanctioners' part that the sanctions in themselves would force Argentina to withdraw its military forces. Therefore, in terms of their limited objective, one can maintain that sanctions were by and large effective.

That sanctions did have impact had been demonstrated during the ministerial conference of the General Agreement on Tariffs and Trade held in Brussels in November 1982. At that meeting, the Argentine government made strong, though unsuccessful, efforts to have a new interpretation placed on Article 21 of the GATT. The article, called 'security exceptions', states that nothing in the GATT prevents a signatory from taking action to protect its security interests. The article allows a nation to abandon the normal trading disciplines when it feels its own security interests are at stake. It is this clause which is used to justify actions like the economic sanctions of Argentina organized by Britain during the Falklands crisis. Argentina was seeking to have stricter procedural guidelines laid down for the application of Article 21 which would cover matters such as taking regard of the interest of third parties and using available consultation procedures. Had sanctions been totally ineffective, the Argentine government would not have bothered to seek such a security switch. It is instructive to compare Argentina's efforts with those of Italy following the imposition of the League's sanctions in 1936 (see page 70).

4　Unilateral Sanctions: One-State Coercive Actions

International law and custom give every sovereign state the right to decide with whom it will or will not trade. States often use this right in pursuing their foreign policies. At times, a sanctioner or a boycotting country may attempt to extend its so-called 'primary' boycott to second or third parties. A nation may avoid trading with another (the 'secondary' boycott) in order not to offend a sanctioner with which it has strong diplomatic or economic ties.

Major powers enjoy not only the ability to impose sanctions, but the power to break them as well. For example, when the Soviet Union imposed trade restrictions against Yugoslavia, the United States and Western Europe went to Yugoslavia's aid. Similarly, ever since the United States imposed its trade boycott on Cuba, the Soviet Union has subsidized the Castro regime to keep it economically viable.

Although the following discussion will focus on the two superpowers' use of economic power to gain political leverage, other states, too, have attempted, at times successfully, to do the same.

Soviet economic coercion practices

The Soviet Union has often used its economic power, particularly foreign aid, to promote its foreign policy. Following the 1917 Bolshevik Revolution, the Soviet government exercised strict controls over a limited amount of foreign trade.[1] At the end of World War II the Soviet Union did not ratify the Bretton Woods Agreements that established the postwar international financial order.[2]

One of the most celebrated cases of Soviet economic coercion occurred in 1948 when Yugoslavia attempted to assert its independence from the Soviet bloc. Moscow placed the Yugoslavians under gradually increasing economic pressure by recalling Soviet technical experts, by reneging on a loan agreement, and finally by cutting off all trade and aid.[3] The other Communist states in Eastern Europe followed suit.[4] At the time, more than half of Yugoslavia's trade was conducted with the Communist countries, and it depended on them completely for technical assistance and credits.[5] But despite Yugoslavia's economic dependence on the Soviet Union, and although the economic rupture certainly did hurt, the Yugoslavian government was nevertheless able to defy its powerful opponent, because others, particularly Western countries, were willing to provide alternative trade outlets and economic aid. To cite other cases: As a result of a dispute over a Soviet deserter, the Soviet Union in 1954 switched its large wool purchases from Australia to South Africa.[6] When in June 1960 Albania openly backed Peking against Moscow, the Soviet Union cancelled all economic aid to Albania and by the end of 1961 all trade relations had come to an end. Albania, a weak, very poor nation, 'was highly dependent economically on the USSR and hence vulnerable to economic pressure.'[7] Consequently, Albania 'suffered acute economic distress' and 'had to cut back her industrialization program.'[8] And the dispute between the Soviet Union and China led Moscow to abruptly cut off economic aid and to withdraw Soviet technical experts in mid-1960.[9]

The Soviet Union also uses economic and military aid to the Third World to attempt to win it over to Communism and to protect the Communist parties operating there.[10] On several occasions after the Suez crisis the Soviet Union complained to Egypt about the harsh treatment of Egyptian Communists, resulting in the deterioration of relations between the two countries.[11] In 1963 Soviet economic and military aid to Algeria was provided both as an incentive for Algerian president Ben Bella to allow a number of Algerian Communists to participate in his regime and as an encouragement to nationalize a sizable portion of Algeria's agricultural land and industry.[12] Considerable economic loans to Egypt and Algeria seemed also to have been aimed at gaining the USSR admission to the second Bandung Conference of Afro-Asian states, which was scheduled to be held in Algeria in 1965. To block Soviet admission to the conference, Communist China offered loans of its own.[13]

American economic coercion practices

The role of economic coercion in American foreign policy-making dates back to the war of 1812, when the United States resorted to economic sanctions to bring pressure to bear on Britain.[14] In contrast to Western Europe, Japan, China, and even the Soviet Union, the United States has had a strong proclivity to use economic measures as instruments of foreign policy due to self-sufficiency and monopolistic powers. Francis A. Beer's book *Peace Against War* (1981) describes some practices of economic coercive diplomacy employed by the United States during World War II:

> The United States in July 1940 placed an embargo on 'aviation fuel and topgrade scrap iron' to Japan. In December the United States began 'unobtrusive selective licensing of . . . exports to Japan.' In June there were more 'unobtrusive U.S. embargoes.' In July the United States froze Japanese economic assets. These U.S. actions helped precipitate the Japanese attack on Pearl Harbor.[15]

In 1951 the Battle Act, or Mutual Defense Assistance Control Act restricted export to the Eastern bloc — from third-party countries as well as from the United States — of items which incorporated American components or American know-how.[16] In this legislation, Congress stipulated that the President of the United States may not give any economic, financial or military aid to any nation which did not cooperate in specified ways with the United States in its trade discrimination against 'the Union of Soviet Socialist Republics and all countries under its domination.'[17] Since the United States's aid in the early 1950s to Western Europe was several times greater than the turnover of East-West trade, this law was of crucial importance for West European governments. It is still in force and is used in relations with those underdeveloped nations that receive United States foreign aid.[18]

Another form of economic leverage used by the United States is the most-favored-nation (MFN) trade status it awards to certain countries. A much-publicized example was the attempt of Senator Henry Jackson to link American trade with the Soviet Union to the loosening of Soviet restrictions on Jewish emigration to Israel. The Trade Reform Act of 1974 was finally approved following a compromise that made MFN status for Communist countries conditional upon free emigration, but permitted the President under certain conditions to waive this requirement for up to eighteen months. Any extension beyond that period was to be authorized by concurrent resolutions passed by both houses of Congress.[19] As a reprisal measure aimed at the members of the Organization of Petroleum Exporting Countries (OPEC), an additional provision denied duty-free treatment (for eligible products) to those states withholding supplies of vital materials or, through monopolistic pricing, 'unreasonably' raising the price of a given commodity.[20]

The history of American attempts to 'regulate' exports to the socialist nations for political reasons is now more than a quarter of a century old. The first decisions to use the embargo as a weapon in the cold war were made in the United States in the second half of 1947. Since then, most nonsocialist nations have been involved, to a greater or lesser degree, in politically motivated trade discrimination against socialist countries.[21] But in its trade with Cuba, the Communist countries of Indochina, and mainland China, the United States's strategic embargo policy reflected the economic cold-warfare view in its most extreme form; the ban on United States exports to these countries (though not to the rest of the Communist bloc) was a total one. Since the governments of these countries were regarded as being irreversibly opposed to the United States, all exports to them were necessarily 'strategic exports.' Consequently, the United States implemented a complete trade embargo against these countries. Only recently did it ease trade restrictions with China.

To this day, the United States continues its unilateral trade embargo against Cuba. This embargo has been in effect since 1962, since approximately three years after Fidel Castro assumed power. Acting under the authority of Section 620(A) of the Foreign Assistance Act of 1961, President Kennedy in February 1962 ordered a ban on almost all trade with Cuba 'to deprive Cuba of an annual income of about $35 million, roughly a third of her dollar income from non-Communist countries.'[22] His proclamation barred all trade with Cuba as well as the importation of Cuban goods 'no matter how they might be routed toward the United States.'[23] Premier Castro described the trade ban as an 'attempt to create poverty, shortage of materials and a series of difficulties for the Cuban people in order to force them to their knees by despicable tactics.'[24] The United States followed up its embargo on trade with the Cuban regime, and only recently did it ease the embargo by allowing foreign affiliates of American companies to do business with Cuba, though special licenses for such trade are still required.

Washington still imposes a strict embargo against commercial relations with the countries of Indochina. Trade sanctions have been in effect for years against North Korea and North Vietnam; they were extended to South Vietnam and Cambodia when their pro-Western governments fell. The United States rejected all signals from the Vietnamese Communists, who are interested in exploiting their rich agricultural areas and timber in the South and coal in the North, and in investigating the possibility of producing offshore oil. The State Department was opposed to ending the embargo, and in mid-November 1975 President Ford reinforced that stand by notifying Congressional leaders that the United States had removed Vietnam and Cambodia from the list of nations eligible for special tariff concessions. In mid-May 1975, acting under the Export Administration Act of 1969 which allowed the use of export controls to further American foreign policy, the administration placed South Vietnam and Cambodia under its strictest limits – called Category Z. This combination of restrictions, which were at the time already in effect for North Vietnam and North Korea, made it illegal for American businessmen to buy Vietnamese or Cambodian goods or to export their own products to those countries, even through a neutral middleman. The reasons for the United States embargo were, of course, political and had little to do with the amount or kind of trade with Indochina.

For more than two decades a plenary embargo on American trade with Communist China was maintained. The embargo had teeth because under the Battle Act of 1951, the President of the United States was empowered to cut off American aid to any country trading with China.[25]

By revisions to the Export Administration Regulations, effective 16 February 1978, the United States imposed a virtually total embargo on exports and reexports of commodities and technical data of US origin for use by or for military or police entities in the Republic of South Africa or in Namibia. The regulations were intended to further US foreign policy regarding the preservation of human rights by denying the South African and Namibian military access to such commodities and technical data, and were also intended to strengthen UN Security Council Resolutions Nos. 181 and 182 of 1963 and Resolution No. 418 of 1977 regarding arms and munitions exports to South Africa.

In its economic battles the United States enjoys the benefit of another economic weapon, foreign aid,[26] which is disbursed as direct grants or in the form of loans (usually tied to purchases in the United States with payment demanded as the economic condition of the recipients improves). Since World War II, the foreign-aid program has gained importance, although its purpose has radically changed since its inception. The Marshall Plan was clearly intended to help Europe recover from the devastating effects of World War II. Economic and military assistance in the early 1950s for the underdeveloped and developing countries was aimed at helping those countries build their economies and political systems, thus enabling pro-Western regimes to stifle Communist tendencies or temptations. Other motivations for giving aid were commercial, geopolitical, and occasionally altruistic. But with time and the cold war, economic aid came to be employed as an instrument of foreign policy designed to help and keep allies and friends, to tempt and buy neutrals, and also to pressure both of these, as well as adversaries, by attaching strings to the aid packages. Thomas L. Brewer in *American Foreign Policy* (1980) outlines some of the political objectives of US economic assistance:

> The United States has also used economic aid to try to achieve specific political objectives in individual cases — sometimes to solicit support for a particular diplomatic initiative, sometimes to strengthen or weaken a particular government's internal political position, sometimes to try to change a government's internal or foreign policies.[27]

Emerging nations, trying to assert their independence, reacted with increasing hostility. Slogans such as 'Yankee Go Home' scrawled on the walls of buildings in those countries made the average American citizen, who had thus far accepted foreign aid as something desirable — an act of unselfish charity consistent with Christian ethics — feel uneasy. Growing popular doubts about the benefits of foreign aid caused the US Congress to decrease it, though not to go so far as to abolish it.

United States economic aid was not used as an economic weapon against independent states alone, but also against international organizations and agencies. For example, the United States used this aspect of its foreign diplomacy on the United Nations and its agencies to influence it to revise its practices and general policies. In October 1971 the Senate defeated the 1971 Foreign Aid Bill. In part, the vote came in reaction to a rebuff suffered by the US in the China vote one week before at the United Nations.[28] The White House, in an effort to change the course of the action, had announced that the China vote could adversely affect US support for the United Nations. On another occasion, the United States withdrew its financial aid from the International Labor Organization (ILO) as a result of what Washington termed 'the politicizing of the ILO.' However, it later rejoined the organization.

Concentrated in the Agency for International Development (AID), a semiautonomous division of the State Department, US economic and technical assistance became one of the most potent instruments of

American foreign policy. At times, it was used to penalize recipients of aid who expropriated American property, such as Argentina. In a statement issued in January 1972 President Nixon announced that the United States would not extend new bilateral economic assistance, and would oppose multilateral loans, to nations expropriating American interests without taking 'reasonable steps' toward compensation.[29] The weapon of withholding economic and technical assistance was also used against nations which discouraged private enterprise, such as Indonesia and Peru; or those which declared a state of war against friends of the United States, such as Egypt and Syria. When India invaded East Pakistan in early 1972, the United States suspended economic-aid deliveries to India. This action was explained thus by a spokesman for the Department of State: 'The United States is not making a short-term contribution to the Indian economy to make it easier for the Indian government to sustain its military effort.'[30] Or the weapon could be used against those who voted against the United States too often in the United Nations, such as the Philippines. In January 1976 the *New York Times* reported that Secretary of State Kissinger had initiated a policy of selecting for cutbacks in American economic aid those nations that had voted against the United States's position on the General Assembly's resolution to condemn Zionism. Two particular states were singled out as possible targets: Tanzania and Guyana.[31] Other targets were Third World countries that insisted on pursuing a nonalignment policy in international affairs, such as India and Egypt in the 1950s, or allies who pursued policies which were not consistent with American views. For example, in an effort to force Israel out of the Sinai following the Suez crisis of 1956, Eisenhower 'publicly avowed his intention of cutting off U.S. assistance to Israel as well as eliminating tax loopholes for private American contributors to Israel's welfare. On 1 March 1957 the Israelis gave way and withdrew.'[32] Britain, which since World War II had received an enormous amount of American financial aid, was in February 1964 deprived of assistance 'as a rebuke for persisting in trading with Cuba against the wishes of a United States Congress.'[33] Also, in a study of the American-Israeli relations between 1973–5, Mitchell Cohen found that 'inducements, as opposed to overt linkages and coercion as a mode of economic leverage proved most effective in American-Israeli relations between 1973 and 1975.'[34] Aid was at times given as a reward for nations that followed American political leads. In 1974, for example, the Nixon administration asked Congress for hundreds of millions of dollars in economic assistance appropriations for Israel, Syria,

Jordan, and Egypt, following negotiations on disengagements between Syrian and Israeli troops.[35] In 1978 and 1979 the Carter administration used the promise of economic assistance to Israel as an inducement to obtain Israel's endorsement of a peace treaty with Egypt.[36]

The United States has also used economic aid to strengthen pro-Western regimes faced with economic crises: the Dominican Republic and Colombia in 1962, Brazil in 1964, Iran in 1967.[37] It used its enormous trading power to strike better bargains with its trading partners. While Nixon imposed a temporary embargo on grain exports to the Soviet Union 'to negotiate Soviet acceptance of certain rules that were to govern future purchases,'[38] Ford imposed, in 1975, a three-month embargo on wheat sales to the Soviet Union 'in order to muster bargaining power for the negotiation of a grain purchase agreement with that country.'[39]

The United States also uses its enormous economic power to influence other nations through the international financial institutions to which it contributes. For example, in 1968 when Peru expropriated the International Petroleum Corporation (IPC), owned jointly by Standard Oil and Shell, the economic assistance that Peru had been receiving from a number of international financial institutions was cut off. Direct economic sanctions were not invoked, as Peru held a number of American firms hostage by holding the threat of expropriation over their heads. Consequently, as Jessica P. Einhorn puts it in her book *Expropriation Politics* (1974), 'Peru was pushed, but never strangled,' by US economic pressure.[40] In response, the Peruvian government expropriated a number of American firms.[41]

 The Carter administration extended the range of issues on which it was ready to impose economic sanctions, both against countries found in violation of human rights and against countries perceived to support international terrorism. Thus it reflected the persistent tendency to resort to economic sanctions. But it was the administration's grain embargo against the Soviet Union which received the most attention and interest.

Case study: the US grain embargo

The stage for a major economic diplomacy effort by the Carter administration against the Soviet Union had been set long before Jimmy Carter took office as the thirty-ninth President of the United States.

In 1945, the Export-Import Bank Act restricted the US Export-Import Bank from participating in financing exports to the Soviet Union. This was followed in 1949 by the Export Control Act, which imposed strict restrictions on sales to the Soviet Union and the Communist bloc. Under this act, for example, zipper sales were banned (apparently on the premise that you can't aim a rifle while holding up your pants). In 1969, brassières intended for East Germany were considered a 'strategic' export.

But it was the Trade Reform Act of 1974 which clearly linked international economic relationships to noneconomic considerations. The sale of any controlled commodities that might be turned to 'strategic' advantage by the Soviet Union – from motor vehicles to oil-drilling equipment – came to require by US law special federal licenses.

When Carter took office in 1977 a heated debate arose regarding US economic policy toward the Soviet Union. On one end of the spectrum were the hardliners who argued that the United States should deny the Russians not only items of potential military value but also anything that could significantly improve the Soviet Union's economic efficiency and growth. On the other end were those who believed that such 'destructionist' tactics would backfire both diplomatically and politically. In the middle were those who called for short-term tightening up on sales to the Soviets, but wished to preserve a framework for long-term trade if US-Soviet relations improved.

In the fall of 1978, Harvard political scientist Samuel P. Huntington urged that President Carter regulate US trade with the Soviet Union according to the degree of Soviet cooperation on matters of human rights and military adventurism. 'Economc detente and military adventurism cannot go hand-in-hand for long,' Huntington affirmed. 'At some point the Soviets will have to make a choice.'[42] Huntington was sensitive to the risks involved in a general embargo:

> A strategy of pure denial could deprive the United States of an opportunity to use its economic advantages either to compete more effectively with the Soviet Union or to induce desirable Soviet action on matters of common interest.[43]

Consequently, his proposal is to unite politics and economics:

> What is needed instead is a new approach of conditioned flexibility in which changes in the scope and character of U.S.-Soviet economic

relations are linked to and conditioned by progress in the achievement of U.S. political and security objectives.[44]

Epigrammatically, Huntington concludes that 'if war is too important to be left to the generals, surely commerce is, in this context, too salient to be left to bankers and businessmen.'[45]

A proposed sale of sophisticated American oil technology to the Soviet Union raised the question whether such a sale could boost Soviet oil production, thus improving the Soviets' strategic position. The proposed transaction involved the sale by Dresser Industries of Dallas of a $144 million plant for manufacturing oil-drilling bits. The issue was temporarily settled when the Carter administration confirmed the sale in mid-September 1977. However, the argument raised the two issues that determine when economic diplomacy can prove effective. First, the volume of trade between the sanctioner and the target at the time sanctions are contemplated: a relatively large volume of exports from the sanctioner to the target is necessary for sanctions to have an appreciable effect. Second, it is necessary to enlist the full cooperation of other suppliers in the decision to impose economic sanctions or a commodity embargo. An overriding importance is attached to getting all suppliers to act in unison, so as to deny the target alternative-supply options and at the same time to insure that competitors will refrain from moving in to take over projects that the sanctioner's companies have had to abandon.

The opportunity to test the power of economic coercion materialized in late 1979 when the Soviet Union intervened in Afghanistan. Feeling the need for a sharp response short of military action, President Carter moved to impose three forms of economic and financial sanctions on the Soviet Union:

1. a US grain embargo;
2. restrictions of high-technology sales; and
3. the curtailment of trade credits and guarantees.

Of these three measures, the grain embargo proved to be the most controversial and most complicated to pursue at home and abroad, because of its adverse effect on the domestic economies of the United States and its allies joining the embargo. Back in 1976 when the Ford administration threatened to halt grain shipments to the Soviet Union as a result of Soviet involvement in the Angolan civil war, American farmers, who stood to lose most, succeeded in aborting the idea.

Objectives of the grain embargo

In a nationally televised address on 4 January 1980 President Carter denounced the Soviet military intervention in Afghanistan, describing it as
'an extremely serious threat to peace' and 'a callous violation of international law and the United Nations Charter.'[46] Since no action could
be taken by the Security Council due to the Soviets' veto power, the
President declared that trade with the Soviet Union 'will be severely restricted' to express America's 'deep concern.' In pursuing this policy
Carter announced the following measures:

> I have decided to halt or to reduce exports to the Soviet Union in
> three areas that are particularly important to them. These new poli-
> cies are being and will be coordinated with those of our allies.
> – I have directed that no high technology or other strategic items
> will be licensed for sale to the Soviet Union until further notice,
> while we revise our licensing policy.
> – Fishing privileges for the Soviet Union in United States waters
> will be severely curtailed.
> – The 17 million tons of grain ordered by the Soviet Union in ex-
> cess of that amount which we are committed to sell will not be de-
> livered. This grain was not intended for human consumption but was
> to be used for building up Soviet livestock herds.
> I am determined to minimize any adverse impact on the Ameri-
> can farmer from this action. The undelivered grain will be removed
> from the market through storage and price support programs and
> through purchases at market prices. We will also increase amounts of
> grain devoted to the alleviation of hunger in poor countries and we'll
> have a massive increase of the use of grain for gasohol production
> here at home.
> After consultation with other principal grain exporting nations, I
> am confident that they will not replace these quantities of grain by
> additional shipments on their part to the Soviet Union.
> These actions will require some sacrifice on the part of all Ameri-
> cans, but there is absolutely no doubt that these actions are in the
> interest of world peace and in the interest of the security of our own
> nation, and are also compatible with actions being taken by our own
> major trading partners and others who share our deep concern about
> this new Soviet threat to world stability.[47]

Analysis of President Carter's speech allows us to identify a number of policy goals that the administration hoped to achieve:

First, to protest against the Soviet invasion of Afghanistan and express 'deep concern' over Soviet military intervention against an independent, sovereign, nonaligned country.

Second, to express solidarity with the Afghani people in their struggle against the Soviet occupation and to let them know that they do not stand alone.

Third, to demonstrate to the Soviet Union that such actions are not cost-free. The American administration wanted to signal to the Soviets that it would not do business as usual as long as the Soviet leaders continued to embark on aggressive policies and that it was willing to disrupt US-Soviet trade, even if that meant a heavy economic burden, to make that point.

Fourth, to put pressure on the Soviet Union to withdraw from Afghanistan and restore the country's independence.

Fifth, to deter aggression (represented by the Soviet attempt to crush a small independent country) by retaliating with countermeasures. As Carter said, 'History teaches perhaps very few clear lessons. But surely one such lesson learned by the world at great cost is that aggression unopposed becomes a contagious disease.'[48]

Sixth, to protect US national security, which had been threatened by the Soviet move due to Afghanistan's strategic importance. In the analysis of Carter, 'A Soviet-occupied Afghanistan threatens both Iran and Pakistan and is a steppingstone to possible control over much of the world's oil resources.'[49] Consequently, by imposing the embargo Carter was attempting to prevent the Soviet army from moving westward towards the oilfields of the Persian Gulf. The message is clear: having exhausted all nonmilitary options, the chances are high that a similar move by the Soviet Union into another nonaligned independent nation would spark a military response from the United States.

Seventh, to preserve the peace, which was seriously threatened by the Soviet actions. As Carter declared,

this invasion is an extremely serious threat to peace — because of the threat of further Soviet expansion into neighboring countries in Southwest Asia, and also because such an aggressive military policy is unsettling to other people throughout the world.[50]

Eighth, to take a step, short of military intervention, that would serve notice on the Soviet Union that its aggressive policies would not be tolerated by the United States. A more coercive step would have meant many more sacrifices on the part of the American people. Carter did not want the Soviets to construe his soft handling of Iran as the norm and thus conclude that America had weakened and lost the initiative. Therefore, by taking a new get-tough stance with the Soviets, Carter hoped to represent the US as strong and determined.

Ninth, to focus world attention, which had thus far been absorbed by the two months' ordeal of the fifty hostages in Iran, on what the Carter administration considered a 'more important and potentially far more dangerous confrontation between the United States and the Soviet Union.'[51]

Tenth, to incite the world's anger and rally other nations around the United States, causing them to look to the US for guidance and inspiration and thus to assert the leadership role of the United States in world affairs. The move aimed to reassert to the world community America's commitment to peaceful norms of international behavior.

It is important to note the Carter administration's limited objectives in its embargo decision. No one was under any illusion that the embargo by itself would lead to Soviet withdrawal from Afghanistan. As Carter told several members of Congress on 8 January, just a few days after he made his announcement to suspend grain exports:

> We anticipate that this withholding of grain to the Soviet Union will not force them to withdraw their troops from Afghanistan. . . . But we hope that we . . . let them know that they will indeed suffer now and in the future from this unwarranted invasion.[52]

Furthermore, the Carter administration was fully aware that Soviet leaders would 'view such efforts as interference with domestic affairs.'[53] and, as a result, they would downplay its effects and make sure that they would make no major policy changes on Afghanistan which could be construed as yielding to the embargo pressure.

Immediate problems facing the embargo

To become effective the embargo needed to overcome several major obstacles. Among these were the following:

First, strong resistance was expected from farmers, because the embargo would place a heavy economic burden on only one sector of the economy — agriculture. Holding 17 million tons of grain could cause a glut on the domestic market, resulting in a substantial drop in prices. With storage and interest costs rising, lower grain prices meant less income for farmers. Furthermore, storage would adversely affect the cash-flow situation. Farmers who had held their wheat crop off the market from the year before in hopes that market prices would improve feared most the implications of the embargo decision.

To mitigate potential losses to the farmer, the Carter administration purchased the embargoed wheat and expanded its grain reserve program. At the same time, the government offered to provide loans to farmers hit hard by the effects of the embargo, which was expected to reduce overall US exports from the 1979 grain crop by 8 per cent. However, the farmers were deeply concerned over loan payments they were already committed to pay. According to Dr James M. Howell, chief economist of the First National Bank of Boston, 'The 1975–78 period was one of the sharpest expansions of farmers' equipment and operations felt in the post-World War II period.'[54]

Second, the Carter administration sought to prevent a collapse of the market as a result of failure of American grain companies to meet export contracts. According to Secretary of Agriculture Bob Bergland,

> creditors who financed the exporters would have required that undelivered grain and forward contracts for delivery of grain be resold to minimize losses. The effect would have been a cascading of panic sales as creditors of local elevators and producers would have forced additional sales.[55]

To avert this collapse, the Carter administration offered to assume the contractual obligations for the undelivered grain. To make sure that the suspension of Soviet grain shipments should not alter supply and demand fundamentals, the administration removed from the market all grain destined for the Soviet Union: 'There is no more grain available for trade than there would have been had the grain been delivered.'[56]

To tighten the available supply and exert upward pressure on prices, the administration promoted sales of agricultural products to other countries such as Mexico and China, announced that it would offer part of it as food aid to some Third World nations, and earmarked another part for a stepped-up gasohol program. Furthermore, to give the industry time to adjust to the embargo decision, the administration suspended all trading in grain futures for two days — a move that had never before been necessary in peacetime.

Third, Carter sought to alleviate the economic burden on the tax-payer which had resulted from the government's efforts to offset the effects of the suspension by itself purchasing the embargoed grain, ex-panding its grain reserves, and offering subsidies to the farmers. This cost 'between $2.5 to $3.0 billion for the combined fiscal years 1980 and 1981'.[57] However, the general public stood to benefit, as lower grain prices would eventually mean lower food prices for consumers.

Fourth, there existed general skepticism whether such measures would actually harm the Soviets or force them to make any substantial foreign policy changes. Given the autonomy of the Soviet economy, the embargo was not expected by many observers to have a particularly dis-ruptive impact on the Soviet Union, nor was it expected to make the Soviet government yield on Afghanistan. By contrast, the Carter admin-istration judged that the grain embargo would put significant pressure on the Soviet Union, which had depended on American shipments to make up for previous dismal grain harvests. In the words of Bob Bergland:

> These actions could not have come at a worse time for the Soviet Union. The Soviet agricultural plant is particularly vulnerable to weather-related caprices, and this last year's grain crop was an es-pecially disappointing 179 million tons. That is 58 million tons be-low the previous year's record, and 48 million tons below what their plans called for.
>
> The Soviets have been depending on the United States for two-thirds of their grain imports. A grain suspension, together with a cut-off of high-technology imports needed for industrial production, and curtailed fish supplies, is likely to spell more difficulty for an already troubled domestic situation.[58]

Bergland's optimism was based on a number of factors. Among those were (a) dry weather in the Soviet Union in early 1979 which reduced the Soviet grain harvest well below production targets, and (b) other major suppliers seemed reluctant to assist in meeting the Soviet grain demand. This optimism was reinforced by CIA studies which showed 'that without U.S. corn, the Kremlin's schedules for increasing meat output would be set back a decade.'[59] The CIA study pointed out 'that President Leonid Brezhnev stressed livestock production in the current Soviet Five Year Plan and that the embargo represents "a marked set-back to Brezhnev."'[60]

Fifth, there was fear that the embargo might jeopardize the US's trade position with other customers, labeling it as an unreliable supplier of foodstuffs and eventually causing it to lose important markets. Customers relying on the United States for grain supplies would be aware that the US was willing to use its food weapon for political purposes leading them to seek to reduce any vulnerability which could result from depending on supplies from the United States. 'What we term linkage, or "conditioned flexibility," the Soviet leaders interpret as questionable reliability,' wrote William Verity in the *New York Times* in early January 1979.[61] In a similar vein, economist Sung Won Son told *Time* magazine a year later, 'Some countries will get the message through to the Soviets that they, not the U.S., are reliable suppliers. Then the U.S. will get only residual sales.'[62] When President Nixon imposed cutbacks on exports of soya beans to Europe and Japan in 1973, and President Ford in 1975 imposed a temporary halt of further grain sales to the Soviet Union and Poland, Brazil had exploited the embargoes to win a larger share of the world soya bean trade. There were fears that this time Argentina might imitate Brazil, and establish itself as a reliable major supplier by increasing its grain exports at the expense of the United States.

Sixth, the embargo decision had political ramifications for Carter's reelection campaign, because it represented a drastic change from his earlier views. In the 1976 primaries Carter consistently promised farmers he would never embargo grain unless the nation's security demanded it. He had said in 1976, 'The singling out of food as a bargaining weapon is something that I would not do. If we want to put economic pressure on another nation under any circumstances . . . I would not single out food.'[63]

The embargo move posed the greatest political problems in farm states, particularly in Iowa, where Carter faced a crucial challenge from his rivals in the state's Democratic presidential caucuses scheduled for 21 January 1980. Senator Edward Kennedy, Carter's main opponent, was quick to capitalize on this issue. He made a number of statements accusing Carter of 'lurching from crisis to crisis,' maintaining that he opposed the embargo because 'it's going to hurt the American farmer and taxpayer more than the Soviet aggressor.'[64] Other Democratic and Republican rivals denounced the embargo as 'unfair' and 'ineffective.' Carter's advisors feared that these criticisms would soon be translated into opposition votes in the Iowa caucuses and in early primary elections.

On the international front, Carter sought to enlist the support of all other grain suppliers so that they would not make up for the Soviets' loss of American grain. Representatives from Canada, Argentina, Australia, and the European Community, the world's major grain-exporting nations, met in Washington in the second week of January 1980. An official joint statement issued after the meeting stated that they agreed (though with varying degrees of enthusiasm) that their governments 'would not directly or indirectly replace the grain that would have been shipped to the Soviet Union prior to the actions announced by President Carter.' Argentina, a major grain exporter which had earlier indicated that it would not go along with the United States, agreed not to 'take trade advantages' from the embargo or to shift markets. However, none of those major grain exporters agreed to cancel any existing contracts.

The impact of the grain embargo

The US grain embargo proved to be a classic example of a sanction in which the cost to the target country was much less than the cost to the sanctioner. This resulted from a number of complex, interrelated factors. The following is a concise assessment of the embargo's impact.

First, the full economic cost of the embargo to the United States is hard to measure. Nevertheless, agriculture economists have estimated these costs as including the following:

Government purchases of grain originally intended for the Soviet Union at a cost of $2.5 billion.

Restrictions on this year's production, with the Government required to pay farmers more than $2 billion to induce them to divert cropland from cultivation of grain crops.

A loss of about $2.5 billion in returns on foreign trade, in addition to whatever reduction may result from lower prices that other overseas customers may pay.

Additional tax costs if lower farm prices require greater subsidies as a result of programs that guarantee producers at least $2.20 a bushel for corn and $3.40 for wheat. A bill passed by the Senate would increase those guarantees to farmers to $2.35 for corn and $3.60 for wheat. Farm prices had been generally above current. guarantees before President Carter delivered his jolt to the grain trade, but many recent quotations have been below the Government targets.

The impact on farm income if grain prices remain depressed, in addition to the cost of heavy machinery acquired to cultivate larger acreages than they will be planting.

The impact on suppliers of machinery, seeds and fertilizer as a result of reduced needs by farmers.

A long-term reduction of Soviet demand for grain if this year's cutoff results in a reduction of Soviet livestock herds.

On the other hand, the economists said, although there is likely to be little immediate impact on consumer prices, livestock herds could be increased and meat prices reduced if grain prices continue at currently depressed levels.[65]

Furthermore, the immediate impact of the grain-suspension announcement was to send grain prices plunging on the commodities market. Government purchases of surplus grain failed to alleviate the negative impact on prices, as the grain held by the federal agency was viewed as a superabundance of the commodity, which itself had a depressing effect on prices.

Second, the embargo 'graphically illustrated American agriculture's increasing dependence on grain exports, particularly those to the Soviet Union.'[66]

Third, no reliable economic data are available to help us assess precisely the effect of the grain embargo on the Soviet Union. But in general the suspension of US shipments of grain, which the Soviet Union imported to feed livestock, had only a limited impact. The Soviets were able to mitigate the damage in a number of ways:

a. By leaning on their reserve grain stocks to maintain livestock herds.

b. By increasing their grain imports from Argentina, Canada, Australia, and the European Community, whose governments initially had agreed to cooperate with the embargo, but later found it difficult to resist the economic windfall. Grain was also imported from South Africa, India, Thailand, and Brazil.

c. By increasing meat imports, thus reducing any threats of shortages in meat supply.

d. By increasing flour imports, since flour was overlooked in the agreement between the United States and the major grain-exporting countries. This helped the Soviet Union to free an equivalent amount of cheap Soviet wheat to be fed to animals.

e. By increasing soybean meal imports from the European Community, either directly through Soviet ports or indirectly through
   Eastern Europe. The meal has five times the protein value of corn.
f. By reducing grain shipments to the Eastern bloc, which, to make
   up the deficiency, increased its imports from the major grain-
   importing countries, particularly the United States.
g. By organizing leakage of the embargo by filtering grain to the
   Soviet Union through the manipulation of export destinations.
   Shipments leaving for one port would end up at another, either a
   Soviet or an Eastern-bloc port.

However, though the Soviet Union was able to circumvent the grain
embargo and obtain supplies from other sources, it did so at a cost. It
was being charged up to 20 per cent above American prices by other
suppliers such as Argentina and Canada. In addition, it had to cope with
severe shipping difficulties.

The grain embargo also stimulated the Soviet Union to increase its
own grain output by again attempting to achieve self-sufficiency in ani-
mal feeds, by trying to bring very marginal land into production.[67]
This effort had been abandoned in 1975 when the Soviets negotiated
the grain agreement with the United States and decided to rely instead
on American imports. But the embargo put a strain on the Soviets, forcing them to attempt to be more self-sufficient.

Fourth, the embargo created divisiveness within the imposing powers,
causing a rift between the United States and its allies. It accelerated the
gradual secession of Europe from the US-dominated Atlantic Alliance.
Europe, seeing its political and economic interests as separate from
those of the United States, declined to follow the American lead, particularly with weak leadership in Washington. Carter's frequent changes
of mind made US allies hesitate to follow a policy initiative which might
be abandoned after a short while. The Europeans feared that, at their
expense, Carter's efforts at sanctions were aimed more at getting himself reelected and at rallying support in the Democratic primaries than
at altering the Soviets' behavior.[68] Moreover, they saw the need to maintain good trade relations with the Soviet Union as a means of pursuing
détente.

Fifth, the practice of manipulating trade for political ends sent nervous tremors through the world's multinational banks and corporations,
as it brought uncertainty to all trade and financial dealings. The fear existed that the Soviet Union might renege in making paymens on its loans.

Sixth, the embargo consolidated the US's reputation as an unreliable supplier. As a former Assistant Secretary of Commerce for Trade, Frank A. Weil, asserted in an interview in the *New York Times* on 27 January 1980:

> The essence of a businessman's philosophy is grounded on three words: Predictability, dependability, and consistency . . . . Every time we reach for the on-off switch, we are doing grave damage to our dependability, predictability and consistency.[69]

Seventh, the embargo dispelled the illusion about 'food power' that had been circulating for a while in the United States.[70] Originally the idea had been to initiate a policy of selective grain embargoes against OPEC countries; 'A Bushel for a Barrel, or 'Cheaper Crude or No More Food,' was the theme. The lessons learned from the grain embargo against the Soviet Union were: (1) that OPEC would have little difficulty purchasing food indirectly from other grain-exporting countries, and (2) the limitations of imposing unilateral food embargoes against the Soviet Union.

Factors that weakened the embargo's effectiveness

First, the grain embargo was imposed 'quite suddenly,' and 'with little preparation'; consequently, there were no detailed plans or organization ready to carry it out effectively and speedily.

Second, the Carter administration failed to coordinate its embargo policy with other major grain exporters prior to the announcement of the decision. This left America's allies without clear signals as to where the embargo policy was heading, what was to be expected of it, and under which circumstances it was to be terminated. Given previous cases where the American administration shifted its position radically without prior warnings, those allies were reluctant to follow the American lead. Examples of this 'switch diplomacy' abound, but one salient example is Dresser Industries' contract to build a drill-bit plant in the Soviet Union. To protest against Soviet treatment of dissidents, a number of Presidential advisers urged the President to veto the sale.

July 17: The President places all American exports of oil technology to the Soviets under government control.

August 9: The Commerce Department (reportedly with the

President's blessing) approves Dresser's export license, enabling the company to go ahead with the sale.

August 25: A special review panel convened at the request of the Defense Secretary advises against the 'technology transfer.'

August 30: The President's senior advisers vote by a 3-to-2 margin to stop the deal.

September 6: The President reaffirms the decision to allow the sale.[71]

Relations between the United States and the European states were already exhibiting strains, as the Europeans had come to perceive the United States 'as only a first among equals, rather than as a superpower-architect of Western policy.'[72] Changing economic conditions, reflected in increased trade between Western Europe and the Soviet Union, only complicated the matter.

Third, the Carter administration underrated Argentina's importance in the world grain market. When Argentina, whose exportable crop was enough to compensate substantially for the grain embargoes by the United States, refused to participate in the embargo, it undermined tremendously the Carter administration's efforts to enforce the embargo.

In early 1977 the Carter administration pinpointed the military government of Argentina as one of the world's chief violators of human rights. This led Argentina to end its traditional military relationship with the United States, choosing to purchase arms from France, Israel, and Czechoslovakia instead rather than submit to a State Department review of the human rights situation as required by Congress for all countries receiving US military aid.[73]

The US embargo decision seems to have given an advantage to Argentina. From the beginning Argentina indicated that it would not go along with the United States, but at the same time the Argentinian government agreed not to 'take trade advantages' from the situation or to shift markets. The United States made some attempts to enlist Argentina's aid on the embargo,[74] but failed. Argentina was hoping that if it would soften its position on the embargo, the Carter administration would soften in return its position on human rights or military aid. But the American government made it clear that the United States would not trade its human rights policy 'for cooperation on grains,' and so was not prepared to resume arms sales or mute its criticisms of human rights violations. Unable to get something tangible in return, Argentina was left with no concrete motive for supporting the embargo. Consequently, it continued its sales of grains and soybeans to the Soviet Union, as well as to third party countries such as Hungary and Poland which were buying the grain to supply the Soviet Union. In this respect, it is important to note that even if Argentina had been willing to cooperate with the American embargo, Argentine exporters were not required by law to report the destination of their shipments. As a result, the enforcement of the embargo would have been most difficult. Initially the United States

> assumed that Argentina would not be in a position to supply much of the Soviet demand because it was believed that Argentina's traditional grain customers would take most of this year's crop.
>
> But . . . it now appears that virtually all of Argentina's 12 million tons could find their way to Russia. . . . Argentina's traditional buyers are rushing to buy American grain, which is cheaper because of a drop in prices after Carter's initial announcement of the embargo.[75]

To make good on its highly profitable grain deals with the Soviet Union, Argentina exported less to its traditional customers — Chile, Peru, Spain, Italy, and Japan. But those nations did not suffer because they were able to replace Argentinian grain with the cheaper, embargoed American grain. It was belatedly recognized by the Carter administration that Argentina's refusal to participate in the embargo could make it largely ineffective.

Fourth, the Carter administration failed to control leakage. Grain kept finding its way to the Soviet Union 'through a variant of the sanctions-busting middleman who kept the Rhodesian economy afloat during the 15 years of unilaterally declared independence.'[76] A number of European merchants began to divert to the Soviet Union grain destined for Western European buyers.

Lifting the embargo

When Ronald Reagan took office in January 1981, it seemed that a new hard line towards the Soviet Union would be initiated, in which economic sanctions would play an essential role. However, despite stiff opposition, in particular from Secretary of State Alexander Haig, on 24 April Reagan issued a statement lifting the United States limitation on agricultural sales to the Soviet Union. He explained that he did so in keeping with his 1980 campaign charge that 'American farmers had been unfairly singled out to bear the burden of this ineffective national policy.' He further maintained that he waited three months, until he was certain that 'the Soviets and other nations would not mistakenly think it indicated a weakening of our position.' Reagan ended his statement by asserting:

> The United States, along with the vast majority of nations, has condemned and remains opposed to the Soviet occupation of Afghanistan and other aggressive acts around the world. We will react strongly to acts of aggression wherever they take place. There will never be a weakening of this resolve.[77]

US economic sanctions and the extraterritorial reach

In the late 1970s the use of economic sanctions as instruments of foreign policy by the United States brought to light a dimension that had seldom presented itself this forcefully before: the power of one state to reach beyond its territorial borders and assert hegemony over property, licensing rights, and technical know-how advantages held by its nationals abroad, extending in this case to the imposition of economic sanctions against a target nation through the subsidiaries of the sanctioner's multinational operations. The result was a protracted, bitter, and as yet unsettled debate over the question of legal 'sovereignty' of host countries over subsidiaries of multinational companies — a hornet's nest that, as far as economic sanctions were concerned, had been left undisturbed. The issue involved determining which has legal jurisdiction over a subsidiary or a branch of a multinational corporation: the host country or the home government.

This controversy was precipitated by two major cases: (1) the freezing of all official Iranian financial assets in the United States and in American banks abroad by the Carter administration on 14 November 1979, in its efforts to force release of the American hostages seized by Iranian radicals, and (2) the banning of exports of oil and gas equipment to the Soviet Union by the Reagan administration in response to the imposition of martial law in Poland in December 1981.

(1) The Iranian asset freeze

In the Iranian case, the United States was responding to Iran's threat to withdraw its funds from US bank accounts. These funds amounted to nearly $12 billion of assets; their withdrawal could have led to a major disruption of financial markets, bringing about a weakening of the dollar. The freeze was not, therefore, aimed so much at punishing Iran for taking the hostages as it was triggered by 'fear that a sudden withdrawal of those assets might set off a major currency and banking crisis for the United States.'[78] The blocking of assets was also, and secondarily, aimed at protecting 'the property claims of U.S. individuals and corporations against Iran.'[79]

The vulnerability of the US financial system to the threat that petro-dollars might be used as a political weapon had already stimulated a major debate in the United States. The amassing of billions of dollars by major oil-producing states following the 1973-4 quadrupling in oil prices had led those countries to seek 'safe havens' in which to invest their money. But neither US policymakers nor Middle Eastern experts expected the threat to come from Iran — a staunchly pro-American, non-Arab country that had increased its oil production during the 1973-4 Arab oil embargo to compensate for the Arabs' cut.

The Arab oil embargo was fresh in the minds of the Senate committee members investigating the impact on the American financial system of the concentration of OPEC deposits in American banks. Their main concern was that these assets might be used by Gulf states, particularly Saudi Arabia, as a political weapon to influence US foreign policy vis-à-vis Israel. At the time it was maintained that 'the really large depositors would not suddenly move against the dollar, because converting substantial amounts from dollars to nondollar denominated accounts . . . could have exchange market effects unfavorable to their holdings.'[80] Such arguments assumed rational behavior on the part of the depositors, who, it was presumed, would be prevented from withdrawing their funds for fear of having their deposits devalued — a step no 'prudent' investor would take. This led to the false assumption that deposits were immune to emotional, religious, and political pressures. It was assumed that no country would seek to disrupt foreign exchange markets at the risk of reducing the value of its foreign assets. Major financial institutions, which stood to benefit greatly from petrodollar deposits, therefore underplayed the potential threat to the financial systems and 'continued to paint a picture of a financial world populated only by prudent bankers, rational depositors, and responsible debtors.'[81] Continual Saudi assurances that they would not use their financial deposits as a political weapon helped to maintain this rosy illusion.

Abroad, the freezing of Iranian assets produced different effects. In countries that had huge US deposits there was concern over the assets' safety. The ruling hierarchy in Saudi Arabia feared that, should the Iranian scenario repeat itself in their country, they would have no access to their massive holdings in Western banks. In major western European nations, the news of the freeze was received with a reserve of hope that such nonmilitary countermeasures might help to forestall war, or at least delay military actions long enough for a political compromise to be reached. As the impasse continued, however, the Carter administration took for granted that the freeze would include US subsidiary branches in Europe. This had an added significance, for the postrevolutionary Iranian government tended to deposit its oil income in European subsidiaries of US banks, particularly in Britain, France, West Germany, and Switzerland. In an article published in *Foreign Policy* (Fall 1981), Karin Lissakers, deputy director of the State Department's Policy Planning Staff, 1979-80, judged the freeze not only to have 'violated traditional rules of national sovereignty,' but also to have challenged 'the supranational status that the Eurocurrency operations of private banks had always enjoyed.'[82]

The United States justified its actions on the grounds that 'every country has a right to legislate and exercise power over its nationals wherever they may be.'[83] Furthermore, the structure and operation of the international banking and payment systems required that all transactions of US bank subsidiaries located outside the United States be cleared through New York.[84] This procedure allowed the United States to reject the inference that it was intruding on the jurisdiction of the host governments, as payments of deposits were held not on the host governments' territories but rather in New York, which obviously falls under American jurisdiction. The European governments rejected this rationalization but did not strongly challenge it, because the case involved the sensitive issue of the American hostages. The Europeans did not want to seem unsympathetic to the American cause, nor to seem to undermine American efforts to win the release of the fifty-two hostages. Moreover, the Europeans felt uneasy about involving themselves directly in the Iranian dispute. Consequently, European capitals did not press the issue of their national sovereignty over American subsidiaries operating within their territorial boundaries in order not to antagonize the

United States, allowing subsidiary banks to argue that 'Iran's Euro-dollar deposits were subject to U.S. law rather than the law of the host country.'[85] Both parties, however, exerted great efforts to insure that a final judgment on the issue would not be reached. This strategy insured that they would not find themselves in a position where such a final ruling would cause a radical rift among them and divert the focus from the hostage issue to the issue of extraterritoriality.[86]

On 19 January 1981, as part of the agreement for the release of the American hostages, the US committed itself to 'ensure the mobility and free transfer' of all Iranian assets blocked and agreed to release them to Iran through the Algerian Central Bank as escrow agent.[87] The settlement of the hostage situation, along with the release of the Iranian assets, laid to rest the problem of extraterritoriality as related to the issue of economic sanctions. But it was not long before the conflict was vividly resurrected, when the Reagan administration imposed economic sanctions against the Soviet Union in reaction to the Polish crackdown.

In contrast to the Iranian asset freeze, where United States interests did not diverge significantly from those of its Western allies, the pipeline embargo controversy dramatically illustrates how, when the interests of the United States fail to coincide with those of its European allies, the sanctions policy carries broader international political implications. In the pipeline case, the West Europeans showed considerably more resolve to protect their rights from the American extraterritorial reach.

(2) The Siberian pipeline embargo

In response to the Polish government's declaration of martial law on 13 December 1981, and the crackdown on Solidarity, the independent trade union, President Reagan in his Christmas message delivered on 23 December 1981 declared that if the outrages in Poland did not ease, the United States could not and would not conduct 'business as usual' with Poland. In his statement, the President announced that the US would be taking immediate action (a) to suspend major elements of US economic relationships with the Polish government; (b) to halt the renewal of the Export-Import Bank's line of export credit insurance to the Polish government; (c) to suspend Polish civil aviation privileges in the US; and (d) to suspend the right of Poland's fishing fleet to operate in American waters. The President made it clear that these actions 'are not directed against the Polish people. They are a warning to the

Government of Poland that free men cannot and will not stand idly by in the face of brutal repression.'[88] The President laid a major share of the blame for the developments in Poland on the Soviet Union 'through its threats and pressures.' He announced that he had sent a letter to President Brezhnev,

> urging him to permit the restoration of basic rights in Poland as pro-vided for in the Helsinki Final Act. In it, I informed him that, if this repression continues, the United States will have no choice but to take further concrete political and economic measures affecting our relationship.[89]

Subsequently, on 29 December 1981, President Reagan declared economic sanctions against the Soviet Union for their continued 'heavy and direct responsibility for the repression in Poland.' The President an-nounced that President Brezhnev's response to his letter had made clear the Soviet Union's lack of understanding of the seriousness of US con-cern and of its own obligations under both the Helsinki Final Act and the UN Charter. As the Soviets were perceived to be the 'real instigators' of the martial law declaration, a number of retaliatory measures were taken against them. The sanctions included:

- Barring new licenses for oil and gas equipment, while honoring existing export licenses for such products;
- Suspending the issuance and renewal of export licenses for elec-tronic equipment, computers and other high-technology items;
- Postponing negotiations on a new long-term grain agreement to replace an accord that expired in September 1982;
- Requiring Soviet ships seeking permission to dock at US ports to give fourteen days' notice, instead of four days' notice;
- Suspending landing rights in the US for Aeroflot, the Soviet Air-line, which flies from Moscow to Washington twice a week;
- Closing the Soviet Purchasing Commission, the agency that nego-tiates trade deals with the US;
- Refusing to renew US-Soviet exchange agreements in the fields of energy, science and technology.

Reacting to US sanctions, the Soviet news agency Tass declared on 30 December 1981, 'The Soviet Union . . . will never allow anyone to speak the language of blackmail and *diktat* to it.' The following day, it added that the measures would backfire: 'American workers producing manufacturing equipment whose shipments have been banned will be adversely affected. . . . The U.S. reputation as an unreliable, whimsical trading partner will stick.' In addition to stepping up efforts to produce domestic equivalents of the equipment embargoed by the United States, the Soviet Union said it would reply to the US trade limitations with a concerted shift toward further substitution of non-American imports, and toward adopting a policy of buying licenses and technology to develop related industries, rather than purchasing ready-made equipment.

European reaction

In general, the European governments, though concerned about the Polish situation, refrained from giving the American measures their full support. Different perceptions of the Soviet threat and how to counter it accounted for the difference in perspectives. On basic principles – the existence of the Communist threat – there was little disagreement, but there were fundamental differences on how to contain it.

In particular, the European governments were apprehensive that the imposition of sanctions would weaken or even destroy détente – a concept in which they had come to put much more faith than the Reagan administration. They also worried that a rupture of Western economic relations with Eastern Europe would strain their economies. At the same time, they did not believe that the Soviet Union was vulnerable to economic sanctions.

Within the European countries, however, there was a wide rift over the sanctions policy. Britain, at one end of the spectrum, gave some support for the American action. The British government imposed restrictions on Soviet and Polish diplomats, reduced landing rights for the Polish national airline LOT, and imposed tougher standards for technology transfer to the Soviet Union and Eastern Europe. Although France gave assurances that French businessmen would not be allowed to undermine the American sanctions, the French government signed a major contract with Moscow in late January for a share in construction of the Siberian gas pipeline.

At the other end of the spectrum was West Germany, which opposed the imposition of sanctions and planned to go ahead with its aid and trade commitments to Poland. The German government described the imposition of martial law as essentially an internal Polish affair, 'necessary' to avert a direct Soviet invasion. Along with West Germany went Austria, Greece, and Denmark.

Extension of sanctions

One immediate impact of the US sanctions against the Soviet Union was to cast doubts over Moscow's pipeline construction schedule. Though contracts for equipment to build the pipeline had been signed in October 1981 (after six years of talks between the Soviet Union and the European governments), the rotor shafts and blades driving the gas turbines for the forty-one compressor stations along the 3,500-mile line were made by General Electric Co., a US company that was now prohibited from supplying them. The only possible substitute was the French company Alsthom-Atlantique, which could make the shafts and blades under license from General Electric. But initially neither the French government nor the giant corporation seemed willing to step in because of the political risks and industrial difficulties. However, pressure from other European governments made the French government reconsider its position.

On 18 June 1982, the Reagan administration decided to take additional measures to close this loophole and make the sanctions more effective. Using powers granted by the Export Administration Act of 1979,[90] President Reagan ruled that foreign subsidiaries of American companies, and foreign companies using American technology under license, would not be able to participate in the pipeline project. His statement read:

> I have reviewed the sanctions on the export of oil and gas equipment to the Soviet Union imposed on December 30, 1981, and have decided to extend these sanctions through adoption of new regulations to include equipment produced by subsidiaries of U.S. companies abroad, as well as equipment produced abroad under licenses issued by U.S. companies.

> The objective of the United States in imposing the sanctions has been and continues to be to advance reconciliation in Poland. Since December 30, 1981, little has changed concerning the situation in Poland; there has been no movement that would enable us to undertake positive, reciprocal measures.

> The decision taken today will, we believe, advance our objective of reconciliation in Poland.[91]

It was hoped that this measure would delay the construction of the Siberian pipeline — expected to be finished by 1984 — for up to three years, in the hope of imposing a substantial economic cost on the Soviet

Union. This was a significant step as it stretched American laws outside the territories of the United States. Companies not abiding by this law were liable, under American law, to be prohibited from receiving any goods or data from the United States and to criminal penalties up to a maximum of $100,000 per item for goods involving 'foreign policy' considerations. Nearly twenty companies were affected by the restrictions. Thirteen of these operated under licenses; the rest were subsidiaries of American companies. The US maintained that such restrictions must be honored by the European companies, as there was a clause in all contracts for the sale of American goods and know-how abroad which required foreign companies to obey American export laws when they reexport.

The Europeans were furious over the sales restriction. While *The Economist* of London conceded on 26 June 1982 that the US administration had the right to enforce its sanctions abroad, the independent *Westdeutsche Allgemeine* of Essen wrote on 23 June 1982, 'Despite . . . international commitments, Reagan has transcended national borders and interfered in the transactions of Western firms. Such interference . . . must be rejected by America's allies.' The conservative *Il Globo* of Rome saw the issue from a different perspective. In its opinion, the embargo did not warrant all the controversy it had generated. On 23 June 1982, *Il Globo* wrote, 'Western Europe will receive its Soviet gas, although somewhat later.' European governments moved to defy the American sanctions and to order their companies to honor their commitments and fulfill their contracts.

The subsidiaries' dilemma

On 22 July 1982, the French government announced that it intended to compel the French companies to fulfill their contracts for the pipeline. The government cited rulings from a high court which asserted the primacy of French law when it conflicts with foreign laws. There was also a precedent seventeen years ago when a French company applied for and got a court order to fulfill its contract with the People's Republic of China against a US embargo. On 20 August the French government invoked a decree issued by General de Gaulle in 1959 to requisition the services of a subsidiary of a US company. Under this law the directors of the subsidiary become responsible to the French government and not to the US parent company. In addition, the government threatened to invoke emergency powers if necessary to requisition the equipment. Concurrently Britain, on 2 August, gave similar instructions to British companies. Under the Protection of Trading Interests Act, passed by Parliament on 20 March 1980, it was illegal for companies based in Britain — even those relying on American technology — to comply with American sanctions.[92]

The companies were caught in the middle. If they abided by the sanctions, they would face severe penalties from the host governments. If, on the other hand, they defied the sanctions, the US parent company would face severe penalties under the US Export Administration Act. But as European commercial affairs are closely tied to government policy, the companies opted to defy the US directives and comply with their governments' orders.

The US administration retaliated against the six European firms that violated the ban on the delivery of embargoed equipment to the Soviet Union — two French, one Italian, one British, and two West German.* The initial penalties against the firms barred them from importing equipment or technology of any kind from the US. However, these measures were later revised and softened to bar the companies from receiving only US exports of oil and gas equipment and technological information.

In this context, international law is not clear as to which has primacy, domestic laws or foreign laws. The issue is further complicated by the fact that American laws also are not clear on the matter. In *Avigliano v. Sumitomo Shoji American, Inc.* an American court ruled on 9 January 1981 against the Japanese company, ordering it to obey American laws with regard to civil rights.[93] The case involved hiring senior managers for the Japanese subsidiary in the United States. An agreement between the American side and the Japanese gave the parent company the right to appoint whomever they wished. But the court overruled that contract and ordered the Japanese subsidiary in the United States to conform to American laws.

The court explained that through its incorporation in New York, Sumitomo had become an American company and thus was not a 'national or company' of Japan. The central question put to the court to answer was: 'Can a treaty provision [the 1953 Treaty of Friendship, Commerce and Navigation between the US and Japan] insulate US-incorporated subsidiaries that are fully owned by their Japanese parents from the impact on their hiring decisions of US civil rights laws?' Both

---

*Those companies were: Dresser (France) SA and Creusot Loire, both based in France, Nuovo Pignone of Italy, John Brown Engineering Co. of Britain, and AEG-Kanis and Mannesmann Anlagenbau AG, both of West Germany.

the district court and the court of appeals answered the question in the *negative*.[94] The court pointed out that in *United States v. R. P. Oldham* (1957),

> a case involving this same treaty but arising out of an antitrust viol-
> ation, it was held that an American subsidiary, incorporated in the
> United States, had no more rights or immunities than would other
> American corporations and had no standing to invoke an article of
> the Treaty as a defense to an antitrust indictment.[95]

In another case, *Linskey v. Heidelberg Eastern, Inc.* (1979), a similar issue was raised with respect to a provision in the 1951 FCN Treaty between the US and Denmark. The district court decided at the time that the Treaty did not exempt the American-incorporated subsidiary of a Danish company from liability.[96] The implication of these rulings was that since Japanese subsidiaries in the United States must obey American law, American subsidiaries in France, for example, ought to obey French laws.

However, a similar case was decided differently by the US Court of Appeals. In *Spiess v. C. Itoh & Co.* (24 April 1981),[97] the court held that FCN treaties are binding domestic law of their own. The question put to the court was: 'Does the 1953 Treaty of Friendship, Commerce and Navigation between the United States and Japan provide American subsidiaries of Japanese corporations with the absolute right to hire managerial, professional and other specialized personnel of their choice, irrespective of American law proscribing racial discrimination in employment?' Surprisingly, and in spite of precedents, the court of appeals, reversing the decision of a district court, answered this question in the *affirmative*. The court held that '[s]uch treaties are "the supreme law of the land," and supersede inconsistent state law. . . . Thus, . . . it is our duty to implement the treaty rights.' Consequently, and in view of the discrepancy between the two rulings, the issue remains to be settled by the US Supreme Court.

The European case received a setback when on 24 August 1982 a federal judge in Washington refused a request by Dresser Industries, an American company, for a temporary restraining order that would prevent the American government from penalizing the company and its French subsidiary.[98] Justice Thomas Flannery accepted the government's argument that the case 'involves a very serious area of foreign affairs' and that Dresser had not proved that it would suffer 'immediate and irreparable harm' if its sales of $2 million worth of compressors were blocked.[99] However, a technicality seemed to undermine the American case: contracts for reexport of the relevant goods were signed in October 1981, two months before the American sanctions were imposed. At that time there was no ban on the transfer of American equipment to the Soviet Union, so the clause relating to obeying American law was honored and the relevancy of that clause was terminated following the signing of the contracts. To support their case, the Europeans cited an important legal precedent: the ruling of US federal courts when the Carter administration imposed sanctions on the Soviet Union in 1979 which stated that all signed contracts should be honored and completed.

The Soviets encouraged the European companies to capitalize on this loophole to make delivery of urgently needed equipment for the early stages of construction. For its internal consumption, the Soviet press gave wide coverage to the ongoing construction of the pipeline. In a full-page report published on 19 August 1982, *Izvestia* said that 310 miles of the nearly 3,500 miles had been laid, and that work was proceeding at a rate of nine miles a day. The paper stressed that the pipeline was to be completed by the end of 1983 — with or without foreign help. In an interview with *Izvestia* on 21 August 1982, the Soviet Minister of Construction of Oil and Gas Enterprises, Boris Shcherbina, denied US reports that Washington's sanctions would delay the pipeline. 'Gas will start flowing in January 1984,' he asserted.

Realizing that there was little it could do to stop or seriously delay the construction, the US shifted its efforts to seek a firm commitment from the Europeans not to contract for a second strand of the pipeline in return for lifting the sanctions against the companies.

Pipeline sanctions repealed

Following weeks of intensive negotiations, President Reagan announced on 13 November 1982, that he was lifting sanctions against American and other foreign companies participating in the Soviet natural gas pipeline to Western Europe. The decision made it possible for US companies or their subsidiaries to resume shipments of oil and gas equipment to the Soviet Union immediately. Reagan stated that his decision was made after the US and its major allies reached 'substantial agreement' on new guidelines for tightening East-West trade policies. In language that paralleled that of the June 1982 Versailles communiqué, Reagan maintained that the US and its allies agreed 'not to engage in trade arrangements which contribute to the military or strategic advantage of the USSR or serve to preferentially aid the heavily militarized Soviet economy.'

European nations with companies affected by the sanctions – West Germany, Britain, and Italy – welcomed Reagan's reversal of policy, but reservedly. Britain announced that the European governments had made 'no concessions' in return for the 'unilateral decision' by the American administration. West German officials privately described the accord as an attempt to let Reagan abandon the sanctions without loss of face in his dispute with the allies. But the French government reacted sharply to Reagan's announcement. Upset at the American President's linking the lifting of sanctions (which it had earlier described as an 'obnoxious American problem') to the accord, France declared that it 'is not a party' to any such agreement. The initial French reaction took Washington by surprise. On 14 November 1982, in a statement expressing their displeasure, the French government openly contradicted President Reagan's statement, describing the US announcement of a new East-West trade accord as 'premature.' The statement asserted, 'Progress has been made in these talks, but no definite conclusions have been reached.' Furthermore, it reaffirmed the French position that 'a sharp distinction' must be drawn between discussions on future economic ties with the Eastern bloc and the lifting of sanctions.

The trade agreement, which was endorsed by negotiators from the US, Britain, West Germany, Italy, Japan, Canada, and the Common Market, set broad strategies for energy, credit, and technological trade policies with the Soviet Union. The US and its allies agreed to monitor Western trade and financial dealings with the Eastern bloc nations more firmly, and to work to expand the list of strategic materials banned from sale to the Soviet Union beyond military goods to include high-technology items with national-security implications. However, the accord involved no major European concessions, and the individual points only called for new studies of pending East-West trade issues; furthermore, no reference was made to earlier US demands that the Europeans commit themselves to the cancellation of plans to build a second stage of the pipeline. No mention was made of the martial law in Poland with which the sanctions had been linked initially. The only apparent new ground broken was an understanding that the European countries would neither sign nor approve new contracts to buy Soviet natural gas pending the completion of studies on the possibility of using such alternative Western sources of energy as US coal. No time limit was set for the preparation of these studies, but they were expected to be ready by the next economic summit meeting, to be held in Williamsburg, Virginia, in June 1983.

Conclusions

A report drawn up by European Economic Community energy experts in late July 1982 criticized the US sanctions as largely ineffective, counterproductive, damaging to Western Europe, and unable to stop the flow of Soviet natural gas. Instead, the report said the ban would encourage the Soviet Union 'to increase its already considerable efforts and achievements in energy technology independence.'[100]

In a similar vein, another report on East-West trade released on 8 September 1982 by the Trilateral Commission maintained that the sanctions had little discernible effect other than to strain US relations with the Western alliance. In a highly critical tone, the report described sanctions as having caused confusion among the allies and lacking widespread support. The report recommended that trade relations with the Soviet bloc be increased in the future, as 'expanded trade within the limits of prudence would not add significantly to the military capabilities of the Soviet Union or Eastern European countries.' It concluded, 'Experience has shown that the Soviet Union is better able than the West to withstand economic strains, while pursuing political ends.'[101]

These two reports reflect general feelings among scholars and politicians alike about the US sanctions. There is no doubt that the effectiveness of the sanctions was hampered by complex factors such as (1) the reputation that they had acquired as 'ineffective,' 'counterproductive,' etc.; (2) the conflict of interest among the major parties; and (3) the continued effort even by neutral governments to undermine the use of sanctions in the resolution of international conflicts. Nevertheless, it is hard to assess the sanctions' effects upon Soviet actions in Poland, Afghanistan, or elsewhere, because it is nearly impossible to judge what intentions the Soviets had and to what extent they were restrained.

What is certain is that the severe strain in the US's relations with its European allies may have been highlighted by the sanctions, but they were not caused by them. Rather, sanctions had the positive effect of forcing the US and its allies to address broad and fundamental questions that had previously been ignored. One such issue is the lack of a general economic policy on Western trade with the Eastern bloc. Another significant issue is the extraterritorial rights which the US, unlike the Europeans, asserts to be part of its prerogatives and considers to be consonant with international law.

For future sanctions to become effective, a general trade strategy needs to be drafted in which the policy of sanctions is clearly outlined and the conditions under which they operate are unanimously agreed upon. Until then, sanctions as a US political deterrent against Soviet perceived aggressions and violations of international law will remain only partially effective.

5 Conclusions

The paradox of economic sanctions: failure as a function of success

In an article entitled 'On Misreading History,' published in *L'Espresso* on 21 April 1976, the Italian scholar Antonia Gambino wrote:

> The debate between those who see 'History' as an infallible teacher and those who believe little can be learned from the past has gone on for centuries. The fact is that history should provide a lesson, not an example, and certainly not a rigid 'law.'

Failure to recognize this truth has seriously flawed our understanding of economic sanctions. Though it behooves us to take careful note of historical events, these ought not to misguide us into believing that history repeats itself, and that consequently the future will bring only replays of the past. The history of sanctions has led some observers to conclude that sanctions are 'ineffective,' or at best 'symbolic'; on historical grounds, current social science tends to discredit the idea, dominant in the 1920s and 1930s, that sanctions constitute an effective coercive weapon in international politics.

This consensus has been derived from studies of cases in which sanctions against a target nation failed to achieve the political objectives for which they were initially implemented. Several major cases are cited repeatedly: the League's sanctions against Italy in 1935, the UN's sanctions against Rhodesia in 1965, the OAPEC oil embargo of 1973-4, the US boycott of Cuba, the Arab boycott of Israel, and the US grain embargo of the Soviet Union.

Our conclusions from examining these and many other cases are contrary to the dominant paradigm accepted by scholars in the field. In our view, economic sanctions are effective and useful even if we do not explore all their complex potentials. But paradoxically, the apparent failure of sanctions is often a necessary concomitant of their actual success.

Apprehensive of pushing Mussolini into the arms of Hitler (which eventually took place anyway), neither the League nor the major powers leading it were willing to impose stringent sanctions against Italy for its invasion of Ethiopia. Nevertheless, even the partial measures that were imposed severely strained the chronically weak Italian economy, resulting in high unemployment. Similarly, with Rhodesia there was never any serious effort to make sanctions work. Most of the countries that voted for sanctions did not bother to implement them and declined to join in efforts to make them more effective. Nevertheless, even these partial sanctions affected the Rhodesian economy (for example, the tobacco industry) and, along with other factors, led to the end of the Smith regime.

In neither of these cases is there concrete evidence or reliable statistical data available to substantiate the claim that sanctions were totally ineffective. Both the Italian and Rhodesian governments suppressed relevant data and censored governmental figures to conceal the impact of sanctions. Without such information it is nearly impossible to evaluate the effects of sanctions accurately. In retrospect, both the Italo-Abyssinian and Rhodesian experiences prove nothing except the folly of half-hearted measures, for full implementation of the sanctions clearly could have produced quicker and more drastic results.

In a similar vein, no one can deny the profound impact on the world's economy and the international distribution of power of the OAPEC 1973–4 oil embargo. As far as Cuba is concerned, the mass exodus to the United States in the flotilla of 1979 is the best evidence that the Cuban economy is hurting from the US economic boycott. If the Arab boycott of Israel is not hurting, why did the Israeli government in the mid-1970s find it imperative that the US Congress enact antiboycott laws? And although the Soviet Union was able to circumvent the US embargo by buying grain from Canada and Argentina, it did so only by paying much higher prices and accepting serious shipping delays.

Even should sanctions prove incapable of achieving the goals initially set to them by sanctioners, they need not necessarily be discarded as totally ineffective. Sanctions may not have the power to topple governments, change political systems or even induce drastic foreign policy changes, yet they have the power to cut fresh inroads, impose heavy sacrifices on the target, and inflict deep internal cleavages in the political fabric of the target regime — cleavages hard for the untrained eye to see on initial impact. A sustained boycott could produce such economic dislocation that the industries and trades usually dependent on exports

could be gravely injured. In addition to making the
higher prices for the embargoed goods, economic coer
it to part with a large portion of cherished gold suppl
ing the country's ability to invest abroad and crippli
power for a long time to come. Only the superpower:
bear such sacrifices in the short run but it will be at the expense of
economic prosperity at home.

Some general conclusions

The concept of sanctions developed originally out of a fear of war, and,
in our times especially, all-out nuclear war, with its suicidal impact on
both sides. Sanctions applied by international organizations were seen
as a legitimate collective use of force to uphold the authority of international law. Thus, historically, the real questions are not whether
economic sanctions have been successful in the past, nor to what extent
they have been successful in forcing target nation or nations to comply,
but rather whether they prevent the outbreak of wars, and if so, how
and to what extent, and whether in the event of a conventional war,
they can accelerate the termination of hostilities. The researchers' conclusion is that the answer to both of these questions is yes. Sanctions
do forestall the use of force by performing seven functions:

1. Maintaining the perception that sanctions are inflicting damage
   on the target;
2. Expressing morality and justice;
3. Signifying disapproval or displeasure;
4. Satisfying the emotional needs of the sanctioners;
5. Maintaining the sanctioner's positive image and reputation;
6. Relieving domestic pressure on the sanctioner;
7. Inflicting symbolic vengeance.

The imposition of economic sanctions absorbs the initial public reaction that something needs to be done. This gives way to a transitional
period, during which a compromise solution is attempted. Should the
compromise fail, and sanctions be maintained, a second set of medium-
term objectives is envisioned:

1. To cause economic inconvenience;

2. To use the target states as examples, so that third states are deterred from following them;
3. Restoring the sanctioner's self-confidence and self-image.

The effectiveness of sanctions has come to be measured by the economic deprivation it imposes on the target, and by the impoverishment and hardships the target community faces.

The long-range objective of sanctions is to secure total compliance, or, at most to cause so much economic damage that the target government is overthrown in favor of a more responsive regime. Though this is the most sought-after result of sanctions, it is also the least likely to happen (Figure 2).

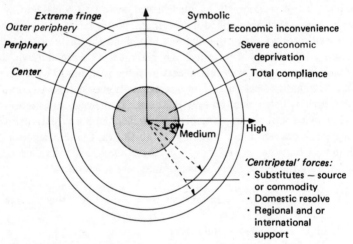

Figure 2: Bull's-eye diagram

The application of sanctions raises problems of extreme complexity. Their function, however, hinges on the precise purpose or goals set by the sanctioners as well as on the economic relationship between the sanctioner and the target at the time sanctions are imposed.

As disturbances continue to emerge from the unequal distribution of social, economic, political, and military power, economic coercion in the form of sanctions, embargoes, and blockades will recur. The economic and political effect of future coercion will very much depend on the conditions under which it is introduced and each episode needs to be evaluated on its own merits. Whether it will have a strong effect depends on circumstances, and generalizations based on other examples are not advisable. With this in mind, the following nine conclusions are offered in response to the six propositions advanced in the introduction of the present study.

First, the prevalent opinion that economic sanctions have no coercive value, or only symbolic value, due to the difficulties of enforcing them and the everlasting presence of suppliers eager to fill the gap, needs reexamination. Under the proper conditions, economic coercion can be a most formidable weapon, which seriously interferes with the prosperity of the target state and the comfort of its population. Although they may not seem to have achieved the high political goals set them, economic sanctions can have a considerable economic impact on the target. How much is difficult to measure, as the data are limited and not fully reliable.

Moreover, it is politically naive to ignore the power of some commodities, preeminently oil. Oil, used as an instrument of Arab foreign policy against importing nations, is a two-edged sword: its dull edge creates some economic inconvenience to the exporting nation, but its sharp edge can seriously hurt an embargoed target's economy, particularly if that nation is highly dependent on imported oil. In an increasingly interdependent world, the more nations rely on imported products essential to their prosperity, the more intolerable peacetime economic sanctions become.

Furthermore, it seems that any military superiority possessed by an embargoed nation does not constitute a serious restraint on a producer who opts to curtail production or stop exports of his commodity. This is particularly true in the case of oil, where a military effort to control an invaded country's oil-producing facilities is vulnerable to sabotage. Furthermore, even if a military operation is successful, holding and securing the oil installations in a hostile country will prove to be a formidable task.

Second, policy-making elites who use sanctions need to consider the following factors:

1. Are there other sources of supply ready, able, and willing to provide the goods (financial aids, essential commodities, technology, finance, loans, etc.) which the sanctioner is now denying?
2. Are there other substitutes or close alternatives which could make up for the loss of supply from the sanctioner?
3. Are there any vital counter-leverages which the sanctioned

country can employ in retaliation? Is the target a first-class military power?

4. Are there any domestic backlashes which the sanctioner must consider before imposing sanctions?
5. Is the target a trade-dependent country?
6. Are its reserves of gold and foreign-exchange assets limited?
7. What are the key components of the target's dependence on foreign trade?

For instance, if the target is an industrial nation, then a general embargo on shipments of raw materials will definitely hurt it. But if the target is an underdeveloped country, then a general embargo on the shipment of finished goods will be more effective. This needs to be coupled with a limitation of the ability of the target nation to purchase the goods on the spot market at higher prices by denying it loans and credits and interdicting its exports.

Theoretically, economic sanctions are most effective politically in cases where suppliers are limited, the supplied goods are in high demand, and the supply interruption is critical to the embargoed country.

Third, sanctions do not work quickly; they are attritional. For sanctions to be effective, the sanctioner needs to adopt realistic expectations. The sanctions policy must be carried out in the right proportions, with the proper methods, and be given adequate time to mature.

A long embargo may result in having the commodity embargoed 'leak' to international markets. But even if this occurs, the embargoed commodity will cost the target more. Consequently, the sanctioner achieves its aim of hurting the target's economy.

Fourth, sometimes it is more effective to hint at sanctions than to impose them. However, the effectiveness of this approach is a function of how the demands are formulated and presented and to what extent they can be negotiated. Sanctioners taking this course are well advised to employ 'salami tactics,' i.e., demands are cut into small pieces which the target can meet without serious loss of public image or international prestige. Once some short-term demands are met, medium-term demands will follow. Nevertheless, such a policy cannot be applied indefinitely, lest the target react negatively. It must be pursued in such a manner that nationalist feelings are not disturbed. The target ought not to seem to bow to foreign pressure, but rather to be acting in its own best interest.

Unless a sanctioner is in a position to carry through, it is not useful to employ the threats of economic sanctions, particularly if these are explicit. Economic sanctions poison the atmosphere between the nations concerned, and complicate their arrival at other solutions. Sanctions should be the last resort, for if the sanctioner is forced to carry out its threat but fails to do so, this could result in a loss of prestige and a decrease in latitude for subsequent actions.

Fifth, the initiator of a total trade embargo or full economic sanctions needs to be conscious of the price paid in economic, political, and human terms. In the first place, assuming that the target government does not give in and remains in power, sanctions will not be conducive to abate mutual hostilities. Furthermore, though most targets are governments and the most effective sanction is the one that would result in a *coup d'état* favourable to the sanctioner, such a policy cannot be pursued without first imposing severe hardships on the people of the target nation.

Sixth, depending on the world market in the embargoed commodity, the refusal of large and powerful nations rich in raw materials to join the embargo alliance may not severely impair the effect of the sanction. A production cut would lead to shorter supplies, pushing prices up and so indirectly hurting the target.

Seventh, the application of economic sanctions brings in its train friction which may result in enmity. It tends to create friction between the sanctioner and his allies, whose domestic prosperity may depend on international trade.

The most important and interesting aspect of the concept of economic sanctions is the ties between the 'state component' and the 'international component' in matters of economic strategy. An economic showdown between two adversaries constitutes a serious development for all nations. Consequently, efforts to impose an economic sanction must be coordinated with other countries not directly involved.

Moreover, embargo measures inflate prices. Consequently, it is harder to restrain other producing nations from violating the embargo alliance, since self-interest prompts other nations to take advantage of the situation and increase their production and exports. The embargo alliance has no means to prevent trading.

Eighth, the use of economic sanctions may erode the trading position of the sanctioning nation, since other nations may view the sanctions as evidence that the producer cannot be counted on as a reliable supplier. Even a threat of denial may give the supplier a reputation for unreliability, which consequently enhances the will and determination of importers to decrease or, even better, to eliminate their dependence and seek other sources of supply.

Ninth, consumers' defensive measures against politically motivated cutbacks in raw materials supply, and efforts to reduce the risk of economic boycott, may result in:

1. Encouraging exploration and production of raw materials in new areas and consequently increase sources of supply;
2. Stimulating conservation and so reduce demand;
3. Developing a variety of substitutes.

These developments will have a long-term impact on the economic relationship between producers and consumers.

The effectiveness of economic sanctions applied by international organizations

The discussion of the practices of the League of Nations and the United Nations brings to light the practical problems which must be solved before any economic sanctions applied by an international organization become effective. From the experiences of the League of Nations and the United Nations one can extract the following lessons and observations.

First, sanctions directed by individual nations do not carry with them the moral power of sanctions directed by international organizations.

Second, states find it difficult to take a broad view and rise above their own narrowly conceived national interests. Nations tend to preserve their sovereignty carefully and find it intolerable to subordinate their sovereignty to some supranational authority. Target nations assert their sovereignty by withdrawing from the international organizations. States called upon to participate in sanctions assert their sovereignty by refusing to join or by joining in accordance with their own whims and desires. Powerful nations do not find it in their national interest to have a strong world community to which their national objectives are subordinated.

Third, member states in general, and violating members against whom the General Assembly has resolved to impose sanctions and members who are candidates for such treatment in particular, are not interested in seeing sanctions become an effective weapon. They are concerned that should sanctions prove effective, they will be resorted to more often. Furthermore, controversial members are worried that one day they will become the General Assembly's 'Italy,' 'Rhodesia,' or 'South Africa' much more than they are concerned that they would become someone's 'Ethiopia' or 'Manchuria.'

Fourth, as noted previously, big nations do not find it in their best interest to subordinate their national objectives to a powerful world community. On their part, small states do not find it in their best interest to commit themselves to the application of economic sanctions against powerful nations, particularly if the target nation is their neighbor. Moreover, those nations find that should they participate in economic sanctions, the economic drain would prove to be much, as opposed to big states who will be damaged less by participation. Economic aid provided to help them deal with this problem is either not enough or causes them to become dependent on nations providing that aid. States are reluctant to apply sanctions to nations against whom they had no previous enmity.

Fifth, the effectiveness of sanctions depends on the adherence of all member states to their application. This aspect deserves particular attention as member states tend to be reluctant to obligate themselves should they feel that the measures taken will not be applied unanimously.

Sixth, for sanctions to be most effective they need to be collective. International organizations not only need to ensure their members' compliance with sanctions resolutions, but also to see to it that nonmembers, too, comply. This is hard to accomplish, because members do not set good examples themselves for nonmembers to follow. Moreover, nonmembers feel no obligation to abide by sanctions decisions. The situation is particularly aggravated when participation of nonmember nations in sanction measures is vital to ensure effectiveness.

Seventh, piecemeal economic sanctions applied in a gradual fashion lose their effect. The approach utilized in applying sanctions against target nations is characterized by gradual escalation from *selective optional* sanctions through an intermediate stage of *selective mandatory* sanctions and culminates in *comprehensive mandatory* sanctions. This slow process is time-consuming and results in giving the target time to overcome the difficulties caused by the sanctions and to reorganize his markets and sources of supply.

The 'bull's-eye' fallacy

Objectively speaking, therefore, a case can be made that sanctions are useful and effective, even if, like the case against sanctions, it cannot be based on hard, reliable statistical evidence.

The questions this raises are (1) How did this 'scientific revolution,' in Thomas Kuhn's terminology, come about? and (2) What led the 'scientific community' to adhere to it?

The answer lies in what we identify as the 'bull's-eye fallacy,' i.e., the erroneous idea that unless economic sanctions succeed in achieving their publicly stated initial demands, they have failed. The consensus regarding the ineffectiveness of sanctions has resulted from a discrepancy between what the sanctioner initially demanded and what the sanctions finally achieved. In peacetime, sanctioners who are not in a position to use military power usually formulate their demands in such a way as to allow room for compromise on both sides. Consequently, sanctions that result in compromise resolutions, or those whose fruits are not obvious because the target nation suppresses economic data, are by no means necessarily failures, though they are often judged to be so.

Failure to achieve the ultimate political objectives set by sanctioners is often the result of a complex combination of irresolution, political compromise, personal frailty, ineffective leadership, private greed, official timidity, and international mistrust. To appraise the effectiveness of economic sanctions, each case needs to be judged on its own merits. It is unrealistic to view the political utility of economic sanctions simply in terms of their having failed to force Mussolini to withdraw from Ethiopia in 1936, or the Israelis from Arab occupied territories in 1973, or the Soviets from Afghanistan in 1980, or in terms of their failure to force Ian Smith to renounce the Unilateral Declaration of Independence in 1965 within a few months. Sanctions should not be judged useless because they failed to rescue the American hostages from Tehran or overthrow Third World leaders like Mossadeq of Iran, Nasser of Egypt, Castro of Cuba, Idi Amin of Uganda, or Qaddafi of Libya. Here we are asking the pistol to inflict damage of which only the cannon is capable.

In this respect, it is important to realize that the fascinating power of economic sanctions lies in their ability to creep in on a target nation and, given enough time, to weaken it beyond measure. Like cancer, international economic sanctions kill minute cells within the economic structure of the target nation which are hard for the naked eye to detect at first. But an accumulation of these dead cells leads to the eventual corruption of the eco-political ability of the sanctioned nation to meet its domestic daily demands, weakening its integrity and eventually causing its collapse. Should sanctioners need to compress the time interval and achieve maximum political effectiveness, sanctions must be complemented by other, more coercive measures.

The gap between our expectations of what sanctions ought to do and their actual performance needs to be bridged. Economic sanctions could very well play the role of heavy bulldozers cutting fresh inroads and causing deep internal cleavages in the target nation's political system, preparing the way either for a military intervention, as was the case in the Dominican Republic in 1962 and Uganda in 1979, or for a diplomatic reconciliation, as was the case in Iran in 1981. Though sanctioners often deliberately overplay their rhetoric, suiting it to their real objectives or not as circumstances demand, political scientists and other observers should not be misled by this aspect of the sanctioners' tactics. Rather, recognition of the 'bull's-eye fallacy' may help us understand the real power of economic sanctions.

The 'bull's-eye fallacy' resulted in a tendency to underrate the power of economic sanctions and to downplay their importance. This gave rise to the universal acceptance of the paradigm that sanctions are ineffective. Once this paradigm became dominant, it influenced greatly the works and views of most practitioners in the field. Few have attempted to challenge this paradigm, as it is always easier to follow suit and accept the prevailing values than to reject or question them. As Kuhn has pointed out, most scientists are trained to do 'normal' science, that is, to apply without much questioning the prevailing paradigms of their science.

Table 1 *Cases of economic sanctions*

Sanctioner	Target	Date
A. *Universal sanctions:* *Punitive actions by world* *organizations*		
1. *League of Nations*	Yugoslavia	1921
	Paraguay	1934
	Italy	1935-6
2. *United Nations*	Spain	1946
	China	1951
	North Korea	1951
	South Africa	December 1963
	Rhodesia	November 1965– December 1979
B. *Multilateral sanctions:* *Multiple-state collective* *actions*		
1. *Loose coalitions*		
a. Western nations (led by Britain) in support of multinational oil companies	Iran	1951-3
b. Arab states	Companies owning business property in Israel	1955–
c. Arab oil producing countries	United States, Britain and West Germany	June 1967– September 1967
2. *Regional alliances*		
a. Inter-American Treaty of Mutual Assistance	Dominican Republic	August 1960
b. Organization of American States (OAS)	Dominican Republic Cuba	1961 December 1963– July 1975

Sanctioner	Target	Date
c. Organization of African Unity (OAU)	South Africa	1963
	Portugal	July 1964
	Rhodesia	October 1965
	Israel	November 1973
d. Arab League (AL)	Israel	1948–
e. Organization of Arab Petroleum Exporting Countries (OAPEC)	United States, South Africa, The Netherlands, Portugal, Rhodesia	October 1973– March 1974
f. Coordinating Committee on Export Controls (Co-Com)	Communist Bloc	1947
g. Council for Mutual Economic Assistance (Comecon)	Western Alliance	1949
	Albania	1962
h. European Economic Community (EEC)	Iran	April 1980– January 1981
	Argentina	April 1982– June 1982

C. *Unilateral sanctions: one-state punitive actions*

1. *Soviet Union*	Yugoslavia	1948 and 1957
	Australia	1954
	Israel	1956
	Finland	1959
	China	1959–60
	Albania	1960–1
2. *Unites States*	Japan	1941
	Dominican Republic	1960–2
	Cuba	1960–
	Indonesia	September 1963– October 1965
	United Arab Republic	1965

Table 1 (*cont*.):

Sanctioner	Target	Date
	India	1965-7
	Chile	January 1972
	India	January 1972
	Angola	1976
	Uganda	October 1978
	Iran	1979-80
	Soviet Union	January 1980–April 1981
	Poland	1982
	Argentina	1982
3. *Britain*	Soviet Union	1933
	Rhodesia	1965-79
	Argentina	1982
4. *Nigeria*	Biafra	1967
5. *India*	Hyderabad	1948
	Goa	1954-61
6. *China*	United States	1905
	Britain	1925-6
	Japan	1931-2
7. *Japan*	Russia	1907

Table 2 *Effectiveness of sanctions*

Effectiveness	Probability of success	Objective of sanctions
Low	Very high	*Symbolic* – to maintain the illusion that the sanctioner is inflicting damage on target – to express morality and justice – to signify disapproval or displeasure
	Extreme fringe	– to satisfy emotional needs – to maintain sanctioners' positive image and reputation – to relieve domestic pressure
Medium	High	*Economic inconvenience* – to inflict vengeance
	Outer periphery	*Obstruct economic growth* – to restore self-confidence and self-image – to deter third states from following the example set by target nation
	Medium	*Severe economic deprivation*
	Periphery	*Impoverishment and hardships*
High	Low	*Total compliance*
	Very low	*Overthrow of target's government*
Bull's eye	Center	*Change of target's political system*

Appendix I:
The Political Utility of Economic
Sanctions: The Old Paradigm

Alexander Berkenheim, Vice-President of the All-Russian Central Union of Consumers' Societies, Moscow (1919):

The continuance of the blockade of Russia renders helpless the quite innocent population, engenders in the people of Russia a feeling of hostility to the allies, and only serves to intensify the disordered state of the country. Only the raising of the blockade can mark the starting-point for the restoration of normal life, and it alone can strengthen the internal forces capable of restoring calm and stable forms of life.[1]

The League of Nations, Assembly Resolutions, Sec. 3 (1921):

The unilateral action of the defaulting state cannot create a state of war (presumably against members of the League other than its victim); it merely entitles the other members of the League to resort to acts of war or to declare themselves in a state of war with the covenant-breaking State; but it is in accordance with the spirit of the Covenant that the League of Nations should attempt, at least at the outset, to avoid war, and to restore peace by economic pressure.[2]

Bruce Williams (1927):

While their application [economic sanctions] is not clearly provided for, the implied responsibility of individual states to the international community and the expressed interest of that community in whatever concerns peace constitute progress.[3]

Dorothy J. Orchard (November 1930):

Politically powerless, China has discovered and put to effective use an economic weapon, the boycott. Almost continually since 1919, China has been boycotting some foreign power in defence of her sovereignty. The pressure of economic resistance has proved powerful — more powerful for a weak nation like China than resort to arms. Trade has been cut off, shipping dislocated, manufacturing depressed, and the economic life of the boycotted nation severely disturbed. The story of the use of the boycott by the Chinese people is one of the most revealing chapters in modern economic history.[4]

Sir Anton Bertram (1932):

[Describes the boycott to be] the great discovery and the most precious possession of the League.[5]

John V. A. MacMurray (2 September 1933):

The results of Professor Remer's investigations disclose that, while there may well have been warrant for doubt as to the economic effectiveness of the earlier Chinese boycotts, they have been growing in such effectiveness until, in the present campaign against Japanese trade, this method of retaliation (crude and costly though it is) has developed into a weapon capable of inflicting really grave injuries.[6]

Anthony Eden, Minister of Foreign Affairs, Great Britain (18 June 1936):

In any event, I would ask you to remember that there was a very good reason for the League to enforce these sanctions, particularly the ones it chose, because, with its incomplete membership, they were the only ones it could impose, which, by their action alone, it could hope to see effective. . . .

Though the League has not prevailed in preventing the successful accomplishment of a violation of the covenant the government does not regret, and I do not believe our fellow members of the League regret, having made the attempt. We have in common taken all those economic and financial measures on which general agreement could be obtained in the hope that these actions would be effective. We ourselves proposed virtually all the most important of them. Those were the motives with which we did so and in that respect we have nothing to apologize for and nothing to retract.[7]

M. J. Bonn (1937):

Though sanctions were not as efficient as they might have been made, they were the only weapon the League held against Italy. To let it slip before the conclusion of peace between the League and the nation which had violated its Covenant was evident proof of the fact that those in positions of responsibility either did not know how to handle the economic weapon, or did not dare to use it properly, or both.[8]

Albert Elmer Highley (1938):

Must one conclude that economic sanctions organized on a cooperative basis are doomed to failure? Not necessarily. But it certainly seems that the obstacles in their way are gigantic — particularly if they are not supplemented by military sanctions or, at least, by a known willingness to use military sanctions if necessary.

The real key to the successful application of sanctions is loyal and vigorous leadership by the great Powers applying them plus a determination to make them succeed. Otherwise there is no hope of obtaining and retaining the essential cooperation of the lesser Powers and of bringing the aggressor to terms.[9]

Robert McElroy, Professor Emeritus, Oxford University, England (January 1943):

Without sanctions, laws represent only what Alexander Hamilton called 'government by supplication,' which has never proved effective, and never can. And international law is no exception: for it, too, sanctions are essential to success.[10]

Anthony Eden (1943):

Looking back the thought comes again. Should we not have shown more determination in pressing through with sanctions in 1935 and if we had could we not have called Mussolini's bluff and at least postponed this second world war? The answer, I am sure, is yes.[11]

Josef Kunz (1946):

The arguments of laymen and lawyers against the legal character of international law consist mostly in the lack of organization and sanction.[12]

Hans Kelsen (1954):

Economic sanctions may be applied in different degrees. The most important economic sanction consists of prohibiting the commerce in arms, ammunition and the raw materials essential to the production of hostilities between the member states of the security organization and the aggressor. Among these prohibitions an oil embargo is of particular importance. The refusal to accept exports from a state is an economic sanction which may have a remarkable effect on the state against which it is applied. The highest possible degree of an economic sanction is achieved by prohibiting all commerce, which includes prohibiting the nationals of the member states from entering the territory of the aggressor, prohibiting the nationals of the aggressor state from entering the territory of the member states, controlling all transport and international exchanges of goods, and interrupting the diplomatic and consular relations between the member states and the aggressor.[13]

M. Henri Spaak, Secretary General of NATO (1959): ... international organizations will only become fully effective, when it is understood that over and above the will of a nation there exists an international law, deriving its sanctions from the majority and to which all countries, large and small, must submit.[14]

Appendix II:
The Political Utility of Economic
Sanctions: The New Paradigm

Alfred Lilienthal, counsel for the American-Arab Association for Commerce and Industry in the United States (December 1963): the Arab boycott had been 'a real flop.'[1]

Rita Falk Taubenfeld and Howard J. Taubenfeld (April 1964):
The admittedly limited forms of economic sanctions employed to date by general international organizations have failed to accomplish anything significant. . . .[2]
In summary, considering the limited economic potentials and the demanding political prerequisites, economic and financial sanctions, used alone, are a relatively weak and crude tool in a world where less than perfection is to be expected. From the psychological point of view, they have consistently proven to be a potentially dangerous tool, tending to unify opinion in the sanctioned state and to divide and undermine the international community.[3]

Anthony Lejeune (11 January 1966):
Does Harold Wilson really believe that sanctions will produce a white counter-revolution to force Mr. Smith to retract? Probably not. . . .[4]
Economic sanctions have never in the past had much effect on any country except to toughen its resolution and increase its self-reliance. Rhodesia is infinitely better placed than Cuba, for example, to survive a period of isolation and stringency: and Portugal and South Africa are much more capable of helping her than Russia is of helping Cuba.[5]

National Review (8 March 1966):
Congressman John Ashbrook returned from Rhodesia a fortnight ago convinced that economic sanctions alone will not bring down the government of Prime Minister Ian Smith. He reports that the pressures Harold Wilson has brought to bear against Rhodesia have —

as might have been expected — served rather to unite than to fragment the country.[6]

Frank Kearns (21 March 1966):
The oil embargo against Rhodesia appears to be a complete
failure.[7]

Elspeth Huxley (6 September 1966):
July has come and gone. Sanctions have failed; the Smith regime,
rebellious and illegal, as ever, has dug in.[8]

New Republic (17 September 1966):
Today, after 10 months of sanctions, the morale of the Rhodesian
government is high. On the surface the economy is surprisingly
buoyant. Far from deviating from the discriminatory trends of its
racial policies which were the real cause of the break with Britain,
the Rhodesian government is openly following the pattern of South
Africa's apartheid legislation, and has begun to make new and
harsher repressive laws.[9]

Time (2 December 1966):
The Arab world's 15-year-old boycott of Israel — and of foreign
companies that do more than just sell finished goods to Israel — has
up to now produced a lot of political smoke but not much economic
fire. Unevenly applied and quixotically enforced, the blacklist has
up to now proved mostly a nuisance to Israel.[10]

Ian Smith, Rhodesian Prime Minister (19 December 1966):
Question. Turning to mandatory sanctions, how do you hope to
sell your metals and minerals in the face of a U.N. boycott?
Answer. We believe that we are finding more markets, not less
markets, as time goes on. Time is on our side, and I think the longer
any campaign takes and any blockade continues, the natural tendency is for loopholes to become bigger, not smaller.[11]

Newsweek (26 December 1966):
What next? "It will have to be force." commented a Rhodesian
African spokesman in New York. "The Smith regime is based on
force. It will have to be met with force. If neither Britain nor the
U.N. supplies it, we will have to take action ourselves. Maybe then,
if their white 'kith and kin' are threatened, the British will finally
send in troops and settle the matter. The sanctions will not bring
Smith down."[12]

James Burnham (27 December 1966):

U.N. sanctions against South Africa will not change this political position. Military analysts believe effective sanctions against South Africa are impossible. The political-economic coordination to make them effective is unachievable, they say. In addition, the cost of an effective blockade would be prohibitive.[13]

Alexander Eckstein (1966):

... the embargo has only a symbolic meaning. It stands as a symbol of our determination to isolate China, to treat her as an outlaw, and to refuse to have any dealings with her.[14]

Colin Harris (January 1967):

The resort of the British Government to the United Nations for selective mandatory sanctions against Rhodesia is convincing evidence of the failure of the voluntary sanctions policy. Voluntary sanctions have proved ineffective in their twofold aim of demonstrating the economic perils of illegal independence, and applying political pressure for a return to constitutional legality. After a year of subjection to voluntary sanctions, conditions of life for the white Rhodesians are relatively unchanged on the surface and political reaction has been the opposite of what was intended.[15]

A. M. Hawkins (July 1967):

Economic sanctions against Rhodesia have failed. Not only have they failed to achieve their political objective of bringing about the collapse of the existing Government, but they have also failed to depress economic activity to the extent that was intended. After 12 months of voluntary sanctions followed by eight months of mandatory United Nations sanctions there are signs that the economy — far from wilting under the pressure — is beginning to grow once again. It would appear that the worst is past.[16]

Frank Gervasi (1967):

Since 1950, Israel has enjoyed an economic growth rate of 10% annually, one of the world's highest; annual per capita income is $1,000 ... and gross national product has outstripped population growth by 2.38 to 1, an unusually good performance in comparison with other developing nations. Israel's imports have increased from $423,106,000 in 1958 to $826,233,000 in 1964, and exports have risen in the same period from $139,102,000 to $351,821,000. ... [Thus,] far from 'strangling' Israel, the boycott actually may have stimulated the country's economic development by promoting greater self-reliance.[17]

Elspeth Huxley (9 April 1968):
Everyone now admits that sanctions have failed and no one sees any reason why they should not continue to fail.[18]

Timothy R. Curtin (April 1968):
Economic sanctions are unlikely to have an economic, let alone a political effect. 'If it is assumed that exports are reduced to what seems the lowest level that can be reasonably expected, Rhodesia would still be able to import sufficient quantities of the capital and other goods that cannot be produced domestically to permit at least a moderate rate of growth of natural income for many years to come.'[19]

Time (19 July 1971):
In many respects, the boycott and other forms of Arab hostility have strengthened rather than weakened Israel's economy.[20]

Tuvia Arazi, director of the Political-Economic Planning Division of Israel (July 1971):
The Boycott does us infinitesimal harm now. It is so inefficient and ineffective that we simply don't need this division any more.[21]

William D. Coplin and Charles W. Kegley (1971):
His [Peter Wallensteen] general finding is that sanctions have been unsuccessful and often are useful only as acts of protest and condemnation. Our confidence in the findings is increased because they are based on a careful comparison of ten cases.[22]

Financial Times (26 October 1974):
There is a growing feeling among some delegates [to the Seventh Arab summit] already assembled that, with on the one hand the difficulties of enforcing the oil sanction and on the other the willingness of non-Arab oil producers (including, now, Mexico) to try to fil' the gap, the use of the oil weapon as a means of coercion has a limited value.[23]

Chaim Bar-Lev, Israeli Minister of Commerce (1975):
The Arab boycott means nothing to us. It has no effect on Israel.[24]

Derek Bowett (1976):
the concept of economic coercion will prove redundant, either

because coercive tactics are no longer resorted to or, more likely, because the conduct in question will be characterized as 'fair' or 'unfair' under the rules of a general mechanism for regulating trade.[25]

Dan S. Chill (1976):
many Arab Boycott activities . . . have not only failed economically but have been politically disastrous.[26]

Charles F. Doran (1977):
the power of the oil weapon to force an alteration of foreign policies remained for the time being conjectural.[27]

Jerald A. Combs (1978):
Overall, America's wielding of the weapon of embargo has not been notably successful except as a direct adjunct of war. Jefferson's embargo brought serious domestic disaffection and helped bring on the War of 1812. King Cotton diplomacy was a colossal failure. As the United States became an industrial power in the twentieth century, the nation was itself more dependent on foreign trade than its potential opponents. Thus embargoes stood to hurt the United States more than its enemies. Because of this and the historical failures of the embargo, the American government has wielded the weapon more carefully, and usually as a supplement to military operations or as a symbolic gesture when the course of outright military attack was for some reason closed to it.[28]

J. Chal Vinson (1978):
Utopian dreams of stable world peace remain unfulfilled. In an imperfect world sanctions are flawed by difficulties in gaining universal agreement as to issues requiring action and means for achieving general support for the application of sanctions to such issues. This probably will continue to be the case unless, or until, it becomes overwhelmingly clear that international cooperation offers more hope of security than does unrestrained nationalism.[29]

Andrew Young, US former ambassador to the United Nations (1978):
Economic sanctions looked like an easy answer, but South Africa is one of the most self-sufficient nations in the world. It could get along without us. In fact, their economy contributes about a half billion to the U.S. economy yearly. If we cut off investments, we

would lose jobs in this country and we wouldn't necessarily help Blacks in that country.[30]

D. J. J. Botha, Head, Department of Economics, University of Witwatersrand (1978):

With its high propensity to import, however, the harm done to the South African economy in the long run may turn out to be far less than it would appear from quantitative assessments of the kind which the author [Arnt Spandau] has undertaken.[31]

Jean Mayer, president of Tufts University (5 November 1978):

Denial of food in war constitutes a war measure directed almost exclusively at children, the elderly, and pregnant and nursing women. Not only will innocent bystanders be hurt — they will be the *only* ones to be hurt. It is an ineffective weapon that is also a dear and particularly horrible violation of the rights of man.[32]

James Barber (July 1979):

. . . in general seems to be a wide measure of agreement among scholars that economic sanctions alone have seldom if ever achieved their primary aims.[33]

Paul Lewis, *New York Times* (16 December 1979):

As the American hostages in Teheran began their seventh week of captivity, the United States was drafting plans for international economic reprisals. However, on the record of past attempts, many experts in Europe doubted that sanctions could be made to work, even if the United Nations Security Council agreed to invoke them. . . .

There is strong sympathy for the hostages in Europe and Japan and approval of President Carter's restrained response, exhausting diplomatic avenues before threatening force. But there is also widespread skepticism of international sanctions, rooted in memories and national interests. Sanctions are likely to be ineffective, friendly governments argue, risking injury to the sanctioners more than to the sanctioned.[34]

Ann Crittenden (13 January 1980):

The American military action in Korea was eventually successful, but in the opinion of students of the period, the economic war was a bust. It was a constant source of friction in the West, and was only marginally disruptive to the Communist bloc, which probably became even more self-sufficient as a result of it. . . .[35] the 1930's seemed to prove that economic warfare is poor policy, a view shared by virtually all the experts.[36]

Robert G. Gilpin, expert on political economy at Princeton (13 January 1980):
It is true that economic warfare is a way of doing something; an important symbol. But what does it symbolize? Is it really doing something, or does it just demonstrate impotence?[37]

Roger Fisher, Williston professor of law at Harvard University (14 January 1980):
Sanctions may be domestically popular, may divert attention from inflation and may muffle criticism of the President, but history and common sense are persuasive that they will not serve our national interests.

Let us not forget that economic sanctions against the post-revolutionary regimes in the Soviet Union, in China and in Cuba were a total failure. Similarly, League of Nations sanctions against Mussolini's Italy and United Nations sanctions against Rhodesia, far from punishing those countries, led to greater unity, harder work and years of increased production.[38]

Time (21 January 1980):
Economic sanctions have rarely been successful. There are too many middlemen for supplies to be effectively shut off — they can simply be routed through friendly countries.[39]

Frank A. Weil, former Assistant Secretary of Commerce for Trade (27 January 1980):
Question: What the economic and political impact of the embargoes on the Soviet Union is likely to be?
Answer: From the economic point of view, at best, minimal. It is clear the grain embargo would have the most economic and internal political effects. It's also clear that grain is one of the most fungible commodities in the world and could be very difficult to monitor. As for the other aspects of the embargo, it's really de minimis.[40]

James R. Schlesinger, former Energy Secretary (27 January 1980):
The trade sanctions, particularly the grain embargo, and quite possibly the boycott of the Olympics, may make us feel better. But they are strategically marginal at best. . . . I agree that economic

sanctions are a relatively weak tool. They appeal to Americans because they seem to be a substitute for the stiffer measures that may be required.[41]

Roy D. Laird and Ronald Francisco, professors of political science at the University of Kansas (13 February 1980):
There is important evidence to conclude that the embargo will have, at most, a minimal impact on the Soviet food situation. The same evidence strongly points to a speculation that the Kremlin leaders are aware of the fact. Therefore, if in planning the invasion of Afghanistan they considered the possibility of a U.S. grain embargo, they were able to conclude that it would do them little damage.[42]

Forbes (18 February 1980):
Was President Carter wise to invoke economic sanctions against the Soviet Union and Iran? Sanctions are an old American tradition, but they won't work in the modern world and are self-defeating to larger U.S. aims. So argue two Princeton professors, Robert Gilpin and Henry Bienen, who made a major study for a large corporation on the historic impact of this U.S. policy.[43]

Robert Gilpin, professor of political science at Princeton (18 February 1980):
The theory of economic sanctions is that they will cause a split within the leadership and the masses of people. But in almost all cases, it's been the opposite. What you have is really a rallying-around-the-flag response in these countries.[44]

Henry Bienen, professor of political science at Princeton (18 February 1980):
Economic sanctions are frequently potent as symbolic political acts, because they appear to be consequential, whether they are potent as a weapon to coerce is very doubtful. We've looked at the cases of Rhodesia, Cuba and the sanctions imposed by the League of Nations against Italy in 1935, and they all failed. I don't think anyone in the U.S. government really believes — the President stated this himself — that today sanctions would compel the Soviet Union to withdraw from Afghanistan. Nor do I think anyone really believes that this present Iranian government — whoever is making decisions in Iran on the hostages — will be very much affected by economic sanctions.[45]

John A. Schnittker, former Under-Secretary of Agriculture (March 1980):

The embargo has failed as an economic weapon. Its principal effect has been to create a confused market situation and somewhat higher [federal] budget expenditures.[46]

Margaret Doxey (December 1980):

One may conclude that economic sanctions should not be seen as a useful, peaceful weapon of pressure which can be readily employed at low cost. . . . Economic sanctions are not susceptible to 'fine tuning': they are blunt instruments which may miss their true target and can also have a boomerang effect.[47]

Robert L. Wendzel (1981):

The strategic embargoes targeting the Soviet Union and the People's Republic of China had little positive impact. In fact, if anything the embargoes were counter-productive because of the encouragement they gave to (already existing) desires for self-sufficiency, the targets' drive to produce the necessary commodities themselves, and their efforts to develop alternative sources and substitutes.[48]

Daily Telegraph, London (January 1982):

It is argued that Mr. Reagan's sanctions are little more than a pinprick; also, of course, that sanctions never work.[49]

Sidney Weintraub (1982):

One almost unanimous conclusion of past studies is that multilateral economic sanctions rarely achieve their objectives primarily because they do not achieve universality. For this reason, unilateral sanctions are thought to be even less effective than multilateral.[50]

Christopher Dobson, John Miller, and Ronald Payne (1982):

It was understood well enough that sanctions alone never decide wars — they had not worked against Ian Smith's Rhodesia and they had no discernible effect on Russia's intervention in Afghanistan — but with a country whose economy was in such a parlous state as Argentina's they were bound to have some effect even if they were more a display of disapproval than measures which would bring the junta to heel.[51]

Time (11 January 1982):

At the heart of the allied opposition to President Reagan's economic sanctions against Poland and the Soviet Union is the belief that sanctions, no matter how well meaning, do not work. As one Italian politician noted cynically, 'Carter adopted sanctions against the Soviets to get them out of Afghanistan. They still are in Afghanistan.' Said a British trade official: 'Trade is a very difficult sanction to apply; like water, it will always find a way through. . . .'[52]

Time (11 January 1982):
More pragmatically, the Europeans harbor a deep distrust of sanctions, particularly economic ones, as an effective instrument of international pressure.[53]

Otto Wolff von Amerongen, Chairman of the West German Association of Chambers of Commerce (11 January 1982):
Trade embargoes do not help anybody because there is a high potential for circumvention.[54]

The Economist (22 May 1982):
Most countries that have been subjected to sanctions have in fact shown far greater economic resilience and adaptability (for example, in finding alternatives or developing substitutes for embargoed goods) than expected. Economic sanctions did not curtail Mussolini's Abyssinia adventure before the second world war. Nor did comprehensive economic sanctions within the framework of the United Nations bring Mr. Smith's illegal regime in Rhodesia to an end after the unilateral declaration of independence. Hence the frequent assertion that 'sanctions never work.'[55]

George Shultz, Secretary of State (26 July 1982):
As a general proposition, I think the use of trade sanctions as an instrument of diplomacy is a bad idea. . . . Our using it here, there and elsewhere to try to affect some other country's behavior . . . basically has not worked.[56]

Richard Nixon (24 August 1982):
Some people think of economic leverage as the punitive use of economic sanctions, with highly publicized conditions set for their removal. This is highly ineffective, and sometimes counterproductive.[57]

The Economist (4 September 1982):
The history of sanctions against Mussolini's Italy, Mao's China, Castro's Cuba, Smith's Rhodesia, Khomeini's Iran and Galtieri's

Argentina illustrates the limits of economic warfare against dictator-ships.[58]

Harold Brown, Secretary of Defense, 1977–81 (6 September 1982):

. . . economic sanctions should be applied only in situations where military action by the U.S. is either infeasible or too dangerous but where something more than mere moral outrage is required.

Furthermore, when applied, sanctions should be limited in time because they become ineffective after a limited time because of leakage — even if they're effective at the beginning.[59]

Helmut Sonnenfeldt, Counselor of the State Department, 1974–7 (6 September 1982):

As for the arguments about the effectiveness of economic sanc-tions, they are essentially academic: Really airtight policies of denial have proved to be politically infeasible in virtually all countries where they have been attempted over the last several decades.[60]

Anatoli Alexandrov, President, Soviet Academy of Sciences (20 October 1982):

U.S. economic sanctions, on balance, benefited the Soviet Union by speeding improvement of domestic technology.

In retrospect, I am glad about the limitation on technology, in that it provided practical backing for my own wish that we should develop our own computer technology further. . . . It was this U.S. move which facilitated a speeding up of our work.[61]

Carl Marcy, Co-Director, American Committee on East-West Accord (11 October 1982):

. . . economic sanctions generally do not work. Take, for example, the Arab oil boycott of the U.S. a few years ago. What did it ac-complish? Did it make the United States do what the Arabs wanted? No. It forced us to increase fuel reserves and probably had the effect of changing our entire automobile industry from building large cars to building small, fuel-efficient cars.

Or take the case of Germany during World War II. We blockaded the Germans, cut off their rubber supplies, cut off their fuel supplies, and what happened? Germany developed synthetic rubber and syn-thetic fuels. In short, sanctions have unintended effects.[62]

Notes

Introduction

1 Dennis Austin, 'Sanctions and Rhodesia,' *The World Today* 22, no. 3 (March 1966), The Royal Institute of International Affairs, p. 106.

2 Puchala and Fagan, 'International Politics in the 1970's: The Search for a Perspective,' *International Organization* XXVII (Spring 1974), p. 263; see Allan J. Mayer and Rich Thomas, 'Commodities: A Better Idea?' *Newsweek*, 4 April 1977, pp. 57–8; and 'Tougher Talk on Commodity Facts,' *Business Week*, 12 May 1980, pp. 28–9.

3 Robert L. Paarlberg, 'Food, Oil, and Coercive Resource Power,' in *International Security*, vol. 3, no. 2 (Fall 1978), p. 3.

4 Ibid., p. 4; a useful discussion is 'Grain as a Weapon,' *Time*, 21 January 1980, pp. 12–27.

5 Ibid.

6 *Webster's New Collegiate Dictionary* (Springfield, Mass.: Merriam, 1977), p. 1,023.

7 A. R. C. De Crespigny and R. T. McKinnell, 'The Nature and Significance of Economic Boycott,' *The South African Journal of Economics* 28 (December 1960), p. 319.

8 Ibid.

9 Ibid.

10 Gerhard Von Glahn, *Law Among Nations* (New York: Macmillan, 1976), p. 503.

11 Ibid., p. 501.

12 Ibid.

13 Ibid., p. 502.

14 Eric Partridge, *Usage and Abusage*, 3rd edn (Harmondsworth: Penguin, 1973), p. 354.

15 Jack Plano and Milton Greenberg, *The American Political Dictionary* (New York: Holt, Rinehart & Winston, 1964), p. 319.

16 William L. Safire, *Safire's Political Dictionary* (New York: Random House, 1978), p. 548.

17 Ibid.

18 This somewhat whimsical formula is that of Roger Hilsman quoted in William Safire's *Safire's Political Dictionary*, p. 549.

19 William Safire, *On Language* (New York: Times Books, 1980), p. 97.

20   John Austin, *The Province of Jurisprudence Determined and the Uses of the Study of Jurisprudence* (New York: Noonday Press, 1954), p. 15.
21   *International Sanctions: A Report by a Group of Members of the Royal Institute of International Affairs* (London: Oxford University Press for RIIA, 1938), p. 16.
22   Richard Arens and Harold D. Lasswell, 'Towards a General Theory of Sanctions,' *Iowa Law Review* 49 (1964), pp. 233–4.
23   Harold D. Lasswell and Richard Arens, 'The Role of Sanctions in Conflict Resolution,' *Journal of Conflict Resolution* 11 (1967), p. 28.
24   Donald L. Losman, *International Economic Sanctions* (Albuquerque: University of New Mexico Press, 1979), p. 1.
25   Johan Galtung, 'On the Effects of International Economic Sanctions, with Examples from the case of Rhodesia,' *World Politics* XIX (April 1967), p. 379.
26   Richard Stuart Olson, 'Economic Coercion in World Politics, with a Focus on North-South Relations,' *World Politics* XXXI (July 1979), p. 474.
27   Ibid.
28   Ibid.
29   Hanns Maull, *Oil and Influence: The Oil Weapon Examined*, Adelphi Papers, no. 118 (London: International Institute for Strategic Studies, Summer 1975), p. 1.
30   Ibid.
31   Robert L. Allen, 'State Trading and Economic Warfare,' *Law and Contemporary Problems* 24 (1959), p. 259.
32   William Norton Medlicott, *The Economic Blockade* (London: HM Stationery Office, 1952–9, reprinted 1978), cited in James A. Boorman III, 'Economic Coercion in International Law: The Arab Oil Weapon and the Ensuing Judicial Issues,' *Journal of International Law and Economics* 9 (1974), p. 210.
33   Quincy Wright, *A Study of War* (Chicago: University of Chicago Press, 1965), p. 1,483.
34   Geoffrey Blainey, *The Causes of War* (New York: Free Press, 1973), p. 22. See also K. Knorr and F. Traeger (eds), *Economic Issues and National Security* (Lawrence: Regents Press of Kansas, 1977).
35   Losman, *International Economic Sanctions*, p. 2.
36   Michael Haas, *International Conflict* (New York: Bobbs-Merrill, 1974), p. 8
37   Ibid., p. 9.
38   For a clear, concise explanation and review of the basic assumptions of the general theories on sanctions, see Harry R. Strack, *Sanctions, The Case of Rhodesia* (New York: Syracuse University Press, 1978), pp. 11–16; and Richard C. Porter, 'Economic Sanctions: The Theory and the Evidence from Rhodesia,' *Journal of Peace Studies* 3, no. 2 (Fall 1978), pp. 93–110.

1 Economic Sanctions in International Relations

1   See Thomas S. Kuhn, *The Structure of Scientific Revolutions* (Chicago and London: The University of Chicago Press, 1962), p. 10.
2   James A. Bill and Robert L. Hardgrave, Jr, *Comparative Politics, The Quest for Theory* (Columbus, Ohio: Charles E. Merrill, 1973), p. 28.

3 Ibid.
4 Kuhn, *The Structure of Scientific Revolutions*, p. 10.
5 Ibid., pp. 23–4.
6 Ibid., p. 23.
7 Ibid., p. 20.
8 Ibid., p. 8.
9 Robert T. Holt and John M. Richardson, Jr, 'Competing Paradigms in Comparative Politics,' in Robert T. Holt and John E. Turner (eds), *The Methodology of Comparative Research* (New York: Free Press, 1970), p. 28.
10 Kuhn, *The Structure of Scientific Revolutions*, p. 23.
11 Ibid., p. 10.
12 Ibid., p. 42.
13 Willis W. Harman, 'The Coming Transformation' (second part), *The Futurist* XI (April 1977), p. 107.
14 Dennis Pirages, *Global Ecopolitics* (North Scituate, Massachusetts: Duxbury Press, 1978), p. 7.
15 Kuhn, *The Structure of Scientific Revolutions*, p. 91.
16 Ibid., p. 77
17 Ibid., p. 169.
18 Holt and Richardson, 'Competing Paradigms in Comparative Politics', p. 21.
19 Larry Laudan, *Progress and its Problems* (Berkeley: University of California Press, 1977), p. 73.
20 Ibid.
21 Willis, W. Harman, 'The Coming Transformation' (first part), *The Futurist* XI (February 1977), p. 5.
22 Philip Kerr, 'Navies and Peace: A British View', *Foreign Affairs* 8, no. 1 (October 1929), p. 26.
23 Philip Kerr, 'Europe and the United States: The Problem of Sanctions,' *Journal of the Royal Institute of International Affairs* IX, no. 3 (May 1930), p. 289.
24 W. Arnold Forster, 'Sanctions,' *Journal of the British Institute of International Affairs* V, no. 1 (January 1926), p. 1.
25 See Ruth B. Henig (ed.), *The League of Nations* (New York: Harper & Row, 1973), p. 147.
26 Jan C. Smuts, *The League of Nations: A Practical Suggestion* (London: Hodder & Stoughton, 1918).
27 A. E. Zimmern, *The Economic Weapon in the War Against Germany* (New York: George H. Doran, 1918), p. 13.
28 Signor Schanzer, rapporteur for the Special Committee on the Economic Weapon, in a speech to the second Assembly on 21 September 1921, quoted in William E. Rappard, *International Relations as Viewed from Geneva* (New Haven: Yale University Press, 1925), pp. 142–3.
29 D. Mitrany, *The Problem of International Sanctions* (London: Oxford University Press, 1925), p. 73. Mitrany concludes: 'We have said that the economic weapon is at present the only one generally available for the enforcement of peace. It is also the weapon that conforms better to the general development of western civilization and outlook' (p. 76).
30 Quoted in Rappard, *International Relations as Viewed from Geneva*, p. 129.

31   Sir Austen Chamberlain, Speech to the League Council at Geneva, 12 March 1925 (London, Public Record Office, reference number Fo371/11070).
32   W. Arnold Forster, 'Sanctions,' p. 3.
33   Philip Kerr, 'Navies and Peace: A British View,' p. 24.
34   Committee on Economic Sanctions, *Reports of Research Findings*, 1931, p. 222.
35   Raymond Leslie Buell, 'Are Sanctions Necessary to International Organization? Yes,' *Foreign Policy Association*, pamphlet no. 82, series 1931-2 (June 1932), p. 11.
36   Albert E. Hindmarsh, *Force in Peace* (Cambridge, Mass.: Harvard University Press, 1933), p. 6.
37   C. K. Webster, *The League of Nations in Theory and Practice* (Boston and New York: Houghton Mifflin, 1933), p. 144.
38   Charles Cheney Hyde, 'The Boycott as a Sanction of International Law,' *Political Science Quarterly* 48, no. 211 (June 1933), p. 216.
39   C. F. Remer, *A Study of Chinese Boycotts, with Special Reference to Their Economic Effectiveness* (Baltimore: The Johns Hopkins Press, 1933), p. 251.
40   John I. Knudson, *A History of the League of Nations* (Atlanta, Georgia: Turner E. Smith, 1938), p. 11.
41   Norman Angell, *Peace with the Dictators* (New York and London, Harper & Brothers, 1938), p. 136.
42   Sir Charles Webster, *Sanctions: The Use of Force in an International Organization* (London: David Davies Memorial Institute of International Studies, March 1956), p. 16.
43   *Strengthening the United Nations*, Commission to Study the Organization of Peace, Arthur N. Holcombe, Chairman (New York: Harper & Brothers Publishers, 1957), p. 43.
44   See David Hunter Miller, *Drafting of the Covenant*, 2 vols. (New York: G. P. Putnam's Sons, 1928), II, p. 838.
45   *Woodrow Wilson's Case for the League of Nations*, compiled with his approval by Hamilton Foley (Princeton: Princeton University Press, 1923), pp. 67, 71, 72.
46   Evans Clark (ed.), *Boycotts and Peace*, a Report by the Committee on Economic Sanctions (New York and London: Harper & Brothers, 1932), p. 21.
47   Quoted in Knudson, *A History of the League of Nations*, p. 9.
48   Herbert Feis, *The Road to Pearl Harbor* (New York: Atheneum, 1965), p. 12.
49   J. M. Spaight, *Pseudo-Security* (London: Longman, Green & Co., 1928), pp. 28-9. Spaight outlines his attacks on the concept of sanctions in a chapter entitled 'The Pseudo-Sanctions,' pp. 53-73.
50   John Dewey, 'Are Sanctions Necessary to International Organization? No,' *Foreign Policy Association*, pamphlet number 82, series 1931-32 (June 1932), p. 23.
51   C. John Colombos, 'Book Review: *Der Zwang im Völkerrecht* by Hans Widmer,' *International Affairs* (January 1937), pp. 142-3.
52   LeLand M. Goodrich, 'International Sanctions,' in David L. Sills (ed.), *International Encyclopedia of the Social Sciences* 14 (1968), p. 5.

53 Fredrik Hoffmann, 'The Functions of Economic Sanctions: A Comparative Analysis,' *Journal of Peace Research* II (1967), p. 144.

54 Albert E. Hindmarsh, *Force in Peace*, p. 160. See M. Consett, *The Triumph of Unarmed Forces 1914-1918* (London: Williams & Norgate, 1923).

55 Forster, 'Sanctions,' p. 1.

56 Henig (ed.), *The League of Nations*, pp. 9-10. Inis L. Claude in *Swords into Plowshares: The Problems and Progress of International Organization* (New York: Random House, 1956), reflects similar views. He writes that the League system of sanctions was a system of collective security which rested 'upon the proposition that war can be prevented by the deterrent effect of overwhelming power upon states which are too rational to invite certain defeat' (p. 228).

57 Dewey, 'Are Sanctions Necessary to International Organization? No,' p. 23. See also Sir Thomas Holland, 'The Mineral Sanction as a Contribution to International Security,' *International Affairs* 15, no. 5 (September-October 1936), pp. 735-52.

58 Kuhn, *The Structure of Scientific Revolutions*, p. 144.

59 Charles Cheney Hyde, 'The Boycott as a Sanction of International Law,' p. 213.

60 Dewey, 'Are Sanctions Necessary to International Organization? No,' p. 23.

61 C. G. Fenwick, 'The "Failure" of the League of Nations,' *American Journal of International Law* 30 (July 1936), p. 506.

62 Extract from a speech made by Neville Chamberlain, 10 June 1936, to the 1900 Club, reported in *The Times*, 11 June 1936, quoted in Henig (ed.), *The League of Nations*, p. 147. See also 'Failure of the Collective System?,' *Geneva* IX (May 1936), pp. 173-6.

63 Norman Angell, *Peace with the Dictators*, p. 134.

64 'The League Admits Failure,' *Geneva* IX (July 1936), p. 192.

65 Charles Cheney Hyde and Louis B. Wehle, 'The Boycott in Foreign Affairs,' *American Journal of International Law* 27 (January 1933): 9.

66 Quincy Wright, *The United States and Neutrality* (Chicago: University of Chicago Press, 1935). On 31 August 1935 the US Congress adopted the Neutrality Act (ch. 837, 49 Stat. 1081) which authorized the President to control the export of arms, ammunition, or implements of war to any belligerent country during the progress of war between, or among, two or more foreign states. A 1937 amendment to the Neutrality Act authorized the President to place restrictions on 'the shipment of certain articles or materials in addition to arms, ammunition, and implements of war from the United States to belligerent states, or, to a state where civil strife exists . . .' if such restrictions are 'necessary to promote the security or preserve the peace of the United States or to protect the lives of citizens of the United States.' The Neutrality Act of 4 November 1939 provided, in addition, that the President, pursuant to a declaration that there exists a state of war between foreign countries, could restrict the export of any articles or materials to any such countries.

67 Charles Warren, 'Safeguards to Neutrality,' *Foreign Affairs* 14, 2 (January 1936), p. 215. For an informed discussion on neutrality, see Allen W. Dulles

and Hamilton Fish Armstrong, *Can We Be Neutral?* (New York: Harper &
Brothers, 1936). In this book, the authors give the pros and cons of the
various courses open to the United States by which it can avoid being drawn
into wars begun by other countries. Also a detailed analysis and a careful
research work is found in Philip C. Jessup and Francis Deak, *Neutrality:
Its History, Economics, and Law*, 4 vols (New York: Columbia University
Press, 1936). In *American Neutrality 1914–1917* (New Haven: Yale University Press, 1935), Charles Seymour argues that the only reason behind
US entering of World War I was the German submarine campaign, 'the one
cause which if removed would have left us at peace' (p. 171).

68   L. H. Woolsey, 'The Fallacies of Neutrality,' *American Journal of International Law* 30, no. 2 (April 1936), p. 256.
69   Ibid., p. 257.
70   Ibid., p. 258.
71   Ibid., p. 259.
72   Ibid., p. 260.
73   Ibid., p. 261.
74   Edwin Borchard, 'Sanctions v. Neutrality,' *American Journal of International
Law* 30 (January 1936), p. 91. See also Bernard Baruch's article on 'Neutrality' in the June 1936 issue of *Current History* in which he adduces some
of the practical reasons why an embargo on lethal weapons is sustainable,
whereas an embargo or a threatened embargo on raw materials or nonlethal
commodities is dangerous to the United States, to the world, and to the
cause of peace.
75   Benjamin H. Williams, 'The Coming of Economic Sanctions Into American
Practice,' *American Journal of International Law* 37 (July 1943), p. 387.
76   Ibid., p. 386.
77   Ibid., p. 396.
78   Paul Lewis, 'U.S. Urges Iran Sanctions, But Whom Will They Hurt?' *New
York Times*, 16 December 1979, p. 32.
79   Bard E. O'Neill, 'The Analytical Framework,' in Joseph S. Szyliowicz and
Bard E. O'Neill (eds), *The Energy Crisis and U.S. Foreign Policy* (New York:
Praeger, 1975), p. 2. Hartmut Brosche also writes, 'The Arab oil embargo
was one of the most successful weapons introduced into world politics during the last years' ('The Arab Oil Embargo and United States Pressure Against
Chile: Economic and Political Coercion and the Charter of the United
Nations,' *Case Western Reserve Journal of International Law* 7, no. 3 (1974),
p. 6).
80   Ibrahim F. I. Shihata, 'Destination Embargo of Arab Oil: its Legality under
International Law,' *American Journal of International Law* 68 (October
1974), p. 627.
81   Alexander Eckstein, *Communist China's Economic Growth and Foreign
Trade: Implications for U.S. Policy* (New York: McGraw-Hill, 1966), p. 273.
82   Dennis Austin, 'Sanctions and Rhodesia,' *The World Today* 22, no. 3 (March
1966), The Royal Institute of International Affairs, p. 106. Austin further
adds that 'It is probably a fallacy to suppose that they [economic sanctions]
belong to a special category of pacific weapons' (p. 107).

83 Hoffmann, 'The Functions of Economic Sanctions: A Comparative Analysis,' (1967), p. 159.

84 Johan Galtung, 'On the Effects of International Economic Sanctions with examples from the Case of Rhodesia,' *World Politics*, XIX (April 1967), p. 409, reprinted in Robert L. Pfaltzgraff, Jr (ed.), *Politics and the International System*, 2nd edn (Philadelphia: J. P. Lippincott, 1972), pp. 336–8.

85 J. Wilezynski, 'Strategic Embargo in Perspective,' *Soviet Studies* (July 1967), pp. 83–4.

86 James Burnham, 'Do Sanctions Work?' *National Review*, 14 November 1967, p. 1,254.

87 Muriel J. Grieve, 'Economic Sanctions: Theory and Practice,' *International Relations – Journal of Institute of International Studies*, vol. II, no. 6 (October 1968), p. 442.

88 Gunnar Adler-Karlsson, *Western Economic Warfare 1947–1967: A Case Study in Foreign Economic Policy* (Stockholm: Almquist & Wiksell, 1968), p. 9. In fact, the main theme of Adler-Karlsson's book (originally his doctoral dissertation) is that the strategic trade embargo which was maintained throughout the cold war period by the Western alliance had been a failure even on its own premises. This is due to the fact that the embargo had not to any significant degree succeeded in slowing down the economic development of the Soviet Union and its allies. For an analytic review of the book, see Klaus Tornudd, 'Strategic Embargo and Economic Warfare,' *Cooperation and Conflict* 2 (1968), Oslo, Norway, pp. 148–55.

89 Robert McKinnell, 'Sanctions and the Rhodesian Economy,' *Journal of Modern African Studies* 7, 4 (1969), p. 572.

90 Testimony before a Senate Committee by Ota Sik, a top Czech economic planner who went into exile after the Soviet occupation of Czechoslovakia in 1968, as reported in the *New York Times*, 9 December 1970, p. 23.

91 Peter Wallensteen, 'Characteristics of Economic Sanctions,' *Journal of Peace Research* 5, 3 (1968), (p. 262). Reprinted in Coplin, William D. and Charles W. Kegley (eds), *Multi-Method Introduction to International Politics* (Chicago: Markham, 1971), pp. 128–154.

92 Eshmael Mlambo, *Rhodesia, The Struggle for a Birthright* (London: C. Hurst, 1972), p. 291.

93 Margaret Doxey, 'International Sanctions: A Framework for Analysis with Special Reference to the U.N. and Southern Africa,' *International Organization* XXVI (Summer 1972), p. 547. See also M. Doxey, *Economic Sanctions and International Enforcement*, 2nd edn (New York: Oxford University Press, 1980) in which Doxey concludes that 'in none of the cases analyzed in this study have economic sanctions succeeded in producing the desired results.'

94 George W. Baer, 'Sanctions and Security: The League of Nations and the Italian-Ethiopian War, 1935–1936,' *International Organization* XXVII. (Spring 1973), p. 179.

95 Larry W. Bowman, *Politics in Rhodesia: White Power in an African State* (Cambridge, Mass.: Harvard University Press, 1973), p. 110.

96 Klaus E. Knorr, *Power and Wealth: The Political Economy of International Power* (New York: Basic Books, 1973), pp. 156, 197.

97   F. D. Holzman, 'East-West Trade and Investment Policy Issues: Past and Future,' in *Soviet Economic Prospects for the 70s*, Joint Economic Committee, US Congress (27 June 1973), p. 663.

98   Leonard T. Kapungu, *The United Nations and Economic Sanctions Against Rhodesia* (Lexington, Mass.: Lexington Books, 1973), p. 129.

99   Sheikh Rustum Ali, *Saudi Arabia and Oil Diplomacy* (New York: Praeger, 1976). See also Fred S. Singer, 'Limits to Arab Oil Power,' *Foreign Policy* 30 (1978), pp. 53-67.

100 Robert Blake, *A History of Rhodesia* (London: Eyre Methuen, 1977), p. 400.

101 Samuel P. Huntington, 'Trade, Technology, and Leverage: Economic Diplomacy,' *Foreign Policy* 32 (Fall 1978), p. 71.

102 Franklyn Holzman and Richard Portes, 'The Limits of Pressure,' *Foreign Policy* 32 (Fall 1978), p. 89.

103 Robert E. Klitgaard, 'Sending Signals,' *Foreign Policy* 32 (Fall 1978), p. 105.

104 Harry R. Strack, *Sanctions: The Case of Rhodesia* (Syracuse: Syracuse University Press, 1978), p. 237.

105 Martin Meredith, *The Past is Another Country: Rhodesia, 1890-1979* (London: André Deutsch, 1979), p. 57.

106 Penelope Hartland-Thunberg, 'Book Review: *Sanctions: The Case of Rhodesia*, by Harry R. Strack,' *Annals of the American Academy of the Political and Social Sciences* 444 (July 1979), p. 159.

107 Donald L. Losman, *International Economic Sanctions* (Albuquerque: University of New Mexico Press, 1979), p. 128. See also Losman, 'The Effects of Economic Boycotts,' *Lloyds Bank Review* (October 1972), pp. 27-41, and his article 'International Boycotts: An Appraisal,' *Politico* XXXVII (December 1972), pp. 648-71.

108 Richard H. Ullman, 'Salvaging America's Rhodesian Policy,' *Foreign Affairs* 57 (Summer 1979), p. 1,112.

109 Milton Friedman, 'Economic Sanctions,' *Newsweek*, 21 January 1980, p. 76.

110 Robert L. Paarlberg, 'Lessons of the Grain Embargo,' *Foreign Affairs* 59 (Fall 1980), p. 145. See also Paarlberg, 'Food, Oil and Coercive Resource Power,' *International Security* 3 (Fall 1978), pp. 3-5, and 'The Grain Embargo,' *New York Times*, 28 September 1980, pp. 2ff. For an opposing view see Emma Rothschild, 'Food Politics,' *Foreign Affairs* 54 (January 1976).

111 Gerald F. Fitzgerald, 'Book Review: *Les Sanctions Privatives de Droit ou de Qualité dans Les Organisations Internationales Specialisées* by Charles Leben (1979),' *American Journal of International Law* 74 (July 1980), p. 709.

112 Judith Miller, 'When Sanctions Worked,' *Foreign Policy* 39 (Summer 1980), p. 118.

113 Kuhn, *The Structure of Scientific Revolutions*, p. 144.

114 Ibid., p. 150.

115 Henig (ed.), *The League of Nations*, pp. 270-1.

116 R. St. J. Macdonald, 'Economic Sanctions in the International System,' *The Canadian Yearbook of International Law* (1969), p. 88.

117 Blake, *A History of Rhodesia*, p. 395. Klaus Knorr in *Power and Wealth: The Political Economy of International Power* shares such views. He writes,

'There is no doubt that the Rhodesian economy has suffered serious harm. Her large tobacco industry was virtually crippled and her agriculture generally was hurt by the inability to import ammonia for fertilizer production. Economic growth was stifled, and inflation became strong' (pp. 156-7).

118 Elaine Windrich, *The Rhodesian Problem: A Documentary Record 1923–1973* (London and Boston: Routledge & Kegan Paul, 1975), p. xxii. For a contrasting view, see Anthony Astrachan, 'Sanctions Fail to Bow Rhodesia,' *The Washington Post*, 19 November 1967, p. 22.

119 Stephen Park, *Business as Usual: Transactions Violating Rhodesian Sanctions* (Washington: Carnegie Endowment for International Peace, 1973), p. 31.

120 Bowman, *Politics in Rhodesia*, pp. 183-4. Bowman writes, 'There was an almost complete statistical blackout in Rhodesia from November, 1965 to early 1967. Since then limited data have been issued but, for instance, detailed trade statistics have been completely withheld' (p. 113). Similarly, it is difficult to have a precise measurement of the effect of League sanctions on Italy as the Italian government suspended publication of all trade statistics and Bank of Italy statements.

121 P. B. Harris, 'Rhodesia: Sanctions, Economics and Politics,' *Rhodesian Journal of Economics* 2 (September 1968), p. 8.

122 See the following articles in the *National Review*: 'Can Britain Stop Rhodesia,' 11 January 1966, p. 22; 'Pretoria's View,' 27 December 1966, p. 1310; 'Naked Emperor,' 6 September 1966, p. 877.

123 See William F. Buckley, Jr, 'Our Leader Strikes Again: Decision Not to Lift Sanctions Against Zimbabwe Rhodesia,' *National Review*, 6 July 1979. p. 878.

124 Dan S. Chill, *The Arab Boycott of Israel* (New York: Praeger, 1976), p. 23.

125 Kuhn, *The Structure of Scientific Revolutions*, p. 146.

126 Ibid.

127 Ibid., p. 147.

128 Willis W. Harman, 'The Coming Transformation,' p. 107.

2 Universal Sanctions: Punitive Actions by the League of Nations and by the United Nations

1 Rita Falk Taubenfeld and Howard J. Taubenfeld, 'The Economic Weapon: The League and the United Nations,' *American Society of International Law*, Proceedings (1964), p. 183. An interesting analysis of the League by a political scientist in Inis L. Claude, *Swords into Plowshares: The Problems and Progress of International Organization* (New York: Random House, 1956).

2 See David Hunter Miller, *Drafting of the Covenant* (2 vols) (New York: G. P. Putnam's Sons, 1928) II, p. 838. This book offers a detailed account of the drafting of the League Covenant at Paris in 1919, by the legal adviser to the American Delegation in Paris.

3 Ruth B. Henig (ed.), *The League of Nations* (New York: Harper & Row, 1973), p. 30.

4   F. P. Walters, *A History of the League of Nations* (London: Oxford University Press, 1965), p. 51. This book is an invaluable source of reference to the League's history and activities.

5   John Spencer Bassett, *The League of Nations* (New York: Longman, Green Co., 1930), p. 15.

6   W. E. Hocking, *Man and the State* (New Haven: Yale University Press, 1926), p. 59.

7   Albert E. Hindmarsh, *Force in Peace* (Cambridge, Mass.: Harvard University Press, 1933), p. 152.

8   Miller, *Drafting of the Covenant*, p. 570.

9   J. M. Spaight, *Pseudo-Security* (New York: Longman Green & Co., 1928), p. 3.

10 See Ferdinand Larnaude, *La Société des Nations* (Paris: Imprimerie Nationale, 1920).

11 Max Huber, 'Die Schweizerische Neutralität und der Völkerbund,' in Peter Munch, *Les origines et l'oeuvre de la société des nations*, 2 vols, 1923 and 1924 (Copenhague Rask-Ors tedfonden, vol, II, 1924), pp. 68–136. Quoted in Titus Komarniki's *La Question de l'Integrité Territoriale dans le Pacte de la Société des Nations* (Paris: Presses Universitaires de France, 1923).

12 See 'Resort to War and the Interpretation of the Covenant During the Manchurian Dispute,' *American Journal of International Law* 43 (1934); also R. L. Buell, 'Weaknesses of Peace Machinery,' *Foreign Policy Reports* (14 September 1932).

13 Walters, *A History of the League of Nations*, p. 53.

14 League of Nations, *Official Journal*, 1921, pp. 521, 1, 182; *Annual Register*, or *A View of the History and Politics of the Year* (Great Britain), 1921, p. 155.

15 See Irving Fisher, *League or War?* (New York: Harper Brothers Publishers, 1923), p. 122. On two other occasions, the threat of imposing sanctions proved effective. The first case was that of Turkey. The Turkish government was asked under the threat of sanctions to cease the export of manufactured narcotic drugs and to take effective measures to suppress the illicit drug traffic. Turkey in 1933 acceded to all demands. The second case of the use of sanctions was that of Bulgaria which was producing heroin. The threat of sanctions made the Bulgarian government take 'the necessary steps to meet the situation.' In both cases sanction provisions were not invoked but the lesson derived was: 'The sanction power in the background has been sufficient to produce effective results.' (Helen Howell Moorehead, 'International Administration of Narcotic Drugs, 1928–1934,' *Geneva Special Studies*, vol. VI, no. 1 (27 February 1935), p. 12.

16 Henig, *The League of Nations*, p. 175.

17 Gaetano Salvemini, *Prelude to World War II* (London: Victor Gollancz, 1953), p. 124.

18 See S. R. Smith, *The Manchurian Crisis: 1931–32* (New York: Columbia University Press, 1948), pp. 139–54; also A. L. Stimson and M. Bundy, *On Active Service in Peace and War* (New York: Harper, 1947), pp. 233–44.

19 Shepard B. Clough *et al.*, *A History of the Western World*, 2nd edn (Lexington, Mass.: D.C. Heath, 1969), p. 1,284.
20 Ibid.
21 Gordon Craig in *Europe Since 1914* (1966) states, 'Although the League of Nations appointed a commission to investigate . . . the democratic states failed to agree to apply sanctions against the agressor or to try by any other means to make it withdraw from Manchuria. Their parliamentarians, and editorial writers in their newspapers, vied with each other in citing economic and military arguments to prove the inexpediency and probable ineffectiveness of sanctions, as well as elaborate proofs that forbearance and understanding would in time solve the dispute to everyone's satisfaction' (p. 696).
22 Clough *et al.*, *A History of the Western World*, p. 1,284.
23 Stimson and Bundy, *On Active Service in Peace and War*, p. 220.
24 Salvemini, *Prelude to World War II*, p. 127.
25 Vera M. Dean, 'The League and the Italo-Ethiopian Crisis,' *Foreign Policy Reports* XI, no. 18 (6 November 1935), (p. 214).
26 Eugene N. Anderson, *Modern Europe in World Perspective* (New York: Rinehart, 1958), p. 478.
27 Ibid.
28 For discussion of the Italo-Ethiopian dispute before 4 September 1935 see William Koren, Jr, 'Imperialist Rivalries in Ethiopia,' *Foreign Policy Reports*, 11 September 1935; also Sir Alfred Zimmern, 'The Testing of the League,' *Foreign Affairs* (April 1936), and 'League's Handling of the Italo-Abyssinian Dispute,' *International Affairs* (November–December 1935). Two highly useful accounts on the operation of League sanctions are Albert E. Highley, 'The First Sanctions Experiment,' *Geneva Studies*, vol. IX, no. 4 (July 1938), and *International Sanctions*, Royal Institute of International Affairs (New York: Oxford University Press, 1938).
29 Henig, *The League of Nations*, p. 117.
30 John I. Knudson, *A History of the League of Nations* (Atlanta: Turner E. Smith, 1938), p. 98.
31 Gerhard von Glahn, *Law Among Nations, An Introduction to Public International Law*, 3rd edn (New York: Macmillan, 1976), p. 502.
32 George W. Baer, 'Sanctions and Security: The League of Nations and the Italian-Ethiopian War, 1935–1936,' *International Organization*, vol. 27, no. 2 (Spring 1973), p. 165. See also John F. Williams, 'Sanctions Under the Covenant,' *British Year Book of International Law* (1936), pp. 130–49.
33 Dean, 'The League and the Italo-Ethiopian Crisis,' p. 214.
34 Knudson, *A History of the League of Nations*, p. 98.
35 Lord Davies, *It Need Not Have Happened*, p. 36, quoted in Alex Millward's 'Only Yesterday, Some Reflections on the 'Thirties' with Particular Reference to Sanctions,' *International Relations* (April 1957), p. 284.
36 Dean, 'The League and the Italo-Ethiopian Crisis,' p. 221.
37 Alex Millward, 'Only Yesterday,' p. 283. Eugene Anderson in *Modern Europe in World Perspective* (1958) maintains, 'From the start the British and French governments had tacitly agreed that the League action would not be pushed to the point of Italy's declaring war on other powers, that is, on either Britain or France' (p. 479).

38 Salvemini, *Prelude to World War II*, p. 36.
39 A. LeRoy Bennett, *International Organizations: Principles and Issues* (Englewood Cliffs, New Jersey: Prentice Hall, 1977), p. 28.
40 Sir Thomas Holland, *The Mineral Sanctions* (London: Oliver & Boyd, 1935).
41 Robert E. Dell, *The Geneva Racket* (London: Robert Hale, 1941), p. 117.
42 Anderson, *Modern Europe in World Perspective*, p. 479.
43 Most experts agree on this point. 'In a report published on February 12 [1936], the oil experts' committee of the League of Nations declared that an oil embargo applied by all League states would curb Italy in three and a half months, provided the United States limited its oil exports to the pre-1935 level,' wrote Vera M. Dean in 'The Quest for Ethiopian Peace,' *Foreign Policy Reports*, vol. XI, no. 26 (26 February 1936), p. 318.
44 Dell, *The Geneva Racket*, p. 117.
45 Robert A. Divine, *Roosevelt and World War II* (Baltimore, Maryland: Penguin, 1969), p. 10; see also by the same author, *The Illusion of Neutrality* (Chicago: University of Chicago Press, 1962).
46 Basil Rauch, *Roosevelt: From Munich to Pearl Harbor* (New York: Creative Age Press, 1950), pp. 28–9; also James MacGregor Burns, *Roosevelt: The Lion and the Fox* (New York: Harcourt, Brace, 1956), p. 257; Brice Harris, Jr, *The United States and the Italo-Ethiopian Crisis* (Stanford: Stanford University Press, 1964), p. 81.
47 Divine, *Roosevelt and World War II*, p. 12.
48 Cordell Hull, *The Memoirs of Cordell Hull*, 2 vols (New York: Macmillan, 1948), I, pp. 432–3.
49 Divine, *Roosevelt and World War II*, p. 12.
50 Ibid.
51 Ibid., quoted in Department of State, *Peace and War: United States Foreign Policy, 1931–1941* (Washington: US Government Printing Office, 1943), p. 293.
52 Harris, *The United States and the Italo-Ethiopian Crisis*, p. 92.
53 Divine, *Roosevelt and World War II*, p. 13.
54 *Christian Science Monitor*, 26 November 1935. The State Department warned against comparing October and November figures on the ground that the October figures included some September shipments, but this made the comparison even more striking.
55 Ibid.
56 Walters, *A History of the League of Nations*, p. 669. Sir Samuel Hoare, on 19 December 1935, told the House of Commons, '. . . supposing an oil embargo were to be imposed and that the nonmember states took an effective part in it, the oil embargo might have such an effect upon the hostilities as to force their termination.' Quoted in Vera M. Dean's 'The Quest for Ethiopian Peace,' p. 323.
57 René Albrecht-Carrie, *Britain and France* (New York: Doubleday, 1970), p. 475.
58 H. R. Wilson, *Diplomat between Wars* (New York: Longman, Green & Co., 1941), p. 319.
59 Anthony Eden, *The Eden Memoirs: Facing the Dictators* (London: Cassell, 1962), p. 387.

60   K. Feiling, *Life of Neville Chamberlain* (London: Macmillan 1946), p. 271.
61   A. J. P. Taylor, *The Origins of the Second World War* (Harmondsworth: Penguin, 1965), p. 127.
62   Henig, *The League of Nations*, p. 168.
63   Dante A. Puzzo, *Spain and the Great Powers 1936-1941* (New York and London: Columbia University Press, 1962), p. 97.
64   Henig, *The League of Nations*, p. 168.
65   Julius W. Pratt, *A History of United States Foreign Policy* (Englewood Cliffs, New Jersey: Prentice-Hall, 1955), pp. 580-1.
66   Cecil V. Crabb, Jr, *American Foreign Policy in the Nuclear Age*, 3rd edn (New York: Harper & Row, 1972), p. 428.
67   Henig, *The League of Nations*, p. 164.
68   Gordon A. Craig, *Europe since 1914*, 2nd edn (New York: Holt, Rinehart & Winston, 1966), p. 706. For more details on the Hoare-Laval plan, see Ian Colvin, *None So Blind* (New York: Harcourt, Brace & World, 1965). Robert Dell in *The Geneva Racket* states that the plan was British in origin contradicting Arnold Toynbee who asserted that the idea was French and that Hoare was reluctantly drawn to it (see Arnold Toynbee, *Survey of International Affairs* II (London: Institute of International Affairs, 1935), p. 300).
69   Anderson, *Modern Europe in World Perspective*, p. 480.
70   Craig, *Europe since 1914*, pp. 706-7.
71   Toynbee, *Survey of International Affairs* II, p. 429.
72   Henig, *The League of Nations*, p. 146.
73   Craig, *Europe since 1914*, p. 707.
74   Anderson, *Modern Europe in World Perspective*, p. 480.
75   Ibid.
76   Craig, *Europe since 1914*, p. 707.
77   Ibid., p. 708.
78   Walters, *A History of the League of Nations*, p. 102.
79   A. LeRoy Bennett, *International Organizations: Principles and Issues*, p. 28.
80   *Geneva*, vol. IX, no. 5 (May 1936), p. 175.
81   Craig, *Europe since 1914*, p. 709.
82   F. P. Walters, *A History of the League of Nations*, p. 101.
83   *Geneva*, vol. IX, no. 7 (July 1936), p. 191.
84   Ibid,; see also George Scott, *The Rise and Fall of the League of Nations* (London: Hutchinson, 1973), p. 318.
85   Ibid.
86   Ibid.
87   Ibid.
88   Henig, *The League of Nations*, pp. 128-9.
89   Norman Angell, *Peace with the Dictators* (New York and London: Harper & Brothers, 1938), p. 135.
90   Salvemini, *Prelude to World War II*, pp. 414-17.
91   Puzzo, *Spain and the Great Powers 1936-1941*, pp. 203-4.
92   For a text of the Rome Protocols, see Hamilton F. Armstrong, *Europe Between Wars* (New York: Macmillan, 1934), pp. 112-15.

93 Angell, *Peace with the Dictators*, p. 133.
94 Alex Millward, 'Only Yesterday,' p. 284.
95 House of Commons Debate, Official Report, vol. 310, column 2482, 6 April 1936.
96 League of Nations, Records, 16th Assembly, 15th Plenary Meeting, 10 October 1935, p. 5.
97 Ibid., p. 49.
98 Ibid.
99 Ibid.
100 Alfred Zimmern, *The League of Nations and the Rule of Law* (New York: Russell & Russell, 1969), reprint of the 1939 edn. (First edn 1936).
101 Maurice Waters, *The United Nations* (London: Macmillan, 1967), p. 27.
102 Ibid.
103 Ibid., p. 26.
104 Josef K. Kunz, 'Sanctions in International Law,' *American Journal of International Law* 54 (April 1960), p. 338, fn. 37.
105 Ibid., pp. 328-9.
106 Leland M. Goodrich and Edward Hambro, *Charter of the United Nations: Commentary and Documents* (Boston: World Peace Organization, 1946), p. 348.
107 Ibid., p. 160.
108 Ibid., p. 345.
109 Ralph Zacklin, *The United Nations and Rhodesia* (New York: Praeger, 1974), p. 45.
110 Ibid.
111 John Halderman, 'Some Legal Aspects of Sanctions in the Rhodesian Case,' *International and Comparative Law Quarterly*, vol. 17, part 3 (July 1968), p. 690.
112 Jorge Castaneda, *Legal Effects of United Nations Resolutions* (New York and London: Columbia University Press, 1969), p. 11.
113 Concerning the practical efficacy of UN resolutions, see Gabriella Rosner Laude, 'The Changing Effectiveness of General Assembly Resolutions,' in R. A. Falk and S. H. Menlovitz, eds, *The Strategy of World Order*, 4 vols, (New York: World Law Fund, 1966), vol. III.
114 A. J. P. Tammes, 'Decisions of International Organs as a Source of International Law,' *Recueil des Cours de L'Académie de Droit International*, XCIV, p. 333.
115 Castaneda, *Legal Effects of United Nations Resolutions*, p. 12.
116 Ibid., p. 78.
117 Hans Kelsen, *The Law of the United Nations* (New York: Praeger, 1950), p. 96.
118 Goodrich and Hambro, *Charter of the United Nations*, p. 161.
119 Alf Ross, *The Constitution of the United Nations* (Copenhagen: Munksgaard, 1950), p. 71.
120 Castaneda, *Legal Effects of United Nations Resolutions*, p. 77.
121 Thomas Hovet, Jr and Erica Hovet, *A Chronology and Fact Book of the United Nations 1941-1979* (Dobbs Ferry, New York: Oceana, 1979), p. 107.

122 D. von Schenck, 'The Problem of the Participation of the Federal Republic of Germany in Sanctions of the United Nations, with Special Regard for the Case of Rhodesia' (Summary in English), *Zeitschrift für ausländisches öffentliches Recht and Völkerrecht* 29, 2 (May 1969); Rudolf Bindschedler, 'The Problem of the Participation of Switzerland in Sanctions of the United Nations, with Special Regard for the Case of Rhodesia' (Summary in English), *Zeitschrift für ausländisches öffentliches Recht and Völkerrecht* 28, 1 (March 1968).

123 Kelsen, *The Law of the United Nations*, pp. 106–10. For still a third view see Boleslaw Boczek, 'Permanent Neutrality and Collective Security: The Case of Switzerland and the United Nations Sanctions against Southern Rhodesia,' *Case Western Reserve Journal of International Law* 1, 2 (Spring 1969), pp. 87–8; and H. Lauterpacht, *International Law: A Treatise by L. Oppenheim* (London: Longman, Green & Co., 1955), p. 407. Both writers argue that while states not members of the United Nations are not obliged to participate in the enforcement measures, they ought to refrain from aiding states against whom the measures are taken.

124 Goodrich and Hambro, *Charter of the United Nations*, p. 155.

125 Ibid., p. 156.

126 Ibid., p. 160.

127 On 18 May 1951 the UN General Assembly recommended that every state impose 'an embargo on the shipment to areas under the control of the Central People's Government of the People's Republic of China and of the North Korean authorities' of many strategic materials including petroleum. This measure resulted in a decrease of Chinese trade with non-Communist countries by almost one-half from $1,170 million in 1950 to $601 million in 1952 (A. Doak Barnett, *Communist China and Asia* (New York: Harper, 1960), p. 233).

128 For a summary of UN-sponsored activities toward South Africa down to the end of the 1960s, see *International Conciliation*, no. 574 (September 1969), pp. 107–10. See also Ronald Segal (ed.), *Sanctions Against South Africa* (Harmondsworth: Penguin, 1964). See also John Seiler, 'South African Response to External Pressures,' *Journal of Modern African Studies* (September 1975).

129 African leaders made many attempts to eject Portugal from international bodies because of its colonial and racial policies. See Donald C. Blaisdell, *International Organization* (New York: Ronald Press, 1966), pp. 101–2.

130 Many books dealt with UN involvement with Rhodesia. Some are Charles B. Marshall, *Crisis over Rhodesia: A Skeptical View* (Baltimore: Johns Hopkins Press, 1967); A. G. Mezerik (ed.), *Rhodesia and the United Nations* (New York: International Review Service, 1966); C. A. Crause, *Rhodesia Independence and the Security Council of the United Nations* (Cape Province: Fort Hare University Press, 1966). For articles see Catherine Hoskyns, 'The African States and the United Nations,' *International Affairs* 40 (1964), pp. 466–80; Rosalyn Higgins, 'International Law, Rhodesia, and the U.N.,' *World Today* 23 (1967), pp. 97–106; J. Leo Cefkin, 'The Rhodesian Question at the United Nations,' *International Organization* 22 (Summer 1968),

pp. 649–69; Ralph Zacklin, 'Challenge of Rhodesia: Toward an International Public Policy,' *International Conciliation*, no. 575 (November 1969), pp. 1–72; George Alfred Mudge, 'Domestic Policies and UN Activities: The Case of Rhodesia and the Republic of South Africa,' *International Organization* 21 (Winter 1967), pp. 55–78; C. G. Fenwick, 'When is There a Threat to Peace? – Rhodesia,' *American Journal of International Law* 61 (1967), pp. 753–5.

131 'Rhodesia' is the common name used to refer to what was known formerly as 'Southern Rhodesia,' but the 'Southern' was dropped from common usage after Northern Rhodesia became independent as Zambia in 1964. Formal British and UN documents have retained the Colonial name, Southern Rhodesia, often followed by 'Zimbabwe,' the name adopted today as the official name by the nationalist government. Throughout this book, the old name 'Rhodesia' is used in order not to confuse the reader with the various titles. The population of Rhodesia was estimated in 1965 as 4,207,300 including 3,970,000 Africans, 12,400 Coloreds (mixed race), 7,900 Asians, and 217,000 Europeans (chiefly British).

132 Emmet V. Mittlebeeler, 'Africa and the Defense of America,' *World Affairs* 121 (Fall 1958), p. 2. In the cases of both Southern Rhodesia and South Africa, American officials disagreed with African governments on three specific points: (1) Washington doubted that racial discrimination in Africa or elsewhere constituted a 'threat to the peace,' enabling the United Nations to take jurisdiction; (2) it had genuine doubts about the effectiveness of boycotts, embargoes, and the like; and (3) it was skeptical that, even if they were successful such sanctions could ultimately benefit black citizens in these countries. See Cecil V. Crabb, Jr, *American Foreign Policy in the Nuclear Age*, p. 303.

133 Security Council Resolution 216 (1965), 12 November 1965 (10–0:1), para. 2, cited in James Crawford, *The Creation of States in International Law* (Oxford: Clarendon Press, 1979), p. 103.

134 Security Council Resolution 217 (1965) (10–0:1), para. 3, cited in Crawford, *The Creation of States in International Law*, pp. 103–4.

135 Martin Meredith, *The Past is Another Country, Rhodesia 1890–1979* (London: André Deutsch, 1979), p. 53.

136 Ibid., pp. 56–7.

137 Larry W. Bowman, *Politics in Rhodesia* (Cambridge, Mass.: Harvard University Press, 1973), p. 111.

138 See J. Kombo Moyana, 'The Political Economy of Sanctions and Implications for Future Economic Policy,' *Journal of South African Affairs* 11 (October 1977), p. 502.

139 Ibid.

140 Meredith, *The Past is Another Country*, p. 54. For the position of the Rhodesian government see J. Belfiglio, 'A Case for Rhodesia,' *African Affairs* 77 (April 1978), pp. 197–213.

141 Ibid., p. 57.

142 A. G. Mezerik, 'Rhodesia and the United Nations,' *International Review Service* XII (1966), p. 64.

143 Robert Blake, *A History of Rhodesia* (London: Eyre Methuen, 1977), pp. 291–2.
144 Mezerik, 'Rhodesia and the United Nations,' p. 1.
145 Speech by Ambassador Apollo K. Kironde of Uganda to the Security Council on 9 April 1966, quoted in *International Review Service* XII (1966), pp. 4–5.
146 Mezerik, 'Rhodesia and the United Nations,' p. 2.
147 Ibid.
148 Ibid., p. 7.
149 Ibid., p. 8.
150 Ibid.
151 Ibid., p. 10.
152 Ibid.
153 Leonard T. Kapungu, *The United Nations and Economic Sanctions Against Rhodesia* (Lexington, Mass.: Lexington Books, 1973), p. 40.
154 S. E. Wilmer *et al.*, *Zimbabwe Now* (London: Rex Collings, 1973), p. 3.
155 Meredith, *The Past is Another Country*, p. 57. For an informative analysis of the reasons and methods used by Rhodesia in reducing the effectiveness of UN sanctions see C. Barnekov, 'Sanctions and the Rhodesian Economy', *Rhodesian Journal of Economics* 3 (March 1969). For literature dealing with the Rhodesian economy and sanctions see John Handford, *A Portrait of an Economy under Sanctions 1965–1975* (Salisbury: Mercury Press, 1976); Curtin and David Murray, *Economic Sanctions and Rhodesia* (London: Institutute of Economic Affairs, 1967); R. B. Sutcliffe *Sanctions Against Rhodesia: The Economic Background* (London: Africa Bureau, 1966); A. Hoogvelt and D. Child, 'Rhodesia: Economic Blockade and Development.' *Monthly Review* (October 1973); A. Hawkins, 'The Rhodesian Economy under Sanctions,' *Rhodesian Journal of Economics* 1 (August 1967).
156 Richard Arens and Harold Lasswell, 'Towards a General Theory of Sanctions,' *Iowa Law Review* 49 (1964), p. 275.
157 Meredith, *The Past is Another Country*, pp. 56–7.
158 Kapungu, *The United Nations and Economic Sanctions Against Rhodesia*, p. 15.
159 Robert B. Sutcliffe, 'The Political Economy of Rhodesian Sanctions,' *Journal of Commonwealth Political Studies* 7, 2 (July 1969), p. 116.
160 Wilmer *et al.*, *Zimbabwe Now*, p. 48.
161 Mezerik, 'Rhodesia and the United Nations,' p. 82.
162 Ibid.
163 Ibid., p. 85. See a study prepared for the United Nations Secretary General by W. J. Levy Inc. entitled *The Economics and Logistics of an Embargo on Oil and Petroleum Products for Rhodesia* (New York: United Nations, 1966); also 'Why the Oil Sanctions Failed,' a report from Salisbury by Frank Kearns telecast on the CBS Evening News with Walter Cronkite, 27 March 1966 (*Africa Report*, April 1966, p. 24).
164 Meredith, *The Past is Another Country*, p. 145. See also Ian Smiley, 'Zimbabwe, South Africa and the Rise of Robert Mugabe,' *Foreign Affairs*, 58 (Summer 1980).

165   John Barratt, 'Southern Africa: A South African View,' *Foreign Affairs* 55 (October 1976), p. 155.

166   Mezerik, 'Rhodesia and the United Nations,' p. 88.

167   Eshmael Mlambo, *Rhodesia: The Struggle for a Birthright* (London: C. Hurst, 1972), p. 271.

168   George Thayer, *The War Business* (New York: Simon & Schuster, 1969), p. 277.

169   Mlambo, *Rhodesia: The Struggle for a Birthright*, p. 270.

170   Meredith, *The Past is Another Country*, p. 217. Some African specialists view Kissinger's program as a change in tactics rather than a fundamental shift in US policy. See Neil O. Leighton, 'A Perspective on Fundamental Change in Southern Africa: Lusaka – Before and Beyond,' *Africa Today* (July–September 1976), p. 17. Included in this article is the text of the central recommendations of the National Security Study Memorandum 39 (NSSM 39) dubbed as the 'tar baby memo' which Kissinger presented to President Nixon in 1970. For a dispassionate analysis of US policy toward Rhodesia see Anthony Lake, *The 'Tar Baby' Option: American Policy Toward Southern Rhodesia* (New York: Columbia University Press, 1976). This book constitutes the first major account of how US African policy is made in terms of bureaucratic policy. Low priority of African issues for US liberals and blacks resulted in a policy designed and carried out by the bureaucracy without constant, high-level supervision.

171   Ibid., p. 218.

172   Public Law 92–156; 85 Stat. 423.

173   See the 1973 US Digest, pp. 413–15 and the 1974 Digest, p. 598.

174   Donald Rothschild, 'Engagement Versus Disengagement in Africa: The Choice for America,' in Alan M. Jones, Jr (ed.), *U.S. Foreign Policy in a Changing World* (New York: David McKay, 1973), p. 229. See also Bruce Oudes, 'Rhodesian Ore: Here's To Thee, Oh "Club 503,"' *Washington Post*, 19 March 1972, p. B2; Gale W. Mcgee, 'The U.S. Congress and the Rhodesian Chrome Issue,' *Issue: A Quarterly Journal of Africanist Opinion* 2 (Summer 1972), pp. 2–7.

175   73 Department of State Bulletin 209 (1975).

176   Richard C. Schroeder, 'African Policy Reversal,' in *U.S. Foreign Policy, Future Directions* (Washington: Congressional Quarterly, 1979), p. 164.

177   Ibid., p. 163.

178   Ibid.

179   Ibid.

180   Public Law 96–60, the Department of State Authorization Act, Fiscal Years 1980 and 1981, approved 15 August 1979; 93 Stat. 395.

181   See Bernard Gwertzman, 'Why Senate Voted to Reject Carter Stand on Rhodesia,' *New York Times*, 15 June 1979, p. A–3.

182   44 Fed. Reg. 67073 (1979).

183   15 *Weekly Compilations of Presidential Documents*, pp. 2119–120, 19 November 1979.

184   Fed. Reg. 74787–8 (1979).

185   Dept. of State File Nos. P80 0016–1422, 1424, 1426 and 1428.

186 UN DOC. S/RES 217 (1965), reprinted in *The American Journal of International Law* 60 (1966), pp. 924-5.
187 Ibid.
188 UN DOC. A/RES/2151 (XXI), 17 November 1966.
189 Hearing before Senate Foreign Relations Committee on S. 1404, 92d Cong., 1st Sess. 12-18 (1971), statement reprinted at 65 Department of State Bulletin 111-15 (1971) and AJIL 66 (1972), pp. 139-41.
190 Robert B. Sutcliffe, 'The Political Economy of Rhodesian Sanctions,' p. 113.
191 Ibid., p. 114.
192 Ibid.

3 Multilateral Sanctions: Multiple-State Collective Actions

1 Frederick L. Schuman, *International Politics, The Western State System and the World Community*, 6th edn (New York: McGraw-Hill, 1958), p. 145.
2 Ibid.
3 Ibid. Louis M. Sears in *Jefferson and the Embargo* (1927) related how US attempts to use economic pressures against Britain and France had failed conspicuously. The US Congress in an effort to force Britain and France to stop interfering with American shipping passed a law closing American ports to commerce with both those nations. A year later, the embargo was withdrawn after having a disastrous impact on the American economy. In 1936 the Supreme Court in the case of *United States v. Curtiss Wright Export Corporation* upheld President Roosevelt's embargo (based on a joint resolution passed by Congress) on the sale of military hardware by United States companies to Bolivia and Paraguay.
4 See Louis Guichard, *The Naval Blockade* (New York: Appleton, 1930); also M. Parmelee, *Blockade and Sea Power* (New York: Crowell, 1924).
5 Samuel P. Huntington, 'Trade, Technology, and Leverage: Economic Diplomacy,' *Foreign Policy*, no. 32 (Fall 1978), p. 65.
6 Robert Oakeshott, 'The Strategic Embargo: An Obstacle to East-West Trade,' *World Today* (June 1963), p. 240. See also Yuan-Li Wu, *Economic Warfare* (Englewood Cliffs, New Jersey: Prentice-Hall, 1952); Peter Wiles, 'Economic War and the Soviet-Type Economy,' *Osteuropa Wirtschaft* (March 1965), pp. 27-42; J. Wilezynski, 'Strategic Embargo in Perspective,' *Soviet Studies* (July 1967), pp. 74-86.
7 Ibid.
8 Ibid.
9 Ibid., p. 242. Co-Com controls extend to Albania, Bulgaria, China, Czechoslovakia, East Germany, Hungary, Mongolia, North Korea, North Vietnam, Poland, Rumania, Tibet, and the USSR. Fifteen nations – Japan and all the NATO allies except Iceland – presently participate in Co-Com.
10 Jean Jacques Duprez, 'The Strategic Embargo: Doctrine and Practice,' *World Today* (September 1963), p. 374.
11 Oakeshott, 'The Strategic Embargo', p. 243.

12   Sheldon Appleton, *United States Foreign Policy* (Boston: Little, Brown and Co., 1968), p. 554.

13   James B. Agnew *et al.*, 'Detente: The Historical Dimension,' in *National Security and Detente* (New York: Crowell, 1976), p. 1.

14   Albert L. Weeks, *The Trouble Détente* (New York: New York University Press, 1976), p. 141. Rationale for the Nixon administration's policy of pursuing détente with the Soviet Union is outlined in Henry A. Kissinger's article, 'Détente with the Soviet Union: The Reality of Competition and the Imperative of Cooperation,' in *Détente and Defense, A Reader* by Robert J. Pranger (ed.) (Washington, DC: American Enterprise Institute for Public Policy Research, October 1976), pp. 153-78.

15   Commission on Foreign Economic Policy, *Staff Papers* (Washington, DC: The Commission, February 1954), p. 450.

16   Comecon was founded on 25 January 1949. A text of the official announcement is printed in the *New York Times*, 26 January 1949. However, its Charter was not officially approved until 1959. For historical accounts of Comecon, see S. Dell, *Trade Blocs and Common Markets* (New York: Knopf, 1963), pp. 306-21; F. L. Pryor, *The Communist Foreign Trade System* (Cambridge, Mass.: MIT Press, 1963), pp. 207-24. A more detailed analysis of Comecon is found in Michael Kaser, *Comecon: Integration Problems of Planned Economies*, 2nd edn (London: Royal Institute of International Affairs, 1967); Andrzej Korbonski, 'Comecon,' *International Conciliation*, no. 549 (September 1964); R. E. H. Mellor, *Comecon: Challenge to the West* (New York: Van Nostrand-Reinhold, 1971).

17   See U. Stehr, 'Unequal Development and Dependency Structures in Comecon,' *Journal of Peace Research* 14 (2), 1977, pp. 115-28.

18   Charles Issawi and Mohamed Yeganeh, *The Economics of Middle East Oil* (New York: Praeger, 1962), pp. 121-2.

19   Harvey O'Connor, *World Crisis in Oil* (New York: Monthly Review Press, 1962), p. 290. For an informative discussion of the nationalization see Hossein Sheikh-Hosseini Noori, *A Study of the Nationalization of the Oil Industry in Iran* (Colorado: Colorado State College, Graduate Division of Education): University Microfilms, 1965); also Richard W. Cotam, *Nationalism in Iran* (Pittsburgh: University of Pittsburgh Press, 1964), pp. 223-30.

20   *New York Times*, 5 January 1954, p. 51.

21   There was a Western tendency to underrate the administrative ability of underdeveloped nations. The Anglo-Iranian Oil Company thought that the Abadan installations would go to pieces under Iranian control; but when the foreign technicians returned they were surprised at the fairly good order in which they had been kept.

22   *New York Times*, 5 January 1954, p. 51.

23   Issawi and Yeganeh, *The Economics of Middle East Oil*, p. 183.

24   See Arthur Krock, *Memoirs: 60 Years on the Firing Line* (New York: Funk & Wagnalls, 1968), p. 262.

25   Ibid.

26   See George W. Stocking, *Middle East Oil* (Nashville: Vanderbilt University Press, 1970), pp. 153-6; also Michael Tanzer, *The Political Economy of*

Oil and the Underdeveloped Countries (Boston: Beacon Press, 1969), pp. 321-6.

27   For a popular account of the American intervention in Iran, see David Wise and Thomas B. Ross, *The Invisible Government* (New York: Random House, 1964). Also for a detailed discussion on how the CIA overthrew Mossadeq and brought the Shah back to power, see Kermit Roosevelt, *Countercoup: The Struggle for Control of Iran* (New York: McGraw-Hill, 1979). Kermit Roosevelt was the CIA operative who ran that 1953 operation whose details remained obscure for more than two decades.

28   Joe Stork, 'Middle East Oil and the Energy Crisis', *Middle East Research and Information Project*, Washington, no. 20 (September 1973), p. 14.

29   P. H. Frankel, quoted in Stocking, *Middle East Oil*, p. 158.

30   Issawi and Yeganeh, *The Economics of Middle East Oil*, p. 122.

31   *New York Times*, 1 November 1954, pp. 1-4.

32   Ibid.

33   Charles L. Roberton, *International Politics Since World War II* (New York: John Wiley, 1966), p. 213.

34   William C. Carleton, *The Revolution in American Foreign Policy: Its Global Range*, 2nd edn (New York: Random House, 1967), p. 297.

35   Walter LaFeber, *America, Russia, and the Cold War 1945-1975*, 3rd edn (New York: John Wiley, 1976), p. 187.

36   Robertson, *International Politics Since World War II*, p. 213.

37   Ann Williams, *Britain and France in the Middle East and North Africa* (New York: St Martin's Press, 1968), p. 121.

38   LaFeber, *America, Russia, and the Cold War 1945-1975*, pp. 188-90.

39   *The Times*, London 27 July 1956, p. 10.

40   A discussion of the Arab boycott from an Israeli perspective is found in Dan S. Chill, *The Arab Boycott of Israel: Economic Aggression and World Reaction* (New York: Praeger, 1976); and from an Arab perspective in Leila Meo *et al.*, *The Arab Boycott of Israel* (Detroit: AAUG, 1976).

41   Nancy Turck, 'The Arab Boycott of Israel,' *Foreign Affairs* 55 (April 1977), p. 472.

42   Ibid., p. 473.

43   Ibid., p. 477.

44   See *New York Times*, 27 February 1975.

45   'Arab Boycott,' *American Journal of International Law* 69 (July 1975), pp. 654-60.

46   Ibid., p. 661. Public Law 91-184; 83 Stat. 841; 50 USC App. 2402.

47   Turck, 'The Arab Boycott of Israel,' p. 489.

48   Fuad M. Itayim, 'Strengths and Weaknesses of the Oil Weapon,' Paper Submitted to the Sixteenth Annual Conference of the International Institute of Strategic Studies, University of Sussex, 12-15 September 1974, p. 5.

49   Juan de Onis, 'Two Countries Balk,' *New York Times*, 19 March 1974. This objective coincides with statements made by a number of Arab officials: the Algerian Minister of Energy, Belaid Abdesselam, maintained that the oil weapon was used in order 'to call the world's attention to the injustices of the situation,' *U.S. News and World Report*, 31 December 1973, p. 21;

the Saudi Arabian Minister of Foreign Affairs, Omar Sakkaf, asserted that the oil weapon was used to put the case to the American people, *New York Times*, 31 December 1973, p. 5, col. 1; Egyptian Ambassador Ghorbal stated that the oil weapon was used 'to gain attention to 25 years of suffering,' *New York Times*, 7 January 1974, p. 1, col. 2. President Sadat declared that the oil weapon 'was only a message to show the whole world that the Arabs after the 6th of October deserve to take their place under the sun,' *New York Times*, 25 February 1974, p. 1, col. 3.

50   UN Doc. S/13735, 10 January 1980.

51   'A Limp Set of Sanctions on Iran,' *Business Week*, 2 June 1980, p. 25.

52   Other European officials shared the same feelings. See the following articles in the *Christian Science Monitor*: 'W. Europeans Stay Aloof on Iranian Crisis,' 27 November 1979; 'U.S. Claims Sanctions Can Free Iran Hostages,' 18 April 1980; 'Europe Puts Large Holes Into Iran Sanctions Net,' 19 May 1980.

53   The text of the Executive Order is published in the 45 Federal Register 24, 099–100 (9 April 1980) and is reprinted in the *American Journal of International Law* 74 (1980), pp. 668–670. The President's message to Congress regarding his exercise of the authority granted under the International Emergency Economic Powers Act of 28 December 1977 is published in 16 *Weekly Compilation of Presidential Documents* 614–15 (14 April 1980). His message to Congress, transmitting a copy of Executive Order 12211 is found on pages 716–17 (21 April 1980) of the same volume.

54   *U.S. News and World Report*, 21 April 1980, p. 27.

55   *U.S. News and World Report*, 28 April 1980, p. 19. By February, US exports to Iran had shrunk to a negligible 1.6 million dollars. This compares with 27 million in October 1979 and an average of 200 to 300 million dollars monthly in 1978 while the Shah was still in power.

56   Text of the agreement is reprinted in the *New York Times*, 20 January 1981.

57   For a discussion of the two diametrically opposed points of view, see M. Kempton 'General Galtieri's Case,' and N. Annan, 'Mrs. Thatcher's Case,' *New York Review of Books* 29 (15 July 1982), pp. 20–3. Other useful articles dealing with different aspects of the Falklands crisis are Elizabeth Young, 'Falklands Fall-Out,' Lawrence Freedman, 'British Defense Policy After the Falklands,' and Gordon Connell-Smith, 'The OAS and the Falklands Conflict,' in *World Today* 38, no. 9 (September 1982), pp. 327–47; see also J. Pearce, 'Falkland Islands Dispute, *World Today* 38 (May 1982), pp. 161–5; J. Fawcett, 'Falklands and the Law,' *World Today* 38, no. 6 (June 1982), pp. 203–6; P. J. Beck, 'Cooperative Confrontation in the Falkland Islands Dispute: The Anglo-Argentine Search for a Way Forward, 1968–1981,' *Journal of Interamerican Studies* 24 (Fall 1982), pp. 37–58.

58   See 'Sanctions: Who'll Call Default?' *The Economist* (10 April 1982), p. 26.

59   See 'Galtieri's Economy: Run on Banks,' *The Economist* (24 April 1982), p. 28.

60   *Weekly Compilation of Presidential Documents*, vol. 18, no. 28 (19 July 1982), pp. 893–4.

61   'Argentine Sanctions: Melting,' *The Economist* (18 September 1982), p. 92.
62   See 'European Political Cooperation Shows Results,' *European Trends*
     (London: *The Economist* Intelligence Unit, no. 71, May 1982), p. 1
63   'Diplomacy: The Other War,' *The Economist* (29 May 1982), p. 20.
64   *New York Times*, 1 May 1982.
65   See 'Penalizing Argentina will Hurt Germany,' *Business Week* (26 April
     1982), pp. 33–4.

4 Unilateral Sanctions: One-State Coercive Actions

1   See J. Quigley, *The Soviet Foreign Trade Monopoly: Institutions and Laws*
    (Columbus: Ohio State University Press, 1974).
2   See A. S. Milward, *War, Economy and Society, 1939–1945* (Berkeley: University of California Press, 1977), p. 364.
3   See Vernon V. Aspaturian, 'The Soviet Union and International Communism,' in Roy C. Macridis (ed.), *Foreign Policy in World Politics*, 4th edn
    (Englewood Cliffs, New Jersey: Prentice-Hall, 1972). For the views of the
    Yugoslavian leaders on their conflict with the Soviet Union, see Milovan
    Djilas, *Lenin on Relations between Socialist States* (New York: Yugoslav
    Inform., 1949), pp. 16, 31. For more on how the Soviet Union employs
    economic coercion see D. Beim, 'The Communist bloc and the foreign aid
    game,' *Western Political Quarterly* 17 (December 1964), pp. 784–799; Leo
    Tansky, 'Soviet foreign aid to the less developed countries,' in *New Directions in the Soviet Economy*, Studies prepared for the Subcommittee on
    Foreign Economic Policy of the Joint Economic Committee, Congress of the
    United States (1966), pp. 947–74; Marshall I. Goldman, *Soviet Foreign Aid*
    (New York: Praeger, 1967); Joseph S. Berliner, *Soviet Economic Aid* (New
    York: Praeger, 1958); Robert L. Allen, *Soviet Economic Warfare* (Washington: Public Affairs Press, 1960); Howard S. Ellis, *Exchange Control in
    Central Europe*, Harvard Economic Studies 69 (Cambridge, Mass.: Harvard
    University Press, 1941).
4   See Victor L. Albjerg and Marguerite H. Albjerg, *Europe from 1914 to the
    Present* (New York: McGraw-Hill, 1951), p. 759.
5   See Robert Owen Freedman, *Economic Warfare in the Communist Bloc*
    (New York: Praeger, 1970), chapter II.
6   Klaus Knorr, *Power and Wealth: The Political Economy of International
    Power* (New York: Basic Books, 1973), p. 150.
7   Ibid., p. 145.
8   Ibid., p. 146.
9   For a discussion of how the Soviet leadership attempted to change Yugoslavian, Albanian, and Chinese policy through manipulation of economic
    and military assistance, see Robert O. Freedman, *Economic Warfare in the
    Communist Bloc: A Study of Soviet Economic Pressure against Yugoslavia,
    Albania and Communist China* (New York: Praeger, 1970).
10 For an examination of Soviet efforts under Krushchev to win over the Third
    World to communism through political support and large amounts of

economic and military aid, see Oles M. Smolansky, *The Soviet Union and the Arab East under Khrushchev* (Lewisburg, Pa.: Bucknell University Press, 1974).

11   Walter Laquer, *The Struggle for the Middle East* (New York: Macmillan, 1969), p. 235.

12   Kurt Mueller, *The Foreign Aid Programs of the Soviet Bloc and Communist China* (New York: Walker, 1967), p. 226; see also David and Marina Ottaway, *Algeria: The Politics of a Socialist Revolution* (Berkeley: University of California Press, 1970).

13   Marshall I. Goldman, *Soviet Foreign Aid*, p. 190. See also Sevinc Carlson, 'China, the Soviet Union and the Middle East,' *New Middle East* 27 (December 1970), p. 34.

14   For an article summarizing American embargo policy, see Jerald A. Combs, 'Embargoes,' *Encyclopedia of American Foreign Policy*, pp. 310–21.

15   Francis A. Beer, *Peace Against War* (San Francisco: W. H. Freeman, 1981), pp. 281–2. See also G. H. Snyder and P. Diesing, *Conflict Among Nations: Bargaining, Decision Making, and System Structure in International Crises* (Princeton, New Jersey: Princeton University Press, 1977), pp. 554–5.

16   Robert Oakeshott, 'The Strategic Embargo: An Obstacle to East-West Trade,' *World Today* (June 1963), p. 245.

17   Gunnar Adler-Karlsson, 'International Economic Power – The U.S. Strategic Embargo,' *Journal of World Trade Law* 6 (1972), p. 503.

18   See William C. Binning, 'The Nixon Foreign Aid Policy for Latin America,' *Inter-American Economic Affairs* 25 (Summer 1971), pp. 31–45.

19   *Review: 1974 Session of the Congress* (Washington: American Enterprise Institute for Public Policy Research, 1975), p. 16.

20   Ibid.

21   Gunnar Adler-Karlsson, 'International Economic Power – The U.S. Strategic Embargo,' p. 502.

22   *Japan Times*, Tokyo, 6 February 1962. Some useful accounts of US economic coercion against Cuba are Edward Boorstein, *The Economic Transformation of Cuba* (New York: Monthly Review Press, 1968); Donald Losman, *International Economic Sanctions* (Albuquerque: University of New Mexico Press, 1979); Anna P. Schreiber, 'Economic coercion as an Instrument of Foreign Policy,' *World Politics* 25 (April 1973), pp. 387–413; *New York Times*, 13 July 1974, pp. 1, 2 and Ann Crittenden, 'The Cuban Economy: How It Works,' *New York Times*, 18 December 1977, section 3, pp. 1, 9; A. Chayes, 'Law and the Quarantine of Cuba,' *Foreign Affairs* XLI (April 1963), pp. 550–7.

23   *New York Times*, 4 February 1962.

24   *Hsinhua News Agency*, Peking, 6 February 1962.

25   In 1958, China decided to cease exclusive dependence on the Soviet Union. However, the United States, failing to recognize the Sino-Soviet split for what it was, 'did all that it could to deny the Chinese access to what they needed . . . willing European sources found themselves severely constrained by an effective U.S. veto of Western technology transfers to China.' (Jack H. Harris, 'Northeast Asia: The Problem of Balancing Power,' in *Foreign Policy*

and U.S. National Security, by William W. Whitson (ed.) (New York: Praeger, 1976), pp. 141–2.

26 For an insightful perspective on the use of foreign aid as a diplomatic weapon, see Thomas G. Paterson, *Soviet-American Confrontation; Postwar Reconstruction and the Origins of the Cold War* (Baltimore: Johns Hopkins University Press, 1973). Paterson argues that the United States had employed its economic power regarding a postwar loan to Russia in an uncompromising way, thereby embittering Soviet-American relations. This view is refuted by Arthur M. Schlesinger, Jr, in his article, 'Origins of the Cold War,' *Foreign Affairs* 46 (October 1967), pp. 22–52. See also Hans Morgenthau, 'A Political Theory of Foreign Aid,' in David S. McLellan *et al.* (eds) *The Theory and Practice of International Relations*, 2nd edn (Englewood Cliffs, New Jersey: Prentice-Hall, 1974); David A. Baldwin, 'Foreign Aid, Intervention, and Influence,' in Romano Romani (ed.), *The International Political System: Introduction and Readings* (New York: Wiley, 1972); Peter A. Toma, 'The Problem of Foreign Aid,' in Peter A. Toma (ed.), *Basic Issues in International Relations* 2nd edn (Boston: Allyn & Bacon, 1974).

27 Thomas L. Brewer, *American Foreign Policy* (Englewood Cliffs, New Jersey: Prentice-Hall, 1980), p. 224.

28 *Jerusalem Post*, Tel Aviv, 31 October 1971.

29 See P. E. Sigmund, 'The Invisible Blockade and the Overthrow of Allende,' *Foreign Affairs* (January 1974).

30 *New York Times*, 9 January 1972, p. 1.

31 *New York Times*, 9 January 1976, pp. 1, 5.

32 James A. Nathan and James K. Oliver, *United States Foreign Policy and World Order* (Boston: Little, Brown & Company, 1976), p. 249. The threat by the US to cease economic aid to Israel was the means whereby the Israeli project for diverting the River Jordan in 1953 was stopped. E. L. Burns, *Between Arab and Israeli* (New York: Obelensky, 1962), p. 11.

33 Nancy Balfour, 'A Generation of U.S. Aid,' *World Today* (July 1964), p. 298.

34 Mitchell Cohen, *International Economic Leverage: United States and Israel 1973–75*, Monographs on National Security Affairs (Providence, Rhode Island: Brown University, October 1979), p. 124.

35 David H. Blake and Robert S. Walters, *The Politics of Global Economic Relations* (Englewood Cliffs, New Jersey: Prentice Hall, 1976), p. 132.

36 Ibid.

37 Joan Edelman Spero, *The Politics of International Economic Relations* (New York: St. Martin's Press, 1977), p. 144.

38 Klaus Knorr, 'International Economic Leverage and its Uses,' in *Economic Issues and National Security* by Klaus Knorr and Frank N. Trager (eds) (Lawrence, Kansas: Allen Press, 1977), p. 111.

39 Ibid., p. 114.

40 See Jessica Pernitz Einhorn, *Expropriation Politics* (Lexington, Mass.: D. C. Heath 1974), p. 25.

41 See Alfred Stepan, *The State and Society, Peru in Comparative Perspective* (Princeton, New Jersey: Princeton University Press, 1978), pp. 250, 258.

42   Samuel P. Huntington, 'Trade, Technology, and Leverage: Economic Diplomacy,' *Foreign Policy*, no. 32 (Fall 1978), p. 66.
43   Ibid.
44   Ibid., p. 67.
45   Ibid., p. 71.
46   'Soviet Military Intervention in Afghanistan, Actions to be Taken by the United States,' Speech by Jimmy Carter, delivered to the Nation, Washington, DC, 4 January 1980, reprinted in *Vital Speeches of the Day*, vol. XLVI, no. 7 (15 January 1980), pp. 194–5.
47   Ibid., p. 195.
48   Ibid.
49   Ibid.
50   Ibid.
51   'Grain Becomes a Weapon,' *Time*, 21 January 1980, p. 12.
52   Quoted by Irwin Ross, 'Who Broke the Grain Embargo,' *Fortune*, 11 August 1980, p. 124.
53   See William Verity, 'Taking Politics Out of Trade With the Soviet,' *New York Times*, 2 January 1979, p. A15.
54   Quoted in 'Grain Cutoff could Benefit Consumer,' *Christian Science Monitor*, 11 January 1980, p. 10. Howell believed that the effect on the American grain farmers 'could be particularly harmful' because many farmers were seriously in debt.
55   Bob Bergland, 'The United States Grain Program: The Effect on the Soviet Union,' *Vital Speeches of the Day*, vol. XLVI, no. 10 (1 March 1980), p. 291.
56   Ibid., p. 293.
57   Ibid.
58   Ibid., p. 294.
59   *Time*, 21 January 1980, p. 221.
60   'The CIA's Embargo Report,' *Newsweek*, 28 January 1980.
61   William Verity, 'Taking Politics Out of Trade With the Soviet,' *New York Times*, 2 January 1979, p. A15.
62   *Time*, 21 January 1980, p. 22.
63   'Grain Becomes a Weapon,' *Time*, 21 January 1980, p. 12.
64   'Embargoes Were the Simple Part,' *New York Times*, 13 January 1980, sec. 4, p. E1.
65   William Robbins, 'High Cost of the Grain Halt,' *New York Times*, 14 January 1980, p. D6.
66   Seth S. King, 'With or Without the Soviets, Farmers Depend on Exports,' *New York Times*, 13 January 1980, p. 4E.
67   'Grain Embargo: Leakage,' *Economist*, 15 March 1980, p. 37.
68   See 'How Europe's Neutralism Harms U.S. Business,' *Business Week*, 28 July 1980, pp. 56–9.
69   Interview with Steven Rattner, 'Trade as Weapon: Picking Ammunition, Target,' *New York Times*, 27 January 1980, p. E5.
70   The idea of using food as a political weapon was seriously discussed during the Arab oil embargo; see United States House Committee on Foreign Affairs: *Data and Analysis Concerning the Possibility of a U.S. Food Embargo*

as a Response to the Present Arab Oil Boycott, 93rd Congress, lst session, Washington, DC, 21 November 1973. Also, see Dan Morgan's articles on the use of US grain exports as a weapon against OPEC in the *Washington Post*: 'Cheaper Crude or No More Food; Using U.S. Wheat Against OPEC: Not so Farfetched as You Think,' 8 July 1979, and 'A Real Foreign Trade Is Taking Root in the Midwest,' 6 May 1979, p. A3; see also Simon Winchester, 'The Politics of Hunger: Food Now Ranks with Oil as a Weapon of Power Diplomacy,' *Manchester Guardian*, 5–7 January 1976; 'A Bushell for a Barrel?' *Washington Post*, 30 July 1979, p. A–12; 'OPEC: The U.S. is Losing its "Food Weapon",' *Business Week*, 26 November 1979, p. 52.

71   George P. Shultz, 'Light-Switch Diplomacy,' *Business Week*, 28 May 1979, p. 24.

72   *Business Week*, 28 July 1980, p. 57.

73   See James Nelson Goodsell, 'Argentina: "No" to Embargo,' *Christian Science Monitor*, 28 January 1980, p. 3.

74   See Charles A. Krause, 'U.S. General Asks Argentine Aid on Embargo,' *Washington Post*, 25 January 1980, p. A16.

75   Ibid.

76   'Grain Embargo: Leakage,' *The Economist* 15 March 1980, p. 36. See also 'America's Leaky Grain Embargo,' *U.S. News and World Report*, 24 March 1980, p. 12; see also Robert L. Paarlberg, 'Lessons of the Grain Embargo,' *Foreign Affairs* 59, no. 1 (Fall 1980), pp. 149–55.

77   'Limitation on Agricultural Sales to the Soviet Union,' Statement on Lifting the United States Limitation, 24 April 1981, published in the *Weekly Compilation of Presidential Documents*, vol. 17, no. 17, 27 April 1981, p. 465. See also 'When Reagan Lifted the Grain Embargo,' *U.S. News and World Report*, 4 May 1981, p. 11.

78   Karin Lissakers, 'Money and Manipulation,' *Foreign Policy* 44 (Fall 1981), p. 107. Other useful studies and articles dealing with the freeze are: E. Gordon, 'The Blocking of Iranian Assets,' 14 *International Law* (1980), pp. 660–73; 'Professor Robert H. Mundheim: Our Man in Algiers,' *University of Pennsylvania Law Alumni Journal*, 2 (Winter 1981); *Iranian Asset Settlement: Hearing Before the Senate Committee on Banking, Housing, and Urban Affairs*, 97th Congress, 1st session (1981); Pardieu, 'The Carter Freeze: Specific Problems Relating to the International Monetary Fund,' 9 *International Business Law* (1981); *Iranian Assets Litigation Reporter* (Edgemont, Pa.: Andrews Publications, 1980); Schneider, 'Problems of Recognition of the Carter Freeze Order by the German Courts,' 9 *International Business Law* (1981); Richard W. Edwards, 'Extraterritorial Application of the U.S. Iranian Assets Control Regulations,' *AJIL* 75, 4 (October 1981), pp. 870–902; M. Sandler, 'Foreign Policy in the Courtroom: The Iranian Litigation,' *Litigation* 8 (Fall 1981), pp. 10–13; A. J. Mikva and G. L. Neuman, 'Hostage Crisis and the "Hostage Act",' *University of Chicago Law Review* 49 (Spring 1982), pp. 292–354; 'Executive Agreements – Presidential Actions Nullifying Attachments, Ordering the Transfer of Foreign Assets, and Suspending American Claims Do Not Exceed Executive Authority,' *Texas International Law Journal* 17 (Winter 1982), pp. 91–101;

'Executive Power — President Has The Power To Block And Transfer Iranian Assets, Nullify Prejudgement Attachments, And Suspend Claims of United States Nationals In Implementing Executive Agreements For Release of Hostages,' *Vanderbilt Journal of Transnational Law* 15 (Spring, 1982), pp. 347–67; 'Iranian Assets Control Regulations and the International Monetary Fund: Are the Regulations "Exchange Control Regulations?",' *Boston College International and Comparative Law Review* 4 (Spring 1981), pp. 203–23.

79   Robert Carswell, 'Economic Sanctions and the Iran Experience,' *Foreign Affairs* 60, no. 2 (Winter 1981/82), p. 249.

80   Lissakers, 'Money and Manipulation,' p. 109.

81   Ibid.

82   Ibid., p. 115.

83   Carswell, 'Economic Sanctions and the Iran Experience,' p. 249.

84   See ibid., p. 250.

85   Lissakers, 'Money and Manipulation,' p. 116.

86   The issue of extraterritoriality has been gaining increasing attention in recent years, particularly so far as legal jurisdiction is concerned. Some useful references are Griffin B. Bell, 'International Comity and the Extraterritorial Application of Anti-Trust Laws,' 51 *Australian Law Journal* (1977); Reese, 'Limitations on Extraterritorial Application of Law,' 4 *Dalhousie Law Review* (1978); Hacking, 'The Increasing Extraterritorial Impact of U.S. Laws: A Cause for Concern Amongst Friends of America,' *Northwest Journal of International Law and Business* (1979); Joseph P. Griffen (ed.), *Perspectives on the Extraterritorial Application of U.S. Antitrust and Other Laws*, American Bar Association Section on International Law (1979); 'Extraterritoriality: Conflict and Overlap in National and International Regulation,' *Proceedings of the Seventy-Fourth Annual Meeting of the American Society of International Law*, Washington, DC, 17–19 April 1980, pp. 30–42; Harold G. Maier, 'Extraterritorial Jurisdiction at a Crossroads: An Intersection Between Public and Private International Law,' 76 *American Journal of International Law*, 2 (April 1982), pp. 280–320; Detlev F. Vagts, 'A Turnabout in Extraterritoriality,' 76 *AJIL* 3 (July 1982), pp. 591–4; V. R. Grundman, 'New Imperialism: The Extraterritorial Application of United States Law,' *International Lawyer* 14 (Spring 1980), pp. 257–66; J. J. Marcuss and E. L. Richard, 'Extraterritorial Jurisdiction in United States Trade Law: The Need for a Consistent Theory,' *Columbia Journal of Transnational Law* 20 (1981).

87   See 'Foreign Assets Control,' 75 *AJIL* 3 (July 1981), pp. 657–58; 'Iranian Hostage Agreement Under International and United States Law,' *Columbia Law Review* 81 (May 1981), pp. 822–901; E. Suy, 'Settling U.S. Claims Against Iran through Arbitration,' *American Journal of Comparative Law* 29 (Summer 1981), pp. 523–9; A. F. Lowenfeld, 'U.S.–Iranian Dispute Settlement Accords: An Arbitrator Looks at the Prospects for Arbitration,' *Arbitration Journal* 36 (Summer 1981), pp. 3–8; J. J. Norton and M. H. Collins, 'Reflections on the Iranian Hostage Settlement,' *American Bar Association Journal* 67 (April 1981), pp. 428–33; 'Effect of Duress on the Iranian Hostage Settlement Agreement,' *Vanderbilt Journal of Transnational*

Law 14 (Fall 1981), pp. 847–90; 'Iranian Hostage Agreement Cases: The Evolving Presidential Claims Settlement Power,' *Southwestern Law Journal* 35 (Fall 1982), pp. 1055–77.

88 *Weekly Compilation of Presidential Documents*, vol. 17 (28 December 1981), p. 1406; also 76 *AJIL* 2 (April 1982), pp. 379–384.

89 Ibid.

90 For an informative discussion of this act see Harold J. Berman, 'The Export Administration Act: International Aspect,' and Jonathan B. Bingham, 'The Export Administration Act of 1979: A Congressional Perspective,' both found in *Proceedings of the Seventy-Fourth Annual Meeting of the American Society of International Law*, Washington, DC, 17–19 April 1980, pp. 82–99. Also, John T. Evrard, 'The Export Administration Act of 1979: Analysis of its Major Provisions and Potential Impact on United States Exporters,' *California Western International Law Journal* 12, 1 (Winter 1982), pp. 1–45. A good analysis and evaluation of past and present US export control law can be found in C. Donovan, 'The Export Administration Act of 1979: Refining Export Control Machinery,' *Boston College International and Comparative Law Review* IV, 1 (Spring 1981), pp. 77–114.

91 'Statement on Extension of U.S. Sanctions. June 18, 1982,' 18 *Weekly Compilation of Presidential Documents* 24 (21 June 1982), p. 820.

92 For an informative discussion on the British Act and its purposes see A. V. Lowe, 'Blocking Extraterritorial Jurisdiction: The British Protection of Trading Interests Act, 1980,' 75 *AJIL* 2 (April 1981), pp. 257–82; Andreas F. Lowenfield, 'Sovereignty, Jurisdiction, and Reasonableness: A Reply to A. V. Lowe,' 75 *AJIL* 3 (July 1981), pp. 629–38; E. Gordon, 'Extraterritorial Application of United States Economic Laws: Britain Draws the Line,' 14 *International Lawyer* (1980); 'Power to Reverse Foreign Judgements: The British Clawback Statute Under International Law,' *Columbia Law Review* 81 (June 1981), pp. 1097–133; 'Section 6 of Great Britain's Protection of Trading Interests Act: The Claw and the Lever,' *Cornell International Law Journal* 14 (Summer 1981), pp. 457–79; D. L. Jones, 'Protection of Trading Interests Act of 1980,' *Cambridge Law Journal* 40 (April 1981), pp. 41–6; M. Brandon, 'Recent Developments in English Law Affecting International Transactions,' *International Lawyer* 15 (Fall 1981), pp. 629–38; 'Enjoining the Application of the British Protection of Trading Interests Act in Private American Antitrust Litigation,' *Michigan Law Review* 79 (August 1981), pp. 1574–606; 'Antitrust-Protection of British Interests From Foreign Antitrust Judgements-Protection of Trading Interests Act, 1980,' *Texas International Law Journal* 16 (Winter 1981), pp. 163–7; 'Protection of Trading Interests Act,' *International Lawyer* 15 (Spring 1981), pp. 213–32; A. K. Huntley, 'Protection of Trading Interests Act 1980: Some Jurisdictional Aspects of Enforcement of Antitrust Laws,' *International and Comparative Law Quarterly* 30 (January 1981), pp. 213–33; 'Protection of Trading Interests Act of 1980: Britain's Response to U.S. Extraterritorial Antitrust Enforcements,' *Northwestern Journal of International Law and Business* 2 (Autumn 1980), pp. 476–516; 'Antitrust: British Restrictions on Enforcement of Foreign Judgements,' *Harvard International Law Journal*

21 (Fall 1980), pp. 727–35. For more detailed discussion of efforts by other Europeans, see 'Extraterritorial Application of the Antitrust Laws and Retaliatory Legislation by Foreign Countries,' *Golden Gate University Law Review* 11 (Spring 1981), pp. 577–608; and 'Foreign Blocking Legislation: Recent Road Blocks to Effective Enforcement of American Antitrust Law,' *Arizona State Law Journal* (1981), pp. 945–75. The French response is discussed in B. C. Toms, 'French Response to the Extraterritorial Application of United States Antitrust Laws,' *International Lawyer* 15 (Fall 1981), pp. 584–614. While it was Britain, Australia, and Canada who took 'the most drastic steps to limit extraterritorial American antitrust enforcement' other nations such as France and South Africa took similar steps. For a comparative review of the salient points in the antitrust laws of the US, EEC, Germany and Japan, see Timothy Grendell, 'The Antitrust Legislation of the United States, The European Economic Community, Germany and Japan,' *International and Comparative Law Quarterly* 29 (January 1980), pp. 64–86.

93 See *American Journal of International Law*, vol. 72 (1979) at pp. 282–4 and vol. 74 (January 1980) at pp. 158–69.

94 See 'Judicial Decisions,' 75 *AJIL* 3 (July 1981), pp. 671–673.

95 'Judicial Decisions,' 74 *AJIL* 1 (January 1980), p. 195.

96 Ibid., p. 672.

97 See 'Judicial Decisions,' 75 *AJIL* 4 (October 1981), pp. 972–4. The decision of the court was mainly based on the views of 'FCN authority Herman Walker,' expressed in his article 'Provisions on Companies in United States Commercial Treaties,' *AJIL* 50 (1956), pp. 380–3.

98 'Europe Drives a Hole Through those American Sanctions,' *The Economist*, 28 August 1982, p. 48.

99 Ibid. President Reagan's decision on 13 November 1982 to lift the pipeline sanctions ended Dresser's court action against the Commerce Department challenging the government's right to apply the sanctions.

100 'Britain Orders Firms to Ignore U.S. Curbs,' *International Herald Tribune*, 3 August 1982, p. 1.

101 See R. Roosa, A. Gutowski and M. Matsukawa, *East-West Trade at a Crossroads* (New York: New York University Press, 1982).

Appendix I The Political Utility of Economic Sanctions: The Old Paradigm

1 Alexander Berkenheim, 'The Economic Blockade of Russia,' *International Review* 1, London (January–June, 1919), p. 250.

2 Quoted in Quincy Wright, 'The Test of Aggression in the Italo-Ethiopian War,' *American Journal of International Law* 30 (January 1936), p. 48.

3 Bruce Williams, *State Security and the League of Nations* (Baltimore: The Johns Hopkins Press, 1927), pp. 230–1.

4 Dorothy J. Orchard, 'China's Use of the Boycott as a Political Weapon,' *Annals of American Academy of Political Science Society* 152, part IV (November 1930), p. 252.

5 Sir Anton Bertram, 'The Economic Weapon as a Form of Peaceful Pressure,' *Transactions of the Grotius Society* XVII (1932) quoted in C. F. Remer, *A Study of Chinese Boycotts* (Baltimore: Johns Hopkins Press, 1933), p. 7.

6 John V. A. MacMurray, 'Introduction,' in C. F. Remer, *A Study of Chinese Boycotts*, p. vi.

7 Anthony Eden, 'The Future of Sanctions and Negotiations with Germany,' Speech in the House of Commons, 18 June 1936, reprinted in *Vital Speeches of the Day*, 11, no. 2 (1 July 1936), p. 621.

8 M. J. Bonn, 'How Sanctions Failed,' *Foreign Affairs* 15, 2 (1937), p. 361.

9 Albert E. Highley, *The First Sanctions Experiment, A Study of League Procedures* (Geneva: Geneva Studies, vol. IX, no. 4, July 1938), p. 127.

10 Robert McElroy, 'International Law's Greatest Need,' *American Journal of International Law* 37 (January 1943), pp. 117-18.

11 Anthony Eden, *Facing the Dictators* (London: Cassell, 1962), p. 311.

12 Josef Kunz, 'The Problem of the Progressive Development of International Law,' *Iowa Law Review* 31 (1946), pp. 544, 546.

13 Hans Kelsen, 'Collective Security Under International Law,' in *International Law Studies* (1954), Naval War College (1957), pp. 106-7.

14 Henri Spaak, 'Problems Facing the West,' *Virginia Law Review* 107 (1959), p. 1095.

Appendix II The Political Utility of Economic Sanctions: The New Paradigm

1 *New York Times*, 22 December 1963. Quoted in Dan S. Chill, *The Arab Boycott of Israel: Economic Aggression and World Reaction* (New York: Praeger, 1976), p. 30.

2 Rita F. Taubenfeld and Howard J. Taubenfeld, 'The "Economic Weapon": The League and the United Nations,' *Proceedings of the American Society of International Law* 58 (1964), p. 187.

3 Ibid., p. 204.

4 Anthony Lejeune, 'Can Britain Stop Rhodesia?' *National Review*, 11 January 1966, p. 22.

5 Ibid., p. 23.

6 'Score at Half Time,' *National Review*, 8 March 1966, p. 196.

7 'Report from Rhodesia: Why the Oil Sanctions Failed,' a report from Salisbury by Frank Kearns telecast on the 'CBS Evening News with Walter Cronkite,' 21 March 1966, reprinted in *Africa Report* (April 1966), p. 24.

8 Elspeth Huxley, 'Naked Emperor,' *National Review*, 6 September 1966, p. 877.

9 'Confident Rhodesians,' *New Republic*, 17 September 1966, p. 16.

10 'Boomerang Boycott,' *Time*, 2 December 1966, p. 93.

11 'Will Sanctions Work? Time is On Our side,' interview with correspondent Peter Webb, *Newsweek*, 19 December 1966, p. 43.

12 'The U.N. vs. Rhodesia,' *Newsweek*, 26 December 1966, p. 30.

13   James Burnham, 'Pretoria's View,' *National Review*, 27 December 1966, p. 1310.

14   A. Eckstein, *Communist China's Economic Growth and Foreign Trade: Implications for U.S. Policy* (New York: Published for the Council on Foreign Relations by McGraw-Hill, 1966), p. 273.

15   Colin Harris, 'Political and Economic Effects of Sanctions on Rhodesia,' *World Today* 23, no. 1 (January 1967), p. 1.

16   A. M. Hawkins, 'The Rhodesian Economy Under Sanctions,' *Rhodesian Journal of Economics*, August 1967, p. 44.

17   Frank Gervasi, *The Case for Israel* (New York: Viking Press, 1967), p. 134.

18   Elspeth Huxley, 'Letter From Rhodesia: To Crush a Mouse,' *National Review*, 9 April 1968, p. 335.

19   Timothy R. Curtin, 'Rhodesian Economic Development Under Sanctions and "The Long Haul",' *African Affairs* 67 (April 1968), p. 109, cited in P. G. Harris, 'Rhodesia: Sanctions, Economics and Politics,' *Rhodesian Journal of Economics*, September 1968, p. 16.

20   'The Superfluous Boycott,' *Time*, 19 July 1971, p. 17.

21   Ibid.

22   William D. Coplin and Charles W. Kegley (eds), *Multi-Method Introduction to International Politics* (Chicago: Markham, 1971), p. 153.

23   'Doubts over Use of Oil Weapon,' *Financial Times*, 26 October 1974.

24   Quoted in Nancy Turck, 'The Arab Boycott of Israel,' *Foreign Affairs* 55 (April 1977), p. 472.

25   Derek W. Bowett, 'International Law and Economic Coercion,' *Virginia Journal of International Law* 16, 2 (Winter 1976), p. 259.

26   Dan S. Chill, *The Arab Boycott of Israel: Economic Aggression and World Reaction*, p. 12.

27   Charles F. Doran, *Myth, Oil and Politics, Introduction to the Political Economy of Petroleum* (New York: Free Press, 1977), p. 32.

28   Jerald A. Combs, 'Embargoes,' *Encyclopedia of American Foreign Policy*, ed. Alexander de Conde (New York: Charles Scribner's Sons, 1978), p. 320.

29   J. Chal Vinson, 'Sanctions,' *Encyclopedia of American Foreign Policy*, ed. Alexander de Conde, p. 934.

30   *Chicago Tribune*, 6 February 1978, p. 1.

31   D. J. J. Botha, 'An Economic Boycott of South Africa?' *The South African Journal of Economics* 46, 3 (September 1978), p. 280. (Review article of Arnt Spandau's *Wirtschaftsboykott gegen Südafrika*. Cape Town: Juta, 1977).

32   Jean Mayer, 'Starvation as a Weapon Should Be Outlawed,' *Washington Post*, 5 January 1978, p. D8.

33   James Barber, 'Economic Sanctions as a Policy Instrument,' *International Affairs* 55 (July 1979), p. 374.

34   Paul Lewis, 'U.S. Urges Iran Sanctions, But Whom Will They Hurt?' *New York Times*, 16 December 1979, p. E2.

35   Ann Crittenden, 'Warfare: Trade As a Weapon,' *New York Times*, 3 January 1980, p. 1F.

36   Ibid., p. F15.

37 Ibid., p. F15.
38 Roger Fisher, 'My Turn: Sanctions Won't Work,' *Newsweek*, 14 January 1980, p. 21.
39 'Grain Becomes a Weapon,' *Time*, 21 January 1980, p. 22.
40 Interview with Steven Rattner, 'Trade as Weapon: Picking Ammunition, Target,' *New York Times*, 27 January 1980, p. E5.
41 Ibid.
42 Roy D. Laird and Ronald Francisco, 'Why Russians Can Ride Out the Grain Embargo,' *Christian Science Monitor*, 13 February 1980, p. 22.
43 'Economic Sanctions: An Obsolete Weapon?' *Forbes*, 18 February 1980, p. 92.
44 Ibid., p. 91.
45 Ibid.
46 'The Grain Embargo Sends Russia Shopping,' *Business Week*, 3 March 1980, p. 24.
47 Margaret Doxey, 'Economic Sanctions: Benefits and Costs,' *World Today* 36, no. 12 (December 1980), p. 488.
48 Robert L. Wendzel, *International Politics: Policymakers and Policymaking* (New York: John Wiley, 1981), p. 248.
49 'Sensible Sanctions,' *Daily Telegraph*, London, reprinted in *Christian Science Monitor*, 11 January 1982, p. 24.
50 Sidney Weintraub (ed.), *Economic Coercion and U.S. Foreign Policy: Implications of Case Studies from the Johnson Administration* (Boulder, Colorado: Westview Press, 1982), p. 3.
51 Christopher Dobson, John Miller, and Ronald Payne, *The Falklands Conflict* (London: Coronet, 1982), p. 92.
52 'Sanctions as a Symbol,' *Time*, 11 January 1982, p. 20.
53 'Reluctant to Follow Reagan,' *Time*, 11 January 1982, p. 26.
54 'Pressuring NATO on the Sanctions,' *Business Week*, 11 January 1982, p. 135.
55 'East-West Trade: An End to Business as Usual,' *The Economist*, 22 May 1982, p. 61.
56 'Shultz Airs His Views on Critical World Issues,' *U.S. News and World Report*, 26 July 1982, p. 25.
57 Richard Nixon, 'West Must Utilize Its Trade Power,' *Herald Tribune*, 24 August 1982, p. 4.
58 'Pipelines Asunder,' *The Economist*, 4 September 1982, p. 14.
59 'How to Deal with Russia,' *U.S. News and World Report*, 6 September 1982, p. 33.
60 Ibid., p. 34.
61 Ned Temko, 'Soviet View: U.S. Sanctions Spur Research,' *Christian Science Monitor*, 20 October 1982, pp. 1, 8.
62 'Pro and Con: Will Sanctions Sway the Soviets? Interviews with Richard Pipes and Carl Marcy,' *U.S. News and World Report*, 11 October 1982, p. 27.

Selected Bibliography

Economic Coercive Diplomacy: Boycotts, Embargoes, and Sanctions

The following list brings together the titles of books, articles, essays, reports, and interviews which deal directly with the use of economic coercion in international relations. It has been compiled in the hope that it will aid as well as stimulate scholars who desire to develop or investigate this vital subject further. An exhaustive effort was made to make this bibliography comprehensive; however, it makes no claim to completeness.

Abbott, Charles C., 'Economic Penetration and Power Politics,' *Harvard Business Review* 26 (1948), pp. 410–24.

Abbott, K. W., 'Linking Trade to Political Goals: Foreign Policy Export Controls in the 1970s and 1980s,' *Minnesota Law Review* 65 (June 1981), pp. 739–889.

Abouchar, Alan, 'The Case for the U.S. Grain Embargo,' *The World Today* 37, 7–8 (July–August 1981), pp. 277–81. (Argues that a continued grain embargo would have forced the Soviets to reassess their military expenditure.)

Abu-Rudeneh, O., 'The Oil Weapon: From Slogan to Reality' (in Arabic), *Shu'un Filastiniyya* (Palestinian Affairs) 43 (March 1975), pp. 33–58.

Adelman, Morris A., 'Is the Oil Shortage Real?' *Foreign Policy* 9 (Winter 1972–3), pp. 69–107.

Adler-Karlsson, Gunnar, *Western Economic Warfare 1947–67: A Case Study in Foreign Economic Policy*, Stockholm: Almqvist & Wiksell, 1968.

Adler-Karlsson, Gunnar, 'International Economic Power – The U.S. Strategic Embargo,' *Journal of World Trade Law* 6 (1972).

Ahrari, Mohammed, 'OAPEC and "Authoritative" Allocation of Oil: An Analysis of the Arab Oil Embargo,' *Studies in Comparative International Development* XIV, 1 (Spring 1979), pp. 9–21.

Allen, Robert, *Soviet Economic Warfare*, Washington: Public Affairs Press, 1960.

Allen, Robert, 'State Trading and Economic Warfare,' *Law and Contemporary Problems* 24 (1959), pp. 256–76.

Aloisi, P., 'America Plays with Fire: What Italy Thinks of Sanctions,' *Forum* 94 (1935), pp. 326–30; 95 (1936), pp. 11–12.

Alpert, Eugene J. and Samuel J. Bernstein, 'Foreign Aid and Voting Behavior in the UN: The Admission of Communist China,' *Orbis* 15 (1971), pp. 963–77.

Alpert, Eugene J. and Samuel J. Bernstein, 'International Bargaining and Political

Coalitions: U.S. Foreign Aid and China's Admission to the UN.' *Western Political Quarterly* 27 (1974), pp. 314–27.

Ali-Raddam, A., 'The Arab Economic Boycott of Egypt,' (in Arabic) *Majalat Markaz al-Dirasat al-Filastiniyah* (Journal of the Institute of Palestinian Studies), 34–5 (July–December 1979), pp. 69–80.

Ali-Raddam, A., 'The U.S. and the Arab Boycott,' (in Arabic) *Majalat Markaz al-Dirasat al-Filastiniyah* 30 (September–October 1979), pp. 5–22.

Amos, John W., 'The Middle East: The Problem of Quarantine,' in William W. Whitson (ed.), *Foreign Policy and U.S. National Security*, New York: Praeger, 1976, pp. 76–93.

'Analysis and Application of the Anti-Boycott Provisions of the Export Administration Amendments of 1977,' *Law and Policy in International Business* 9 (1977), pp. 915–57.

'Anti-Boycott Legislation – The Export Administration Amendments of 1977, pub. 1, no. 95–52. 91 stat. 235,' *Harvard International Law Journal* 19 (Winter 1978), pp. 343–72.

Anti-Defamation League, B'nai B'rith, *Japan's Foreign Trade and the Arab Boycott of Israel*, New York: Anti-Defamation League, January 1968.

'Antitrust as an Antidote to the Arab Boycott,' *Law and Policy in International Business* 8 (1976), pp. 799–828.

'The Antritrust Implications of the Arab Boycott,' *Michigan Law Review* 74, 4 (March 1976), pp. 795–819.

'The [Arab] Boycott – a Two-Edged, Flexible and Powerful Weapon,' *Middle East Economic Digest* (16 January 1976).

'The Arab Boycott: An Instrument of Peaceful Self-Defense,' *Arab Report* (15 January 1976).

'Arab Boycott: The Antitrust Challenge of United States v. Bechtel 897 Antitrust and Trade Reg Rep (BNA) E–1 (N.D. Cal., 5 January 1979) in Light of the Export Administration Amendments of 1977', *Harvard Law Review* 92 (May 1979), pp. 1440–60.

'Arab Boycott and the Bechtel Case,' 11 *Journal of World Trade Law* (1977).

'Arab Boycott's Effects on Britain,' *Middle East Review* (Winter 1975/6), pp. 48–51.

'Arab Boycott and the International Response'. Introduction. Pressures and principles – the politics of the antiboycott legislation. H. J. Steiner, The antiboycott law: the regulation of international business behavior. S. J. Marcuss, The business effects of the antiboycott provisions of the export administration amendments of 1977 – morality plus pragmatism equals complexity. E. A. Ludwig, J. T. Smith, II, The Arab boycott of Israel: the role of United States antitrust laws in the wake of the export administration amendments of 1977. J. M. Johnstone, J. Paugh, Federal tax consequences of international boycotts. C. Estes, II, A comparative study of non-United States responses to the Arab boycott. N. Turck, The extraterritorial application of the export administration amendments of 1977. *Georgia Journal of International and Comparative Law* 8 (Spring 1978), p. 234.

Arad, R. W. and A. L. Hillman, 'Embargo Threat, Learning and Departure From Comparative Advantage,' *Journal of International Economics* 9 (May 1979), pp. 265–75. (Extends the analysis of trade embargo threats to a situation where there is the possibility of lowering the future cost of production of the potentially embargoed commodity as a result of learning.)

Arbour, J. Maurice, 'Aspects Juridiques de la Crise Americano-Iranienne,' *Les Cahiers Droit* 21 (September 1980), pp. 367–97.

Areeda, Phillip, 'Remarks on the Arab Boycott,' *Texas Law Review* 54 (1976), pp. 1432–7.

Arens, Richard, and Harold Lasswell, 'Towards a General Theory of Sanctions,' *Iowa Law Review* 49 (1964), pp. 233–75.

Arens, Richard, 'The Role of Sanction in Conflict Resolution,' *Journal of Conflict Resolution* 11 (1967), pp. 27–39.

Arnold, Guy, *Sanctions Against Rhodesia, 1965 to 1972*, London: The Africa Bureau, 1972.

Arnold, Guy and Alan Baldwin, *Rhodesia: Token Sanctions or Economic Warfare*, London: The Africa Bureau, 1972.

Arnold-Forster, W., *The Blockade, 1914–1919*, Oxford Pamphlets on World Affairs no. 16, Oxford: Oxford University Press, 1939.

Arnold-Forster, 'Sanctions,' *Journal of the British Institute of International Affairs* V, 1 (January 1926), pp. 1–15.

Arsenault, Raymond, 'White on Chrome: Southern Congressmen and Rhodesia 1962–1971,' *Issue* 2 (Winter 1972), pp. 46–57.

Ashford, N., 'South Africa and the Threat of Economic Sanctions,' *Optima* (Johannesburg) 3 (1979), pp. 138–51.

Atkins, James, 'The Oil Crisis: This Time the Wolf is Here,' *Foreign Affairs* LI (April 1973), pp. 462–90.

Atwater, Elton, *Administration of Export and Import Embargoes by Member States of the League of Nations, 1935–1936, With Special Reference to Great Britain, France, Belgium, the Netherlands, Denmark, Norway and Sweden*, Geneva: Geneva Research Centre, 1938.

Austin, Dennis, 'Sanctions and Rhodesia,' *World Today* 22, 3 (March 1966), pp. 106–13.

Baade, Robert A. and J. F. Galloway, 'Economic Sanctions Against the Union of South Africa: Policy Options,' *Alternatives* (New Delhi) 4, 4 (1979), pp. 487–505.

Baer, George W., *The Coming of the Italian-Ethiopian War*, Cambridge, Mass.: Harvard University Press, 1967.

Baer, George W., 'Sanctions and Security: The League of Nations and the Italian-Ethiopian War, 1935–1936,' *International Organization* 27, 2 (Spring 1973), pp. 165–80.

Bahti, James H., *The Arab Economic Boycott of Israel*, Washington, DC: The Brookings Institution, 1967.

Baily, Martin, 'Who Fuels Apartheid?' *Africa* 16 (April 1981), pp. 43–5.

Baily, Martin and Bernard Rivers, *Oil Sanctions Against Rhodesia. A Paper Prepared for the Commonwealth Committee on Southern Africa*, London: Commonwealth Secretariat, 1977.

Baker, D. I., 'Antitrust Remedies against Government-Inspired Boycotts, Shortages, and Squeezes: Wandering on the Road to Mecca,' *Cornell Law Review* 61 (August 1976), pp. 911–49.

Baldwin, David A., 'The Power of Positive Sanctions,' *World Politics* 24 (October 1971), pp. 20–38.

Balfour, Nancy, 'A Generation of U.S. Aid,' *World Today* (July 1964), pp. 298–304.

Balmer, T. A., 'Use of Conditions in Foreign Relations Legislation,' *Denver Journal of International Law and Policy* 7 (Spring 1978), pp. 197–238.

Barber, James, 'Economic Sanctions as a Policy Instrument,' *International Affairs* 55, 3 (July 1979), pp. 367–84.

Barber, James and M. Spicer, 'Sanctions against South Africa – Options for the West,' *International Affairs* 55, 3 (July 1979), pp. 385–401.

Barkun, M., *Law Without Sanctions*, New Haven, Conn.: Yale University Press, 1968.

Barnekov, C. C., 'Sanctions and the Rhodesian Economy,' *Rhodesian Journal of Economics* 3, 1 (March 1969), pp. 44–75. (An informative analysis of the reasons and methods used by Rhodesia in reducing the effectiveness of UN sanctions.)

Barros, James, *The League of Nations and the Great Powers: The Greek-Bulgarian Incident, 1925*, Oxford: Clarendon Press, 1970.

Bartholin, Pierre, *Aspects Économiques des Sanctions Prises Contre l'Italie*, Paris: Vuibert, 1938.

Bartholin, Pierre, *Les Conséquences Économiques des Sanctions*, Préface de M. François Perroux, Paris: Recueil Sirey, 1939.

Beim, D., 'The Communist Bloc and the Foreign Aid Game,' *Western Political Quarterly* 17 (December 1964), pp. 784–99.

Beiser, B. J. 'International Boycotts,' *Tulane Tax Institute* 27 (1977), p. 13.

Belfiglio, V. J., 'United States Economic Relations with the Republic of South Africa,' *Africa Today* 25 (April 1978), pp. 57–68.

Berg, Gracia, 'Human Rights Sanctions as Leverage: Argentina, A Case Study,' *Journal of Legislation* (Ann. 1980), pp. 93–112.

Berkenheim, Alexander, 'The Economic Blockade of Russia,' *International Review* [London] 1 (January–June 1919), pp. 348–352.

Berliner, Joseph S., *Soviet Economic Aid*, New York: Praeger, 1958.

Berman, Harold J. and John R. Garson, 'United States Export Controls – Past, Present, and Future,' *Columbia Law Review* 67, 5 (May 1967), pp. 791–890. (Provides a complete discussion of United States export control legislation and implementation.)

Bertram, Sir Anton, 'The Economic Weapon as a Form of Peaceful Pressure,' *Transactions of the Grotius Society* 17, London (1932), pp. 139–74.

Bess, Demaree, 'China's New Weapon Against Japan,' *Current History* (July 1932).

Bilder, Richard B., 'East-West Trade Boycotts: A Study in Private, Labor Union, State, and Local Interference with Foreign Policy,' *University of Pennsylvania Law Review* 118, 6 (May 1970), pp. 841–938.

Bilder, Richard B., 'Comments on the Legality of the Arab Oil Boycott,' *Texas International Law Journal* 12 (1977), pp. 41–6.

Bingham, T. H. and S. M. Gray, *Report on the Supply of Petroleum and Petroleum Products to Rhodesia*, London: Foreign and Commonwealth Office, September, 1978.

Blot, Michel J., *Les Sanctions de l'Article X du Parte de la Société des Nations et le Gouvernement Français*, Paris: Les Presses Modernes, 1933.

Blum, Yehuda Z., 'Economic Boycotts in International Law,' *Texas International Law Journal* 12 (1977), pp. 5–15.

Boczek, Boleslaw A., 'Permanent Neutrality and Collective Security: The Case of Switzerland and the United Nations Sanctions Against Rhodesia,' *Case Western Reserve Journal of International Law* 1 (Spring 1969), pp. 75–104.

Bonn, M. J., 'How Sanctions Failed,' *Foreign Affairs* 15, 2 (1937): pp. 350–61.

Boorman, James A., 'Economic Coercion in International Law: The Arab Oil Weapon and the Ensuing Legal Issues,' *Journal of International Law and Economics* 9 (1974), pp. 205–222. (Provides a review of the history of international trade embargoes.)

Borchard, Edwin, 'Sanctions v. Neutrality,' *American Journal of International Law* 30 (January 1936), pp. 91–4.

Borchard, Edwin, 'Neutral Embargoes and Commercial Treaties,' *American Journal of International Law* 30 (July 1936), pp. 501–6.

Bornstein, M., 'Economic Sanctions and Rewards in Support of Arms Control Agreements,' *Rhodesian Journal of Economics*, December 1969.

Bouve, C. L., 'National Boycott as an International Delinquency,' *American Journal of International Law* 28, 19 (January 1934), pp. 19–42.

Bowett, Derek W., 'International Law and Economic Coercion,' *Virginia Journal of International Law* 16, 2 (Winter 1976), pp. 245–60.

Bowett, Derek W., 'Economic Coercion and Reprisals by States,' *Virginia Journal of International Law* 13, 4 (1972), pp. 1–12.

Boycotts and Peace: A Report by the Committee on Economic Sanctions, chairman Nicholas Murray Butler, ed. Evans Clark, New York and London: Harper & Brothers, 1932.

Bradley, Phillip, 'Some Legislative and Administrative Aspects of the Application of Article XVI of the Covenant,' *Transactions of the Grotius Society* (1936), pp. 13–29.

Brady, Lawrence J., 'Trade With the Eastern Bloc,' *Vital Speeches of the Day* XLVIII, 2, 1 November 1981, pp. 56–9. (Argues that the West must not, through its economic relations with the Eastern bloc, increase the capacity of the USSR to wage war.)

Brierly, James Leslie, 'Sanctions in International Law,' in Hersch Lauterpacht and C. H. M. Waldock (eds), *The Basis of Obligation in International Law and Other Papers of the Late James Leslie Brierly*, Aalen: Scientia Verlag, 1977 (reprint of the 1958 edition).

Brosche, Hartmut, 'The Arab Oil Embargo and United States Pressure Against Chile: Economic and Political Coercion and the Charter of the United Nations,' *Case Western Reserve Journal of International Law* 7, 3 (1974), pp. 3–35. (Examines whether economic and political pressure may be used in international relations without violating UN Charter and concludes that in both cases studied, the practice of economic and political coercion was inconsistent with the Charter.)

Brown, E. A., 'Boycott in International Law,' *Canadian Bar Review* 11, 325 (May 1934).

Brown, Lester R., *By Bread Alone*, New York: Praeger, 1974.

Brown, W., 'The Oil Weapon,' *Middle East Journal* 36, 3 (1982), pp. 301–18.

Brown, Winthrop G., 'The Use of Foreign Aid as an Instrument to Secure Compliance with International Obligations,' *American Society of International Law*, Proceedings 58 (1964), pp. 210–17. (Criticizes the punitive foreign aid approach as 'blunt' and 'clumsy.')

Brown-John, C. L., *Multilateral Sanctions in International Law: A Comparative Analysis*, New York: Praeger, 1975.

Brown-John, C. L., 'Economic Sanctions: The Case of the O.A.S. and the Dominican Republic, 1960–1962,' *Caribbean Studies* 15 (July 1975), pp. 73–105.

Brück, Otto, *Les Sanctions en Droit International Public*, Paris: A. Pedone, 1933.

Bryan, Dennis W., 'The China Trade: Legal and Economic Considerations for American Lawyers and Businessmen,' *North Carolina Journal of International Law and Commercial Regulations* 3, 1 (Winter 1978), pp. 43–70.

Budd, Josephine E., 'China's Most Effective Weapon,' *Export Trade and Finance*, 12 March 1932.

Buell, Raymond Leslie, 'Are Sanctions Necessary to International Organization?' *Foreign Policy Association*, New York, 82 (June 1932), pp. 3–22.

Buell, Raymond Leslie, *The Suez Canal and League Sanctions*, Geneva: Geneva Research Center, 1935.

Burrell, R. M. 'The Oil Weapon: Who Gains Most?', *Soviet Analyst* 2, 23 (1973), pp. 1–3.

Business International, *Coping with the Arab Boycott of Israel*, Management Monograph no. 19, New York: Business International, 1963.

Butov, A. F., 'Legal and Institutional Forms of East-West Economic Contacts,' *Acta Oeconomica* 9 (3/4 November 1972), pp. 233–41.

Carswell, Robert, 'Economic Sanctions and the Iran Experience,' *Foreign Affairs* 60, 2 (Winter 1981-2), pp. 247–65. (Concludes that it was special circumstances that made the financial sanctions employed against Iran effective.)

Casadio, Gian Paolo, *The Economic Challenge of the Arabs*, London: Saxon House; New York: D. C. Heath, 1976.

Cavare, Louis, 'Les Sanctions dans le Cadre de l'O.N.U.,' *Academic de Droit International*, Recueil des Cours, 1952, I, vol. 80 (1953), pp. 191–291.

Cefkin, J. Leo, 'The Rhodesian Question at the United Nations,' *International Organization* 22 (Summer 1968), pp. 649–69.

Central Intelligence Agency, 1976, 1977, 1978, *Communist Aid to Less Developed Countries of the Free World*, Washington, DC: Central Intelligence Agency, 1976, 1977, 1978 (these are three separate reports for different years).

Chamberlain, J. P., 'Enforcing Economic Sanctions,' *International Conciliation* 220 (1926), pp. 287–91.

Chanda, N., 'Vietnam Drops Americans a Hint,' *Far Eastern Economic Review* 101 (7 July 1978), p. 51.

Chayes, A., 'Law and the Quarantine of Cuba,' *Foreign Affairs* XLI (April 1963), pp. 550–7.

Cheffers, John., *A Wilderness of Spite: or Rhodesia Denied*, New York: Vantage, 1972.

Chettle, John, 'Is There Any Justification for Economic Pressure Against South Africa?', *Issue: A Quarterly Journal of Africanist Opinion* (Waltham, Mass.) 9, 1/2 (1979), pp. 24–9.

Chill, Dan S., *The Arab Boycott of Israel: Economic Aggression and World Reaction*, New York: Praeger, 1976. (Examines the Arab boycott from an Israeli perspective.)

Chip, W., 'United Nations Role in Ending Civil Wars,' *Columbia Journal of Transnational Law* 19 (1981), pp. 15–33.

Chistol, Carl Q. and Charles L. Davis, 'Maritime Quarantine: The Naval Interdiction of Offensive Weapons and Associated Material to Cuba,' *American Journal of International Law* 57 (July 1963), pp. 525–45.

Clark, Evans (ed.), *Boycotts and Peace: A Report by the Committee on Economic Sanctions*, New York: Harper & Brothers, 1932. (Examines the use of economic measures to maintain peace. Packed with valuable research material gathered by a number of authors in various fields of scholarship.)

Clarke, D. G., 'Zimbabwe's Economic Position and Aspects of Sanctions Removal.' *Journal of Commonwealth and Comparative Politics* 18, 1 (March 1980), pp. 28–54.

Claude, Inis L., Jr, 'The Issue of the Autonomy of the OAS in Imposing Sanctions,' *International Conciliation*, 547 (March 1964), pp. 47–60.

Clissold, Stephen, *Yugoslavia and the Soviet Union 1939-1973: A Documentary Survey*, London: Oxford University Press, 1975.

Clute, N. Vander (Chairman), *Legal Aspects of the Arab Boycott*, New York: Practising Law Institute, 1977.

Cohen, Mitchell, *International Economic Leverage: United States and Israel 1973-75*, Monographs on National Security Affairs, Providence, Rhode Island: Brown University, October 1979.

Cohen, Phyllis, 'Constitutionality of New York's response to the Arab Boycott,' *Syracuse Law Review* 28 (Spring 1977), pp. 631–63.

Coleman, Clarence L., Jr, 'Boycott Not Religious Arabs Tell State Department,' *Issue* (Spring 1962), pp. 79–80.

'Collective Security and Sanction,' in Frederick H. Hartmann (ed.), *World in Crisis, Readings in International Relations*, 4th edn, New York: Macmillan, 1973, pp. 229–54.

Combacau, J., *Le Pouvoir de Sanction de L'O.N.U. Etude Théorique de la Coercition Non-militaire*, Paris: Editions Pedone, 1974.

Combs, J. A., 'Embargoes,' *Encyclopedia of American Foreign Policy*, ed. Alexander de Conde, New York, Charles Scribner's Sons, 1978, pp. 310–21.

Comecon and the Economy of Eastern Europe, Vienna: Creditanstalt Bankverein, June 1962.

'Comment, The Use of Nonviolent Coercion: A Study in Legality Under Article 2(4) of the Charter of the United Nations,' *University of Pennsylvania Law Review* 122, 4 (April 1974), pp. 983–1011.

Committee on Economic Sanctions, *Reports of Research Findings*, Geneva: League of Nations, 1931.

Consett, M. W., *The Triumph of Unarmed Forces 1914-1918*, London: Williams & Norgate, 1923.

'Contraband and Blockade,' *Congressional Digest* 9 (January 1930), pp. 13–14.

Coudert, Frederic R., 'The Sanction of International Law,' *University of Pennsylvania Law Review* 61, 1 (November 1912), pp. 234–9.

Cronje, S., 'Sanctions Against S. Africa,' *New Africa* (London) 6 (May 1964), pp. 16–18.

Cross, E. G., 'Economic Sanctions as a Tool of Policy Against Rhodesia,' *The World Economy* 4, 1 (March 1981), pp. 69–78. (Concludes that 'economic sanctions are a comparatively ineffective means of exercising political leverage.')

Crouzet, François, 'Wars, Blockades and Economic Change in Europe, 1797–1815,' *Journal of Economic History* (December 1964), pp. 567–88. (Gives a concise account of the economic impact of blockades.)

Curtin, Timothy R. and David Murray, *Economic Sanctions and Rhodesia*, London: Institute of Economic Affairs, 1967.

Curtin, Timothy R. and David Murray, 'Rhodesian Economic Development under Sanctions and "The Long Haul".' *African Affairs* (April 1968): 100–10.

Curtin, Timothy R. and David Murray, 'Total Sanctions and the Economic Development in Rhodesia,' *Journal of Commonwealth Political Studies* 7 (1969), pp. 126–31.

Dagan, A., 'The Arab Boycott,' in *The Israel Year Book 1966*, Jerusalem: Israel Yearbook Publications, 1966, pp. 252–4.

Dan, Uri, *L'Embargo*, Paris: Editions et Publications Premières, 1970.

Danaher, K., 'U.S. and South Africa: Building the Base for Sanctions,' *Freedomways* 21, 1 (1981), pp. 29–40.

Daoudi, M. S. and M. S. Dajani, 'Sanctions: The Falklands Episode,' *World Today* 39, 4 (April 1983), pp. 150–60.

De Crespigny, A. R. C. and R. T. McKinnell, 'The Nature and Significance of Economic Boycott,' *South African Journal of Economics* (December 1960), pp. 319–36.

De Gara, John P., *Trade Relations Between the Common Market and the Eastern Bloc*, Brussels: College of Europe, De Tempel, 1964.

De Fiedorowicz, G., 'Historical Survey of the Application of Sanctions,' *Transactions of the Grotius Society* 22 (1937), pp. 117–31.

Dell, S., *Trade Blocs and Common Markets*, New York: Knopf, 1963.

Dempsey, P. S., 'Economic Aggression and Self-Defense in International Law: The Arab Oil Weapon and Alternative American Responses Thereto,' *Case Western Reserve Journal of International Law* 9 (Spring 1977), pp. 253–321.

'Development, Scope and Application of the New Anti-Boycott Law of the United States,' *New York University Journal of International Law and Politics* 10 (Fall 1977), pp. 397–439.

Dewey, John, 'Are Sanctions Necessary to International Organizations?', *Foreign Policy Association*, pamphlet number 82–3 (June 1932), pp. 23–39.

De Wilde, John Charles, *Testing League Sanctions*, New York: Foreign Policy Association, 1935.

Divine, Robert A., *The Illusion of Neutrality: Franklin D. Roosevelt and the Struggle Over the Arms Embargo*, Chicago: University of Chicago Press, 1962.

Dodell, Sue Allen, 'United States Banks and the Arab Boycott of Israel,' *Columbia Journal of Transnational Law* 17 (1978), pp. 119–43.

Dougherly, J., 'The Aswan Decision in Perspective,' *Political Science Quarterly* 74 (March 1959), pp. 21–45.

Downey, A. T., 'Prospects for U.S. Trade With Cuba,' *Inter-American Economic Affairs* 30 (Autumn 1976), pp. 93–6.

Doxey, Margaret P., *Economic Sanctions: Past Lessons and the Case of Rhodesia*, Toronto: Canadian Institute of International Affairs, 1968.

Doxey, Margaret P., 'The Rhodesian Sanctions Experiment,' *Year Book of World Affairs* 25 (1971), pp. 142–62.

Doxey, Margaret P., 'International Sanctions: A Framework for Analysis with Special Reference to the U.N. and Southern Africa,' *International Organization* 26, 3 (Summer 1972), pp. 527–50.

Doxey, Margaret P., *Economic Sanctions and International Enforcement*, New York: Oxford University Press, 1971 (second edition, 1980).

Doxey, Margaret P., 'Sanctions Revisited,' *International Journal* 13 (Winter 1975–6), pp. 53–78.

Doxey, Margaret P., 'Economic Sanctions: Benefits and Costs,' *World Today* 36 (December 1980), pp. 484–9.

Drambyants, G., 'The Oil Embargo,' *New Times* (Moscow), 22 March 1967, pp. 20–2.

Dubin, A. L., 'Journey through the Antiboycott Laws,' *Tulsa Law Journal* 14 (1979), pp. 695–743.

Dubois, Louis, 'L'embargo dans La Pratique Contemporaine,' *Annuaire Français de Droit International* XIII (1967), 99–152.

Dulles, J. F., 'Should Economic Sanctions be Applied in International Disputes?', *Annals* 162 (1932), pp. 103–8.

Duncan, Addison Baker, *Economic Sanctions – A Study of the Actions Taken Against Italian Aggression, 1934-36*, Austin, Texas: University of Texas, 1952.

Duprez, Jean Jacques, 'The Strategic Embargo: Doctrine and Practice,' *World Today* (September 1963), pp. 374–9.

Dworkin, Susan, 'The Japanese and the Arab Boycott,' *Near East Report*, Supplement (October 1968), pp. 11–13.

Eban, Abba, 'The Answer to Arab Boycott,' In *The Israel Yearbook 1966*, Jerusalem: Israel Yearbook Publications, 1966, pp. 19–21.

Eckel, E. C. 'Economic Sanctions, Blockades and Boycotts,' *Asia* 32 (1932), pp. 276–83.

'Economic Sanctions: The Lifting of Sanctions against Zimbabwe-Rhodesia by the United States – Executive Order No. 12.183. 44 Fed. reg. 74.787,' (1979), *Harvard International Law Journal* 21 (Winter 1980), pp. 253–9.

'Economic Sanctions [Zimbabwe]' *American Journal of International Law* 74 (April 1980), pp. 429–32.

Eden, Anthony, 'Future of Sanctions,' *Vital Speeches* 2 (1936), pp. 620–3.

Egetmeyer, Richard, *Der Boykott also international Waffe*, Leipzig, 1929.

Einhorn, Jessica Pernitz, *Expropriation Politics*, Lexington, Massachusetts: D. C. Heath, 1974.

Eiseman, P. M., *Les Sanctions Contre La Rhodesia*, Paris, 1972.

Eisenberg, Meyer, 'Actions of Directors Regarding the Arab Boycott of Israel,' *The Business Lawyer* 31 (March 1976), pp. 1409–22.

Ellis, H. S., *Exchange Control in Central Europe*, Harvard Economic Studies no. 69, Cambridge, Mass.: Harvard University Press, 1941.

Engel, S., *League Reform: An Analysis of Official Proposals and Discussions, 1936–1939*, Geneva: Geneva Research Centre, 1940.

Enke, S., 'What Should Sanction Involve?' *Optima* (1964), pp. 183–9.

'Export Controls,' *Yale Law Journal* 58 (1949), pp. 1325–59.

'Export Policy, Antitrust and the Arab Boycott,' *New York University Law Review* (1976), pp. 94–132.

Faaland, Just (ed.), *Aid and Influence: The Case of Bangladesh*, New York: St Martin's Press, 1981. (Presents the case that inequality of economic power between the international donors on the one hand, and the newly emergent Bangladesh government on the other, had permitted the donors to impose their will on that poverty-stricken country.)

Farnsworth, Elizabeth, 'Chile: What Was the U.S. Role? (1) More Than Admitted,' *Foreign Policy* 16 (Fall 1974), pp. 126–41.

Farrell, R. B., *Jugoslavia and the Soviet Union 1948–1956*, Hamden, Conn.: Shoestring Press, 1956.

Feinberg, K. R., 'Economic Coercion and Economic Sanctions: The Expansion of United States Extraterritorial Jurisdiction,' *American University Law Review* 30 (Winter 1981), pp. 323–48. (Examines the strengths and weaknesses of US efforts to expand its extraterritorial jurisdiction and the broader impact of related pending congressional legislation.)

Feinerman, 'Arab Boycott and State Law: The New York Anti-Boycott Statute,' *Harvard International Law Journal* 18 (Spring 1977), pp. 343–63.

Feis, Herbert, *Seen From E. A. [Economic Affairs]: Three International Episodes*, New York: Knopf, 1947. (Provides an informed discussion of the League's oil boycott of Italy.)

Feis, Herbert, *The Road to Pearl Harbor: The Coming of the War Between the United States and Japan*, Princeton: Princeton University Press, 1950. (Gives a full account of the US attempt to use economic sanctions to deter Japanese expansion, yet avoid military action.)

Feith, D., 'The Oil Weapon De-mystified,' *Policy Review* 15 (1981), pp. 19–39. (Discounts the link between politics and oil prices.)

Fenwick, C. G., 'Quarantine Against Cuba: Legal or Illegal?' *American Journal of International Law* 57 (July 1963), pp. 588–92.

Ferguson, Clyde and William R. Cotter, 'South Africa: What Is To Be Done?' *Foreign Affairs* 56, 2 (January 1978), pp. 253–78.

Fingerman, Mark E., 'Skyjacking and the Bonn Declaration of 1978: Sanctions Applicable to Recalcitrant Nations,' *California Western International Law Journal* 10 (Winter 1980), pp. 123–52.

Fitzgerald, Gerald F., 'Book Review: *Les Sanctions Privatives de Droit ou de Qualité dans Les Organisations Internationales Spécialisées* by Charles Leben (1979),' *American Journal of International Law* 74 (July 1980), p. 709.

Flander, 'Foreign Sovereign Compulsion and the Arab Boycott: A State Action Analogy,' *Georgetown Law Journal* 65 (April 1977), pp. 1001-23.

Flynn, Donald, 'Trading with Communists: Use of Foreign Trade for Policy Objectives,' *American Bar Association Journal* 49 (1963), pp. 1092-5.

Flynn, D. and J. F. McKenzie, 'International Boycotts,' *University of Southern California School of Law Tax Institute* 29 (1977), pp. 139-93.

Forster, Arnold, 'The Arab Boycott: An Interim Report,' *ADL Bulletin*, June 1975.

Foster, John W., 'The Chinese Boycott,' *Atlantic Monthly* XCVII (January 1906).

Franck, T. M. (ed.), 'Policy Paper on the Legality of Mandatory Sanctions by the United Nations Against Rhodesia,' Policy Paper, New York: Center for International Studies, New York University, 1969.

Frank, Charles R., Jr., and Mary Baird, 'Foreign Aid: Its Speckled Past and Future Prospects,' *International Organization* 29 (Winter 1975), pp. 133-67.

Freedeman, Robert O., *Economic Warfare in the Communist Bloc: A Study of Soviet Economic Pressure against Yugoslavia, Albania and Communist China*, New York: Praeger, 1970.

Friedman, H. M., 'Confronting the Arab Boycott: A Lawyer's Baedeker', *Harvard International Law Journal* 19 (Summer 1978), pp. 443-533.

Frost, Mervin, 'Collective Sanctions in International Relations: An Historical Overview of the Theory and Practice,' Seminar Paper' Jan Smuts House, Johannesburg.

Galtung, Johan, 'On the Effects of International Economic Sanctions with Examples from the Case of Rhodesia,' *World Politics* 19, 3 (April 1967), pp. 378-416.

Gamarnikow, M., 'Comecon Today,' *East Europe* XIII (March 1964).

'The General Principles for the Arab Boycott of Israel. Part VII,' *Shu'un Arabiya*, 8 (October 1981), pp. 310-16 (in Arabic).

General Principles for Boycott of Israel, League of Arab Countries General Secretariat, Head Office for the Boycott of Israel, Damascus, June 1972.

General Union of Arab Chambers of Commerce, Industry and Agriculture, *Arab Boycott of Israel: Its Grounds and Its Regulations*, Beirut, 1959.

George, Alexander, David K. Hall and William R. Simons, *The Limits of Coercive Diplomacy: Laos, Cuba, Vietnam*, New York: Columbia University Press, 1971.

Gilbert, Felix, *To the Farewell Address: Ideas of Early American Foreign Policy*, Princeton: Princeton University Press, 1961. (An excellent exposition of early American ideas of economic warfare.)

Gilman, E., 'Israel and the Iranian Oil Embargo: The Search for Alternative Sources of Energy,' *Round Table*, 276 (October 1979), pp. 291-307.

Glenn, Gossard, 'War Without Guns,' *The Virginia Quarterly Review* 8 (July 1932), pp. 388-99. (Argues that the national boycott, 'in and of itself, *is* war.')

'Going Against the Grain: The Regulation of the International Wheat Trade from 1933 to the 1980 Soviet Grain Embargo,' *Boston College International and Comparative Law Review* 5 (Winter 1982), pp. 225-70.

Gold, Joseph, 'The "Sanctions" of the International Monetary Fund,' *American Journal of International Law* 66, 5 (October 1972), pp. 737-62.

Goldman, Marshall, *Soviet Foreign Aid*, New York: Praeger, 1958.

Goldman, Marshall, 'A Balance Sheet of Soviet Foreign Aid,' *Foreign Affairs* 43 (January 1965), pp. 349–60.

Gonzalez, H., 'Arms-Sales Policy: The Chilean Case,' *Inter-American Economic Affairs* 34 (Winter 1980), pp. 3–24.

Goodrich, Leland M., 'International Sanctions,' in David L. Sills (ed.), *International Encyclopedia of the Social Sciences* 14 (1968), pp. 5–9.

Gordon, David L. and Royden Dangerfield, *The Hidden Weapon: The Story of Economic Warfare*, New York: Harper, 1947.

Green, Mark and Steven Solow, 'The Arab Boycott of Israel: How the U.S. and Business Cooperated,' *The Nation*, 17 October 1981.

Greene, J. D., 'Economic Sanctions as Instruments of National Policy,' *Annals* 162 (1932), pp. 100–2.

Greene, P. L., 'Arab Economic Boycott of Israel: The International Law Perspective,' *Vanderbilt Journal of Transnational Law* 11 (Winter 1978), pp. 77–94.

Grieve, Muriel J., 'Economic Sanctions: Theory and Practice,' *International Relations – Journal of the Institute of International Studies* II (October 1968), pp. 431–43.

Gross, Franz B., 'The United States National Interest and the United Nations,' in Franz B. Cross (ed.), *The United States and the United Nations*, Norman, Oklahoma: University of Oklahoma Press, 1964. (Discusses American interest in sanctions since World War II.)

Guichard, Louis, *The Naval Blockade*, New York: Appleton, 1930.

Gullet, John S., 'Economic Planning versus Economic Sanction,' *Harvard Business Review* (April 1932).

Gyeke-Dako, K., *Economic Sanctions Under the United Nations*, Tema, Ghana: Ghana Publishing Corporation, 1973.

Hadjicos, D. N., *Les Sanctions Internationales de la Société des Nations*, Paris, 1920.

Hager, Mark, 'International Trade: Legality of Longshoremen Anti-Soviet Boycott,' *Harvard International Law Journal* 21 (Fall 1980), pp. 763–9. (US District Court extends 'into the international sphere the notion that union political activity should be protected, despite its economic side-effects.')

Haight, James T., 'United States Controls Over Strategic Transactions,' *University of Illinois Law Forum*, 1965, 3 (Fall 1965), pp. 337–65.

Haight, James T., 'U.S. Regulation of East-West Trade,' *Business Law* 19 (1964), pp. 875–86.

Halcombe, R. G., 'Strategic Petroleum Reserve,' *Oil and Gas Tax Quarterly* 26 (June 1978), pp. 457–65.

Halderman, John, 'Some Legal Aspects of Sanctions in the Rhodesian Case,' *International and Comparative Law Quarterly* 17, 3 (July 1968), pp. 672–705.

Hamadah, Mustafa, 'A Look at the Arab Boycott of Israel,' (in Arabic) *Shu'un Arabiya* (Arab Affairs) 2, Beirut (May 1981), pp. 107–20.

Hambro, Edward Isak, *L'Éxecution des Sentences Internationales*, Paris: Librairie du Recueil Sirey, 1936.

Handford, John, *A Portrait of an Economy Under Sanctions 1965-1975*, Salisbury: Mercury Press, 1976.

Hansen, R. D., 'The Politics of Scarcity,' in J. W. Howe (ed.), *The U.S. and the Developing World, Agenda for Action*, New York: Praeger, 1974, pp. 51–65.

Hardt, J. P. and George D. Holliday, *U.S.-Soviet Commercial Relations, The Interplay of Economics, Technology Transfer, and Diplomacy*, Committee on Foreign Affairs, US House of Representatives, 10 June 1973.

Harris, C., 'The Political and Economic Effects of Sanctions on Rhodesia,' *World Today* 23 (1967), pp. 1–4.

Harris, P. B., 'Rhodesia: Sanctions, Economics and Politics,' *Rhodesian Journal of Economics* (Salisbury) II, 3 (September 1968), pp. 5–20.

Hartland-Thunberg, Penelope, 'Book Review: *Sanctions: The Case of Rhodesia*, by Harry R. Strack,' *Annals of the American Academy of the Political and Social Sciences* 444 (July 1979), p. 159.

Hawkins, A. M., 'The Rhodesian Economy under Sanctions,' *Rhodesian Journal of Economics* V, I (August 1967), pp. 44–60.

Hawkins, A. M., 'Rhodesian Economy under Siege,' *Bulletin of the Africa Institute of South Africa* 1 (1975), pp. 12–18, 23.

Hewett, Ed A., 'The Pipeline Connection: Issues for the Alliance,' *The Brookings Review* 1, 1 (Fall 1982), pp. 15–20. (Discusses the disagreement between the US and its allies over the gas pipeline deal.)

Hickey, D. R., 'American Trade Restrictions During the War of 1812,' *Journal of American History* 68 (December 1981), pp. 517–38.

Higgins, Rosalyn, 'International Law, Rhodesia and the U.N.', *World Today* (London) 23, 3 (1967), pp. 94–106.

Highley, Albert E., 'The First Sanctions Experiment,' *Geneva Studies* IX (July 1938).

Highley, Albert E., *The First Sanctions Experiment: A Study of League Procedures*, Geneva: Geneva Research Centre, 1938.

Hildebrand, Klaus, *The Foreign Policy of the Third Reich*, London: Batsford, 1973.

Hirschhorn, Eric and Howard Fenton, 'States' Rights and the Antiboycott Provisions of the Export Administration Act,' *Columbia Journal of Transnational Law* 20, 3 (1981), pp. 517–47. (Examines 'whether the EAA preempts statutes enacted by New York State and New York City that bar anyone who has violated the antiboycott provisions of the EAA from contracting with the state and city.')

Hirschman, Albert O., *National Power and the Structure of Foreign Trade*, Berkeley: University of California Press, 1945. Expanded edition, 1980.

Hoffmann, Fredrik, 'The Functions of Economic Sanctions: A Comparative Analysis,' *Journal of Peace Research* 2 (1967), pp. 140–59.

Holcombe, Chester, 'Chinese Exclusion and the Boycott,' *Outlook*, 30 December 1905, pp. 1071–2.

Holland, Sir Thomas H., *The Mineral Sanction As An Aid to International Security*, London: Oliver & Boyd, July 1935. (A valuable study of economic sanctions and the problem of collective security.)

Holland, Sir Thomas H., 'The Mineral Sanction as a Contribution to International Security,' *International Affairs* 15 (September–October 1936), pp. 735–52.

Holzman, Franklin, and Richard Portes, 'The Limits of Pressure,' *Foreign Policy* 32 (Fall 1978), pp. 80–90.

Hoogvelt, A. M. and D. Child, *Rhodesia – Economic Blockade and Long-Term Development Strategy*, Institute of Social Studies, The Hague, Occasional Paper no. 25, January 1973.

Hoogvelt, A. M. and D. Child, 'Rhodesia: Economic Blockade and Development,' *Monthly Review*, October 1973.

Hotaling, E., *The Arab Blacklist Unveiled*, Beverly Hills, California: Landia, 1977.

Hough, Jerry F., *The Polish Crisis: American Policy Options*, Washington: Brookings Institution, August 1982. (Argues that US sanctions against Poland will become both increasingly unproductive and more difficult to remove, and the termination of martial law in Poland might be the appropriate time to end them.)

Hübner-Dick, G. and R. Seidelmann, 'Simulating Economic Sanctions and Incentives: Hypothetical Alternatives of United States Policy on South Africa,' *Journal of Peace Research* 15, 2 (1978), pp. 153–74; reply with rejoinder, W. W. Hill, Jr., *Journal of Peace Research*, 17, 1 (1980), pp. 77–86.

Hufbauer, G. C. and J. G. Taylor, 'Taxing Boycotts and Bribes,' *Denver Journal of International Law and Policy* 6 (Spring 1977), pp. 589–611.

Huntington, Samuel P., 'Foreign Aid, for What and for Whom,' *Foreign Policy* (Spring 1971), pp. 114–34.

Huntington, Samuel P., 'Trade, Technology, and Leverage: Economic Diplomacy,' *Foreign Policy* 32 (Fall 1978), pp. 63–80.

Hurst, Peter F., Jr., 'Economic Sanctions: The Lifting of Sanctions Against Zimbabwe-Rhodesia by the United States,' *Harvard International Law Journal* 21 (Winter 1980), pp. 253–9.

Hyde, Charles C., 'Boycott as a Sanction of International Law,' *Political Science Quarterly*, 48, (June 1933), pp. 211–19.

Hyde, Charles C. and Louis B. Wehle, 'The Boycott in Foreign Affairs,' *American Journal of International Law* 27, 1 (January 1933), pp. 1–10.

'Import Restrictions: Repeal of the Byrd Amendment – Amendment to the United Nations Participation Act of 1945,' section 5, pub. 1, no. 95-12, 91 state. 22, *Harvard International Law Journal* 18 (Summer 1977), pp. 713–17.

International Sanctions, a report by the Chatham Study Group, London: Oxford University Press for the Royal Institute of International Affairs, 1938. (Investigates how far the constitution of a system of sanctions for the enforcement of international legal obligations is a feasible proposition.)

'International Sanctions – United Nations Security Council Resolution – Economic Sanctions against Southern Rhodesia,' SC Resolution 333, UN Doc. S/Res./333; adopted May 1973, *Virginia Journal of International Law* 14 (Winter 1974), pp. 319–29.

'International Trade – the Export Administration Act of 1969 does not Foreclose Release Pursuant to Freedom of Information Act of Exporter Boycott Request Reports', *Virginia Journal of International Law* 18 (Summer 1978), pp. 838–93.

'International Trade: Uganda Trade Embargo,' *Harvard International Law Journal* 20 (Winter 1979), pp. 206–13.

'I.R.C. Section 999: Taxing the Arab Boycott,' *Cornell International Law Journal* 10 (May 1977), pp. 280–306.

Iskander, Marwan, 'Arab Boycott of Israel,' *Middle East Forum* 36 (October 1960), pp. 27–30.

Iskander, Marwan, *The Arab Boycott of Israel*, Beirut: PLO Research Center, 1966.

Itayim, Fuad, 'Arab Oil – The Political Dimension,' *Journal of Palestine Studies* 3, no. 2 (1974), pp. 84–97.

Itayim, Fuad, 'Strengths and Weaknesses of the Oil Weapon,' in *The Middle East and the International System II: Security and the Energy Crisis*, Adelphi Papers, no. 115, London: The International Institute for Strategic Studies, 1975, pp. 1–7.

Jack, D. T., *Studies in Economic Warfare*, London: King, 1940.

Jackson, Barbara Ward, 'Foreign Aid: Strategy or Stopgap?', *Foreign Affairs* 41 (1962), pp. 90–104.

Jaster, R., 'CEMA's Influence on Soviet Policies in Eastern Europe,' *World Politics* XIV, no. 3 (April 1962), pp. 506–8. (CEMA is another abbreviation for COMECON.)

Johnson, David L., 'Sanctions and South Africa,' *Harvard International Law Journal* (Cambridge, Mass.) 19, 3 (1975), pp. 887–930.

Johnson, Ludwell H., 'The Business of War: Trading with the Enemy in English and Early American Law,' *Proceedings of the American Philosophical Society* 118 (October 1974), pp. 459–70.

Johnson, W. A. and R. G. Messick, 'Vertical Divestiture of U.S. Oil Firms: the Impact on the World Oil Market,' *Law and Policy in International Business* 8 (1976), pp. 963–89.

Joseph, M., 'Byrd Amendment: Chrome that Tarnishes,' *Howard Law Journal* 18 (1973), pp. 171–83.

Joyner, Nelson T., *Arab Boycott/Anti-Boycott – The Effects on U.S. Business*, McLean, Virginia: Rockville Consulting Group, Inc., December 1976.

Kaikati, J., 'The Arab Boycott: Middle East Business Dilemma,' *California Management Review* 20, no. 3 (1978), pp. 32–46.

Kaplan, R. L., 'Income Taxes and the Arab Boycott,' *The Tax Lawyer* 32 (Winter 1979), pp. 313–47.

Kapungu, Leonard T., *The United Nations and Economic Sanctions Against Rhodesia*, Lexington Mass.: Lexington Books, 1973. (Discusses the genesis of the Rhodesian crisis and deals with the formulation and implementation of sanctions and their political and economic effects.)

Kaser, Michael, *Comecon: Integration Problems of Planned Economies*, 2nd edn, London: Royal Institute of International Affairs, 1967.

Kato, Masakatsu, 'A Model of U.S. Foreign Aid: An Application of a Decision-Making Scheme' in John E. Mueller (ed.), *Approaches to Measurement in International Relations*, New York: Appleton-Century-Crofts, 1969.

Kearns, Frank, 'Why Oil Sanctions Failed: A Report from Salisbury,' Telecast on CBS Evening News with Walter Cronkite, 21 March 1966, reprinted in *Africa Report* 11 (April 1966), p. 24.

Kelly, J. B., 'Oil and the West,' *Commentary* (August 1975), pp. 18–21.

Kelsen, Hans, 'Sanctions Under the Charter of the United Nations,' *Canadian*

Journal of Economics and Political Science 12, 4 (November 1946), pp. 429-38.

Kelsen, Hans, *The Law of the United Nations*, New York: Praeger, 1950.

Kerr, Philip, 'Europe and the United States: The Problem of Sanctions,' *Journal of the Royal Institute of International Affairs* IX, no. 3 (May 1930), pp. 288-324.

Kestenbaum, Lionel, 'The Antitrust Challenge to the Arab Boycott: Per Se Theory, Middle East Politics, and United States v. Bechtel Corporation,' *Texas Law Review* 54 (1976), pp. 1411-31.

Kestenbaum, Lionel, 'Arab Boycott in U.S. Law: Flawed Remedies for an International Trade Restraint,' *Law and Politics of International Business* 10 (1978), pp. 769-814.

Kimche, Jon, 'The Arab Boycott of Israel: New Aspects,' *Midstream*, September 1964.

Kindleberger, Charles P., 'The Economics of International Politics: Power,' in *Power and Money*, New York: Basic Books, 1970, pp. 56-70. (An excellent discussion of economic power.)

Klare, M. T., 'Corporations That Sell Arms to South Africa,' *Business and Social Review*, no. 35 (Fall 1980), pp. 45-8.

Klare, M. T., 'Evading the Embargo: Illicit U.S. Arms Transfers to South Africa,' *Journal of International Affairs* 35 (Spring/Summer 1981), pp. 15-28.

Knorr, Klaus, 'International Economic Leverage and its Uses,' in *Economic Issues and National Security*, ed. Klaus Knorr and Frank N. Trager, Lawrence, Kansas: Allen Press, 1977.

Knorr, Klaus, 'The Limits of Economic and Military Power,' *Daedalus* 104 (Fall 1975), pp. 229-43.

Koenderman, Tony, 'Sanctions,' *South Africa International* (Johanesburg) (January 1979), pp. 150-8.

Kohl, W. L., 'United States, Western Europe, and the Energy Problem,' *Journal of International Affairs* 30 (Spring 1976), pp. 81-96.

Kohler, Foy D., Goure Leon, and Harvey Mose, *The Soviet Union and the October 1973 Middle East War: The Implications for Detente*, Coral Gables, Fla.: University of Miami, 1974.

Korbonski, Andrzej, 'Comecon,' *International Conciliation*, no. 549, September 1964. (This study traces broadly the development of COMECON from its origin, and sketches its current institutional framework and policies. It also includes some speculations about the organization's future.)

Krasner, Stephen D., 'Domestic Constraints in International Economic Leverage,' in *Economic Issues and National Security*, edited by Klaus Knorr and Frank N. Trager, pp. 160-81. Lawrence, Kansas: University Press of Kansas, 1977.

Krasner, Stephen D., 'The Great Oil Sheikdown,' *Foreign Policy* 13 (Winter 1973), pp. 123-48.

Krasner, Stephen D., 'Oil is the Exception,' *Foreign Policy* 14 (Spring 1974), pp. 68-83.

Kreczko, Alan J., 'The Unilateral Termination of U.N. Sanctions Against Southern Rhodesia by the United Kingdom,' *Virginia Journal of International Law* 21 (Fall 1980), pp. 97-128.

Kuhn, Arthur K., 'The Economic Sanctions and the Kellogg Pact,' *American Journal of International Law* 30 (January 1936), pp. 83-8.

Kunz, Josef L., 'Sanctions in International Law,' *American Journal of International Law* 54 (April 1960), pp. 324-47.

Kurlander, N. S., 'New International Boycott Provisions,' *Taxes – The Tax Magazine* 55 (Spring, 1977), pp. 587-94.

Kurlander, N. S., 'Foreign Boycott Legislation,' *Oil and Gas Tax Quarterly* 26 (March 1978), pp. 253-72.

Kuyper, Pieter J., *The Implementation of International Sanctions: The Netherlands and Rhodesia*, Alphen aan den Rijn: Sitjhoff and Noordhoff, 1978.

Laferrière, J., 'Le Boycott et le Droit International,' *Revue Générale de Droit International Public* XVII (1910).

Lande, Robert H., 'Arab Boycott and Title VII,' *Harvard Civil Rights-Civil Liberties Law Review* 12 (Winter 1977), pp. 181-205.

Laoussine, Nordine Ait, 'The Political Dimension of Oil,' *OPEC Review* III, no. 3 (Autumn 1979), pp. 39-45.

Larus, Joel (ed.). *From Collective Security to Preventive Diplomacy*, New York: Wiley, 1965. (Discusses American interest in sanctions since World War II.)

Lauterpacht, Hersch, 'Boycott in International Relations,' *British Yearbook of International Law* 14, 125 (1933), pp. 125-40.

Leben, Charles, *Les Sanctions Privatives de Droit ou de Qualité dans les Organisations Internationales Spécialisées*, Brussels: Bruylant, 1979 (bibliography, pp. 369-88; English summary, pp. 363-6).

Lee, B. Y., 'Boycott Brings Profit to Chinese Mills,' *China Weekly Review*, 23 July 1927.

Lee, F. J. T., 'Apartheid Demands Effective Sanctions,' *Review of International Affairs* (Belgrade) 15 (5 May 1964), pp. 11-12.

Lee, F. J. T., 'Sanctions Against South Africa,' *Review of International Affairs* (Belgrade) 15 (20 June 1964), pp. 11-13.

Lee, Luke T. and John B. McCobb, 'United States Trade Embargo on China, 1949-70: Legal Status and Future Prospects,' *New York University Journal of International Law and Politics* 4 (Spring 1971), pp. 1-28.

'Legal Impediments to Normalization of Trade with Cuba,' *Law and Policy in International Business* 8 (1976), pp. 1007-54.

'Legitimacy of the United States Embargo of Uganda,' *Journal of International Law and Economics* 13 (1979), pp. 651-73.

Leiss, Amelia (ed.), *Apartheid and United Nations Collective Measures: An Analysis*, New York: Carnegie Endowment, 1965.

Leonard, J. L., 'The Effect of the Employment of Economic Sanctions on National and World Prosperity,' *Proceedings, Institute of World Affairs* (UCLA) 13 (1936), pp. 221-5.

Levinson, S. O., 'Sanctions Mean War,' *Christian Century* 51 (1934), pp. 806-9.

Levitch, Raphaël A., *La Collaboration dans l'Application des Sanctions Prévues à l'Article 16 du Pacte de La Société des Nations*, Préface de Maurice Bourquin, Paris: A. Pedone, 1938.

Levy, Walter, J., Inc., *The Economics and Logistics of an Embargo on Oil and Petroleum Products for Rhodesia*, Report for the Office of the United

Nations Secretary-General, 12 February 1966, New York: W. J. Levy, 1966.

Levy, Walter J. Inc., 'Oil Power,' *Foreign Affairs* 49 (July 1971), pp. 652–68.

Li, Victor H., 'Legal Aspects of Trade with Communist China,' *Columbia Journal of Transnational Law* (1964), pp. 57–71.

Lillich, Richard B., 'Economic Coercion and the International Legal Order,' *International Affairs* 51, 3 (July 1975), pp. 358–71.

Lillich, Richard B. (ed.), *Economic Coercion and the New International Order*, Charlottesville, Va,: Michie, 1976.

Lillich, R. B. 'Economic Coercion and the "New International Economic Order": A Second Look at some First Impressions,' *Virginia Journal of International Law* 16 (Winter 1976), pp. 233–44.

Lillich, R. B., 'The Status of Economic Coercion Under International Law: United Nations Norms,' *Texas International Law Journal* 12 (1977), pp. 17–23.

Lipson, Charles H., 'Corporate Preferences and Public Policies: Foreign Aid Sanctions and Investment Protection,' *World Politics* 28 (April 1976), pp. 396–421.

Liska, George, *The New Statecraft: Foreign Aid in American Foreign Policy*, Chicago: University of Chicago Press, 1960.

Lissakers, Karin, 'Money and Manipulation,' *Foreign Policy* 44 (Fall 1981), pp. 107–26. (Analyses the impact of US freeze of Iranian assets on the international banking system.)

'List of Boycott Recommendations,' *Economic Review of the Arab World* 2 (February 1967).

Loeber, D. A., *East-West Trade: A Sourcebook on the International Economic Relations of Socialist Countries and Their Legal Aspects*, Dobbs Ferry, New York: Oceana, 1977.

'Longshoremen's Embargo of Soviet Goods: A Secondary Boycott or a Political Protest?', *Mercer Law Review* 32 (Spring 1981), pp. 857–72.

Longstreet, James, 'United States v. Bechtel Corporation No. C-76-99 (N.D. Cal., filed January 16, 1976): Antitrust and the Arab Blacklist.' *Vanderbilt Journal of Transnational Law* 11 (Spring 1978), pp. 299–321.

Losman, Donald L., *International Economic Sanctions*, Albuquerque: University of New Mexico Press, 1979.

Losman, Donald L., 'The Effects of Economic Boycotts,' *Lloyds Bank Review* (October 1972), pp. 27–41.

Losman, Donald L., 'International Boycotts: An Appraisal,' *Politico* XXVII (December 1972), pp. 648–71.

Losman, Donald L., 'The Economics of Bloc Aid and Trade with Cuba,' *Marquette Business Review* (Summer 1970), pp. 68–77.

Lowe, Chuan-hua, 'How Effective is China's Boycott Against Japan?', *China Weekly Review* (20 February 1932).

Lowenfeld, Andreas F., 'Sauce for Gander: The Arab Boycott and United States Political Trade Controls,' *Texas International Law Journal* 12, 1 (1977), pp. 25–39.

Lowenfeld, A., *International Economic Law*, vol. III, 'Trade Controls for Political Ends,' New York: M. Bender, 1977. (Discusses the Arab boycott and the US response.)

Luttig, A. J., 'A Survey of Economic Pressure Against South Africa,' in *South African Yearbook of International Law* 3 (1977), Pretoria, Verhoren van Themaat Centre for International Law, Institute of Foreign and Comparative Law, University of South Africa, 1978, pp. 119–26.

Maccaley, S., 'Reprisals as a Measure of Redress Short of War,' *Cambridge Law Journal* 2 (1924), pp. 60–73.

McCarthy, P. and J. F. McKenzie, 'Commerce Department Regulations Governing Participation by United States Persons in Foreign Boycotts,' *Vanderbilt Journal of Transnational Law* 11 (Spring 1978), pp. 193–247.

MacChesney, Brunson, 'Some Comments on the Quarantine of Cuba,' *American Journal of International Law* 57 (July 1963), pp. 592–7.

Macdonald, R. St. J., 'The Resort to Economic Coercion by International Political Organizations,' *University of Toronto Law Journal* 17 (1967), pp. 86–169.

Macdonald, R. St. J. 'Economic Sanctions in the International System,' *Canadian Yearbook of International Law* (1969), pp. 61–91.

McDonell, Neil E., 'Allied International, Inc. v. International Longshoremen's Association: Foreign Commerce Jurisdiction under Section 8(b) (4) of the National Labor Relations Act,' *Columbia Journal of Transnational Law* 20, 3 (1981), pp. 549–79.

McDougal, Myres S. and W. M. Reisman, 'Rhodesia and the United Nations: The Lawfulness of International Concern,' *American Journal of International Law* 62 (January 1968), pp. 1–19.

McDougal, Myres S., 'Soviet-Cuban Quarantine and Self-Defence,' *American Journal of International Law* LVII (July 1963), pp. 597–604.

McKinnell, Robert T., 'Assessing the Economic Impact of Sanctions Against Rhodesia,' *African Affairs* (London) 67 (1968), pp. 227–32.

McKinnell, Robert T., 'Sanctions and the Rhodesian Economy,' *Journal of Modern African Studies* 7 (December 1969), pp. 559–81.

Mallison, W. T., Jr., 'Limited Naval Blockade or Quarantine – Interdiction,' *George Washington Law Review* XXXI (December 1962), pp. 335–98.

Malloy, Michael P., 'Embargo Programs of the United States Treasury Department,' *Columbia Journal of Transnational Law* 20, 3 (1981), pp. 485–516. (Provides an excellent description of US embargo programs, discusses foreign policy objectives and implementation.)

Manning, C. A. W., *Sanctions Under the Covenant*, Montague Burton International Relations Lecture, 1936.

Marcelletti, Mario, *Bibliografia delle Sanzioni*, Florence: G. S. Sansoni, 1937. (Bibliography on sanctions in international law and the Italo-Ethiopian conflict.)

Marcuss, S. and R. Thomas, Chairman, *The Proposed Anti-Boycott Regulations under the Export Administration Act of 1977: Compliance and Understanding*, New York: Law Journal Press, 1977.

Marcuss, Stanley J. and Eric L. Richard, 'Extraterritorial Jurisdiction in United States Trade Law: The Need for a Consistent Theory,' *Columbia Journal of Transnational Law* 20, 3 (1981), pp. 439–83. (Examines the legal basis of US laws regulating international trade and asserts the need for a consistent theory of international legal principles pertaining to jurisdiction.)

Matsubara, K., 'Self-Defense and Reprisals,' *Journal of International Law and Diplomacy* 1-10 (1958), pp. 241-59.

Maull, Hans, 'Oil and Influence: The Oil Weapon Examined,' *Adelphi Papers*, no. 117 (Summer 1975).

May, Ernest R., *The World War and American Isolation, 1914-1917*, Cambridge, Mass.: Harvard University Press, 1959. (On Wilson's consideration of the embargo against the Allies before World War I.)

Medlicott, William Norton, *The Economic Blockade*, London: HMSO, 1959. Revised edition, 1978. (An authoritative study of Allied economic warfare during World War II.)

Meeker, Leonard C., 'Defensive Quarantine and the Law,' *American Journal of International Law* 57, 3 (July 1963), pp. 515-24.

Mehlman, Maxwell J., Thomas H. Milch and Michael V. Toumanoff, 'United States Restrictions on Exports to South Africa,' *American Journal of International Law* 73, 4 (October 1979), pp. 581-603. (Traces the history of the US policy of restricting exports to South Africa and examines in detail the restrictions that are currently in effect.)

Mellor, R. E. H., *Comecon: Challenge to the West*, New York: Van Nostrand-Reinhold, 1971. (Traces the birth and origin of Comecon and evaluates its economic and political influence.)

Meo, Leila, *et al.*, *The Arab Boycott of Israel*, Detroit: Association of Arab-American University Graduates, 1976. (Addresses, essays, and lectures in which the origin, purpose, and rationale of the Arab boycott are analysed and discussed from the Arab point of view.)

Mersky, R. M. (ed.), *Conference on Transnational Boycotts and Coercion: Papers and Documents*, Dobbs Ferry, New York: Oceana, 1978.

Mersky, R. M. and M. L. Richmond, 'Legal Implications of the Arab Economic Boycott of the State of Israel: A Research Guide,' *Law Library Journal* 71 (1978), pp. 68-76.

Mertens, A., 'Les Sanctions Economiques contre l'Italie,' *Revue Economique Internationale* 28 (January 1936).

Mestre, Achille, *Les Sanctions Internationales: Trois Opinions de Juristes*, Paris: P. Hartmann, 1936.

Metthews, Herbert L., *Revolution in Cuba: An Essay in Understanding*, New York: Scribner, 1975. (Strongly questions the legality of US economic sanctions against Cuba.)

Michels, Robert, *Le Boycottage International, Boycottage Economique et Crises Politiques*, Paris: Payot, 1936.

Middlebush, F. A., 'Non-Recognition as a Sanction of International Law,' *Proceedings of the American Society of International Law* 27 (1933), pp. 40-55.

Midlane, M., 'Crisis Facing South Africa: Has the Twelfth Hour Passed?' *Round Table* 274 (April 1979), pp. 107-21.

Miglioli, Carlo, *La Sanzione Illegittima nel Diritto Internazionale*, Roma: Atlantica, 1949.

Miglioli, Carlo, *La Sanzione nel Diritto Internazionale: Problemi e Lineamenti di Guistizia Superstatuate*, Milano: Giuffrè, 1951.

Miller, Judith, 'When Sanctions Worked,' *Foreign Policy* 39 (Summer 1980), pp. 118-29. (Against the Uganda government of Idi Amin Dada.)

Millward, Alex, 'Only Yesterday: some Reflections on the "Thirties" with Particular Reference to Sanctions,' *International Relations* (April 1957), pp. 281-90.

Milward, Alan S., *War, Economy and Society, 1939-1945*, Berkeley: University of California Press, 1977.

Minty, Abdul S., *The Case for Economic Disengagement*, New York: UN Centre Against Apartheid, November 1976.

Mitrany, David, *The Problem of International Sanctions*, London: Oxford University Press, 1925. (A valuable contribution to the subject of economic sanctions whose strongest feature is its emphasis on the interdependence of sanctions and arbitration.)

Mo, Hsu, 'The Sanctions of International Law,' *Transactions of the Grotius Society* 35 (1940), pp. 4-14, 22-23.

'Mobil's Unctuous Silence: Rhodesia's Endless Ordeal,' *Business and Social Review* 24 (Winter 1977-78), p. 36.

Montgomery, John D., *The Politics of Foreign Aid: American Experience in Southeast Asia*, New York: Praeger, 1962.

Montgomery, John D., *Foreign Aid in International Politics*, Englewood Cliffs, New Jersey: Prentice-Hall, 1967.

Moore, John Norton, 'United States Policy and the Arab Boycott,' *Proceedings of the American Society of International Law* (1977), pp. 174-82.

Moorehead, Helen Howell, 'International Administration of Narcotic Drugs, 1928-1934,' *Geneva Special Studies* VI (27 February 1935).

Morgenthau, Hans, *Théorie des Sanctions Internationales*, Brussels: Bureau de la Revue, 1935. (A reprint of two articles which appeared in 1935 in the Belgian *Revue de Droit International et de Législation Comparée*, nos. 3 and 4. Gives a very clear view of sanctions, both in theory and in practice.)

Morgenthau, Hans, 'A Political Theory of Foreign Aid,' *American Political Science Review* (June 1962), pp. 301-9.

Morris, F., 'For a Complete Boycott of South Africa,' *Contemporary Issues* (London) 12 (September 1964), pp. 15-17.

Mourad, Rashad, 'The Arab Boycott – Its Application,' *American-Arab Trade Newsletter* (Spring-Summer, 1966), pp. 5-6. (Provides precise review of the Arab boycott's general principles and regulations.)

Moyana, J. Kombo, 'The Political Economy of Sanctions and Implication for Future Economic Policy,' *Journal of South African Affairs* 11, 4 (October 1977), pp. 493-521.

'Mozambique: Sanctions Against Rhodesia,' *Bulletin of the Africa Institute of South Africa 5 and 6* (1976), pp. 212-14.

Muir, J. Depray, 'The Boycott in International Law,' *Journal of International Law and Economics* 9, (August 1974), pp. 187-204. (Provides a review of the history of international trade embargoes and concludes that the incentive and opportunity for adoption of boycotts will recur in the future.)

Murray, Gilbert, 'Sanctions,' *The Contemporary Review* 152, 860 (August 1937).

Myers, Desaix, *et al.*, *U.S. Business in South Africa: The Economic, Political, and*

Moral Issues, Bloomington: Indiana University Press, 1980. (Examines the pressures on American companies in South Africa and their responses to those pressures.)

Nafziger, J. A. R., 'Diplomatic Fun and the Games: A Commentary on the United States Boycott of the 1980 Summer Olympics,' *Willamette Law Review* 17 (Winter 1980), pp. 67-81.

Nantet, Jacques, *Les Sanctions dans le Pacte de la Société des Nations. Historique et Conditions d'Application*, Paris: Les Editions Domat-Montchréstien, 1936.

Navarro, Christina, 'Cyprus and the U.N.: A Case for Nonmilitary Collective Measures,' *Indiana Law Journal* 54 (Fall 1978), pp. 125-63.

Neff, Stephen C., 'International Trade, Embargoes and Boycotts,' *Columbia Journal of Transnational Law* 20 (1981), pp. 411-37. (Examines 'the extent to which states are entitled to use their economic power to coerce others into complying with their national priorities.')

Nelson, Joan M., *Aid, Influence and Foreign Policy*, New York: Macmillan, 1968.

Nelson, Walter Henry and Terence C. F. Prittie, *The Economic War Against the Jews*, New York: Random House, 1977. (Provides an historical account of the Arab boycott and related measures of economic warfare against Israel from an Israeli perspective.)

'A New and Flexible Approach to the Arab Boycott?', *Middle East Economic Digest* (22 August 1975).

Newcombe, Hanna, 'The Case for an Arms Embargo,' *War/Peace Report* 11, 17 (1971).

Nicholson, M., 'Tariff Wars and a Model of Conflict,' *Journal of Peace Research* (1967), pp. 26-38.

Nur-Allah, N. A., 'Counter-Legislation to the Arab Boycott of Israel,' *Shu'un Arabiya* (October 1981), pp. 7-20 (in Arabic).

Oakeshott, Robert, 'The Strategic Embargo: An Obstacle to East-West Trade,' *World Today* (June 1963), pp. 240-7.

O'Connor, Harvey, *World Crisis in Oil*, New York: Monthly Review Press, 1962.

O'Leary, Michael K., *The Politics of American Foreign Aid*, New York: Atherton Press, 1967.

Olmstead, Cecil J., 'Foreign Aid as an Effective Means of Persuasion,' *Proceedings of the American Society of International Law* 58 (1964), pp. 205-10.

Olson, Richard Stuart, 'Economic Coercion in World Politics, with a Focus on North-South Relations,' *Comparative Politics* 11 (July 1979), pp. 471-94.

Olson, Richard Stuart, 'Economic Coercion in International Disputes: The United States and Peru in the IPC Expropriation Dispute of 1968-71,' *Journal of Developing Areas* 9 (April 1975): 395-414.

Olson, Richard Stuart, 'Expropriation and International Economic Coercion: Ceylon and the "West" 1961-65,' *Journal of Developing Areas* 11 (January 1977), pp. 205-26.

Olson, Richard Stuart, 'Expropriation, Economic Coercion, and Revolution: A Retrospective Look at Brazil in the 1960s,' *Journal of Developing Areas* 13 (April 1979), pp. 247-62.

'On Resumption of Trade with Cuba: The Issue Defined,' Department of

Commerce testimony before the House International Relations Committee, *Inter-American Economic Affairs* 29 (Autumn 1975), pp. 59-78.

Orchard, Dorothy J., 'China's Use of the Boycott as a Political Weapon,' *Annals of the American Academy of Political Science* (November 1930), p. 253.

'Overview of Export Controls on Transfer of Technology to the U.S.S.R. in Light of Soviet Intervention in Afghanistan,' *North Carolina Journal of International Law and Commercial Regulations* 5 (Summer 1980), pp. 555-73.

Paarlberg, Robert L., 'Lessons of the Grain Embargo,' *Foreign Affairs* 59 (Fall 1980), pp. 144-62.

Paarlberg, Robert L., 'Food, Oil, and Coercive Resource Power,' *International Security* 3 (Fall 1978), pp. 3-5.

Palmer, Norman D., 'Foreign Aid and Foreign Policy: The New Statecraft Re-assessed,' *Orbis* 13, 3 (1969), pp. 763-82.

Park, Choon-ho, and Jerome Alan Cohen, 'The Politics of China's Oil Weapon,' *Foreign Policy* 20 (Fall 1975), pp. 28-49.

Park, Stephen, *Business as Usual: Transactions Violating Rhodesian Sanctions*, Washington: Carnegie Endowment for International Peace, 1973.

Parmelee, M., *Blockade and Sea Power*, New York: Crowell, 1924.

Parry, Clive, 'Defining Economic Coercion in International Law,' *Texas International Law Journal* 12 (1977), pp. 1-4.

Patch, Buel W., 'Boycotts and Embargoes,' *Editorial Research Reports* I, no. 11, Washington, DC (1932).

Paterson, Thomas G., *Soviet American Confrontation: Postwar Reconstruction and the Origins of the Cold War*, Baltimore: Johns Hopkins University Press, 1973. (An insightful analysis of the use of foreign aid as a diplomatic weapon.)

Paust, Jordan J. and Albert P. Blaustein, 'The Arab Oil Weapon — A Threat to International Peace,' *American Journal of International Law* 68 (1974), pp. 410-39.

Paust, J. J. and A. P. Blaustein, 'The Arab Oil Weapon: A Reply and Reaffirmation of Illegality,' *Columbia Journal of Transnational Law* 15 (1976), pp. 57-73.

Paust, J. J. *et al.*, *The Arab Oil Weapon*, Dobbs Ferry, New York: Oceana, 1977.

Petersen, John H., 'Economic Interests and U.S. Foreign Policy in Latin America: An Empirical Approach,' in Satish Raichur and Craig Liske (eds), *The Politics of Aid, Trade, and Investment*, New York: Sage Publications, 1976, pp. 63-86.

Phillips, Charlotte A., *The Arab Boycott of Israel: Possibilities for European Cooperation with U.S. Antiboycott Legislation*, Washington: Congressional Research Service, Library of Congress, 1979.

Pieters, Ludovicus Joannes, *Internationale Sancties, 1914-1946*, Leiden: Stenfert Kroese, 1946.

Pindyck, Robert S., 'OPEC's Threat to the West,' *Foreign Policy*, 30 (Spring 1978), pp. 36-52.

Ping, Ho Kwon, 'Poser for the Third World,' *Far Eastern Economic Review* 107 (15 February 1980), pp. 107-110.

Ping, Ho Kwon, 'Thais Defy the Grain Embargo,' *Far Eastern Economic Review* 107 (15 February 1980), pp. 9-11.

Pisar, S., *Coexistence and Commerce: Guidelines for Transactions Between East and West*, New York: McGraw-Hill, 1970.

Polacheck, S. W., 'Conflict and Trade,' *Journal of Conflict Resolution* 24 (March 1980), pp. 55–78.

Polakas, John, 'Economic Sanctions: An Effective Alternative to Military Coercion?', *Brooklyn Journal of International Law* 6 (Summer 1980), pp. 289–320. (Analyses the impact of economic sanctions instituted by the UN Security Council against Rhodesia and concludes that they 'were not the impetus behind the creation of the new state of Zimbabwe.')

'Policy Conflicts in Foreign Trade and Investments: The Anti-Boycott Regulations,' roundtable convened 27 April 1978 with Thomas S. James presiding, *Proceedings of the American Society of International Law* 72 (1978), pp. 80–97.

Politis, Nicholas, *Neutrality and Peace*, translated from the French by F. C. Macken, Washington: Carnegie Endowment for International Peace, 1935.

Polk, Judd, 'Freezing Dollars Against the Axis,' *Foreign Affairs* 20 (1941), pp. 113–30.

Porter, R. C., 'International Trade and Investment Sanctions: Potential Impact on the South African Economy,' *Journal of Conflict Resolution* 23 (December 1979), pp. 579–612.

Porter, Richard C., *The Potential Impact of International Trade and Investment Sanctions on the South African Economy*, Ann Arbor: University of Michigan, Center for Research on Economic Development, 1979.

Portley, M., 'State Legislative Responses to the Arab Boycott of Israel,' *University of Michigan Journal of Law Reform* 10 (Spring 1977), pp. 592-618.

Potter, P. B., 'Sanctions and Guarantees in International Organizations,' *American Political Science Review* 16 (1922), pp. 297-305.

Potter, P. B., *Sanctions and Security: An Analysis of the French and American Views*, Geneva: Geneva Research Center, 1932.

'Price of United States Noncompliance with United Nations Rhodesian Sanctions,' *Georgia Journal of International and Comparative Law* 5 (Summer 1975), pp. 558-69.

Prittie, T., 'The Secondary Arab Boycott and Britain,' *Middle East Review* (Winter 1975/6), pp. 46-7.

Quigley, J., *The Soviet Foreign Trade Monopoly: Institutions and Laws*, Columbus: Ohio State University Press, 1974.

Rai, Kul B., 'Foreign Aid and Voting in the U.N. General Assembly, 1967-1976,' *Journal of Peace Research*, XVII, 3 (1980), pp. 269-77. (Examines the relationship between foreign economic aid and the General Assembly votes for the period 1967-76. The findings indicate that the American aid is more effective as an inducement and the Soviet aid is more effective as a reward or a punishment.)

Raj, K. N., 'Sanctions and the Indian Experience,' in Ronald Segal (ed.), *International Conciliation, Sanctions Against South Africa*, Harmondsworth: Penguin, 1964, pp. 197-203. (Gives an invaluable account of how South Africa was able to get around the Indian boycott launched against it in July 1946, by trading with third parties.)

Ramcharan, B. G., 'Legal Issues before the United Nations Sanctions Committee,' *Dalhousie Law Journal* 3 (October 1976), pp. 540-59.

Reisman, W. Michael, *Nullity and Revision: The Review and Enforcement of International Judgement and Awards*, New Haven: Yale University Press, 1974. (Treats sanctions from the standpoint of international law.)

Remba, Oded, 'The Arab Boycott: A Study in Total Economic Warfare,' *Midstream* 6, 3 (Summer 1960), pp. 40-55.

Remer, Charles F., *A Study of Chinese Boycotts, With Special Reference to Their Economic Effectiveness*, Baltimore: The Johns Hopkins University Press 1933. (A thorough examination of Chinese efforts in the field of 'nonviolent coercion,' providing insights into the relation between the boycott and war.)

Renwick, Robin, *Economic Sanctions*, London: Croom Helm, 1981. (Examines the effect of economic sanctions – principally those imposed on Italy and Rhodesia.)

Report on the Supply of Petroleum Products to Rhodesia (Bingham Report), London: HMSO, 1978.

Richardson, N. R., *Foreign Policy and Economic Dependence*, Austin: University of Texas Press, 1978.

Richardson, N. R., 'Political Compliance and U.S. Trade Dominance,' *American Political Science Review* 70 (December 1976), pp. 1098-109.

Rogers, B., 'Southern Africa and the Oil Embargo,' *Africa Today* 21 (Spring 1974), pp. 3-8.

Root, Elihu, *The Sanction of International Law*, New York: American Branch of the Association for International Conciliation, 1908.

Rosenfeld, S. S. 'The Politics of Food,' *Foreign Policy* 14 (Spring 1974, pp. 17-29.

Roth, A., 'Arab Boycott and the Federal Securities Laws,' *Securities Regulation Law Journal* 5 (Winter 1978), pp. 318-47.

Rothschild, Emma, 'Food Politics,' *Foreign Affairs* 54 (January 1976), pp. 285-307.

Roudot, Pierre, 'Arab Boycott as Myth,' *New Outlook* 6, 5 (June 1963), pp. 17-24.

Rowan-Robinson, H., *Sanctions Begone! A Plea and a Plan for the Reform of the League*, London: Clowes, 1936.

Rowson, S. W. D., 'Modern Blockade: Some Legal Aspects,' *British Yearbook of International Law* 23 (1946), pp. 346-53.

Roxburgh, R. F., 'Sanctions of International Law,' *American Journal of International Law* 14 (1920), pp. 26-37.

Rubenfeld, S. J., 'Legal and Tax Implications of Participation in International Boycotts,' *Tax Law Review* 32 (Summer 1977), pp. 613-52.

Ruffin, Henri E., *L'entr'aide dans l'Application des Sanctions; Paragraphe III de l'Article XVI du Pacte de la Société des Nations*, Paris: Recueil Sirey, 1937. (Reprinted in 1938 with a preface by Georges Scelle.)

Russell, Jeremy, 'Energy Considerations in Comecon Policies,' *World Today* 32, 2 (February 1976), pp. 39-48,

Ruzie, David, 'Les Sanctions Economiques Contre La Rhodésie,' *Journal du Droit International* 97 (1970), pp. 20-56.

Ruzie, David, *Organisations Internationales et Sanctions Internationales*, Paris: A. Colin, 1971.

Saltoun, A. M., 'Regulation of Foreign Boycotts,' *Business Lawyer* 33 (January 1978), pp. 559–603.

'Sanctions,' *Interdependence* 12 (1935).

'Sanctions and a Poland Policy,' *The Brookings Review* 1, 2 (Winter 1982), pp. 24–5.

Sanctions and South Africa, *Harvard International Law Journal* 19 (Fall 1978), pp. 887–930.

Sanctions: The Character of International Sanctions and Their Application, Information Department Paper, no. 17, 2nd revised and enlarged edition, London: Royal Institute of International Affairs, 1935. (A concise and comprehensive study of the question of sanctions. It examines in detail the scope of Article XVI and the various difficulties of interpretation to which it has given rise.)

'Sanctions in the Italo-Ethiopian Conflict,' *International Conciliation*, 315 (December 1935), pp. 539–44.

Schelling, T. C., *Hearings on East-West Trade*, Committee on Foreign Relations, US Senate, November 1964.

Schirman, S., 'The History of the Arab Boycott. 1921–1975,' *Middle East Review* (Winter 1975/6), pp. 40–2.

Schlesinger, James R., 'Strategic Leverage for Aid and Trade,' in David M. Abshire and Richard V. Allen (eds), *National Security*, New York: Praeger, 1963.

Schneider, William, *Can We Avert Economic Warfare in Raw Materials? U. S. Agriculture as a Blue Chip*, New York: National Strategy Information Center, 1974.

Schreiber, Anna P., 'Economic Coercion as an Instrument of Foreign Policy,' *World Politics* 25 (April 1973), pp. 387–413.

Schwartz, Louis B., 'The Arab Boycott and American Responses: Antitrust Law or Executive Discretion?', *Texas Law Review* 54 (Autumn 1976), pp.1260–87.

'Security Council Resolutions: When do they Give Rise to Enforceable Legal Rights?', The United Nations Charter, the Byrd Amendment and a self-executing treaty analysis, *Cornell International Law Journal* 9 (May 1976), pp. 298–316.

Segal, Ronald (ed.), *International Conciliation, Sanctions Against South Africa*, Harmondsworth: Penguin, 1964.

Seiler, John, 'South African Response to External Pressures,' *Journal of Modern African Studies* (September 1975).

Seligman, Eustace, 'The Legality of U.S. Quarantine Action Under the United Nations Charter,' *American Bar Association Journal* XLIX (February 1963), pp. 142–5.

Shamsedin, Ezzedin, *Arab Oil and the United States: An Admixture of Politics and Economics*, Columbia, South Carolina: University of South Carolina, 1974.

Shamsedin, Ezzedin, *The Arab Oil Embargo and the United States Economy*, London: Middle East Economic Digest Monographs, 1974.

Shihata, Ibrahim, 'Destination Embargo of Arab Oil: Its Legality Under International Law,' *American Journal of International Law* 68 (October 1974), pp. 591-627.

Shihata, I. F. I., 'Arab Oil Policies and the New International Economic Order,' *Virginia Journal of International Law* 16 (Winter 1976), pp. 261-88.

Shneyer, P. A. and V. Barta, 'Legality of the U.S. Economic Blockade of Cuba under International Law,' *Case Western Reserve Journal of International Law* 13 (Summer 1981), pp. 451-82.

'Should the United States Impose Economic Sanctions on the South African Government in Order to Promote Majority Rule?', Yes and No Debate between Andrew Young and Robert L. Scheuttinger in Herbert M. Levine (ed.), *Point-Counterpoint: Readings in American Government*, Glenview, Illinois: Scott, Foresman & Co., 1979, pp. 421-34.

Sigmund, Paul E., 'The "Invisible Blockade" and the Overthrow of Allende,' *Foreign Affairs* 52 (January 1974), pp. 322-40.

Siney, Marion C., *The Allied Blockade of Germany , 1914-1916*, Ann Arbor: University of Michigan Press, 1957.

Singer, S. Fred. 'Limits to Arab Oil Power,' *Foreign Policy*, 30 (Spring 1978), pp. 53-67.

Skil, A. G. and C. H. Peterson, 'Export Control Laws and Multinational Enterprises,' *The International Lawyer* 11 (Winter 1977), pp. 29-44.

Slonim, S., '1948 American Embargo on Arms to Palestine,' *Political Science Quarterly* 94 (Fall 1979), pp. 495-514.

Steiner, Henry J., 'International Boycotts and Domestic Order: American Involvement in the Arab-Israeli Conflict,' *Texas Law Review* 54 (1976), pp. 1355-410.

Smith, Stephen N., 'Re "The Arab Oil Weapon": A Skeptic's View,' *American Journal of International Law* 69 (1975), p. 136. (Comment on Paust and Blaustein, 'The Arab Oil Weapon: A Threat to International Peace,' *AJIL* 68 (1974), p. 410.)

Sokol, Albert, 'State Reaction to the Arab Boycott of Israel: Legislative and Constitutional Preemption,' *Boston University Law Review* 57 (March 1977), pp. 335-67.

Soubeyrol, Jacques, 'Les Sanctions Internationales Contre Les Territoires Gouvernés par les Minorités Blanches en Afrique Australe,' *Année Africaine* (Paris) 1973, pp. 137-71.

Spaight, J. M., 'The Pseudo-Sanctions,' in *Pseudo-Security*, London: Longmans, Green and Co., 1928, pp. 53-73.

Spandau, Arnt, 'Economic Boycott Against South Africa: Normative and Factual Issues,' *Kenwyn* (Cape Town), Juta, 1979.

Sporn, Charles M., 'Complicity with the Arab Blacklist: Business Expedience Versus Abridgment of Constitutional Rights,' *Brooklyn Journal of International Law* II, 2 (Spring 1976), pp. 228-49.

Standard, William L., 'United States Quarantine of Cuba and the Rule of Law,' *American Bar Association Journal* XLIX (August 1963).

Stehr, U., 'Unequal Development and Dependency Structures in Comecon,' *Journal of Peace Research* 14, 2 (1977), pp. 115-28.

Stephen, M., 'United Nations and International Law: The Rhodesia Case,' *Contemporary Review* 224 (May 1974), pp. 239-43.

Stephenson, G. V., 'Impact of International Economic Sanctions on the Internal Viability of Rhodesia,' *Geographical Review* 65 (July 1975), pp. 377–89.

Strack, Harry R., *Sanctions: The Case of Rhodesia*, Syracuse, New York: Syracuse University Press, 1978. (Examines the nature and purpose of international sanctions and investigates the extent to which and under what conditions Rhodesia has been able to maintain or establish international relations and thus avoid isolation.)

Strange, Susan, 'The Strategic Trade Embargoes: Sense or Nonsense?', *Year Book of World Affairs* 12 (1958), pp. 55-73.

Strinson, J. W., 'International Sanction and American Law,' *American Journal of International Law* 19 (1925), pp. 505-16.

Sutcliffe, Robert B., *Sanctions Against Rhodesia: The Economic Background*, London: Africa Bureau, 1966.

Sutcliffe, Robert B., 'The Cost of Sanctions to Britain,' *The Listener* (London) (30 March 1967), pp. 417-19.

Sutcliffe, Robert B., 'Rhodesia and the Effects of Sanctions,' *The Listener* (29 June 1967), pp. 839-40.

Sutcliffe, Robert B., 'Rhodesian Trade Since U.D.I.', *World Today* 23 (October 1967), pp. 418-22.

Sutcliffe, Robert B., 'The Political Economy of Rhodesian Sanctions,' *Journal of Commonwealth Political Studies* 7 (July 1969), pp. 113-25.

Swayze, F. B., 'Traditional Principles of Blockade in Modern Practice: United States Mining of Internal and Territorial Waters of North Vietnam,' *JAG Journal* 29 (Spring 1977), pp. 143-73.

Szyliowicz, Joseph S., 'The Embargo and U.S. Foreign Policy,' in Joseph S. Szyliowicz and Bard E. O'Neil (eds), *The Energy Crisis and U.S. Foreign Policy*, New York: Praeger, 1975, pp. 183-232.

Taba, Moriyoshi, 'An Historical Survey of the Anti-Japanese Boycott Movement,' *Far Eastern Review* XXIV (August 1928).

Takayanagi, Kenzo, 'On the Legality of the Chinese Boycott,' *Pacific Affairs* 5, 10 (October 1932), pp. 855-62.

Tanzer, Michel, *The Political Economy of International Oil and the Underdeveloped Countries*, Boston: Beacon, 1969.

Tanzer, Michel, *The Energy Crisis: World Struggle for Power and Wealth*, New York: Monthly Review Press, 1974.

Tate, J. M. and R. B. Lake, 'Taking Sides: An Overview of the U.S. Legislative Response to the Arab Boycott of Israel,' *Denver Journal of International Law and Policy* 6 (Spring 1977), pp. 613-34.

Taubenfeld, Howard J., *Economic Sanctions: An Appraisal and Case Study*, New York: Columbia University, 1958 (mimeo).

Taubenfeld, Howard J. and Rita F. Taubenfeld, 'The Economic Weapon: The League and the United Nations,' *Proceedings of the American Society of International Law* (1964), pp. 183-205.

'Taxation: Anti-Boycott and Anti-Bribery Legislation – Tax Reform Act of 1976, pub. 1, no. 74-455, sections 1061-7, 90 stat. 1649-1654. *Harvard International Law Journal* 18 (Spring 1977), pp. 365-73.

Taylor, R. K., *Blockade: A Guide to Non-Violent Intervention*, Maryknoll, New York: Orbis, 1977.

Teyssaire, J. *Le Blocus Pacifique*, Paris: Beauvais, 1910.

Thomas, John, 'Arab Boycott: A Legislative Solution to Multidimensional Problem, *University of Pittsburgh Law Review* 39 (Fall 1977), pp. 63–86.

Thompson, J. B., 'Rumania's Struggle With Comecon,' *East Europe* XIII (June 1964), pp. 2–9. (Discusses Rumania's defiance of Comecon.)

'Through The Antiboycott Morass to an Export Priority,' *Georgia Journal of International and Comparative Law* 9 (Summer 1979), pp. 357–411.

Tilson, John, *The Embargo on Spain*, New Haven: Tilson, 1939.

Timberg, S., 'Sovereign Immunity and Act of State Defenses: Transnational Boycotts and Economic Coercion,' *Texas Law Review* 55 (December 1976), 1–37.

Tornudd, Klaus, 'Strategic Embargo and Economic Warfare,' *Cooperation and Conflict* 2, Oslo, Norway (1968), pp. 148–55.

'Toward an Effective Oil Embargo of South Africa,' Sanctions Working Group, *Monthly Review* 32 (December 1980), pp. 58–62.

Tuomi, H., 'The Food Power: The Position of Main Exporting Countries in World Food Economy,' *Instant Research on Peace and Violence* 5, 3 (1975), pp. 121–37.

Turck, Nancy, 'The Arab Boycott of Israel,' *Foreign Affairs* 55 (April 1977), pp. 472–493. (An excellent examination of the Arab boycott and the effects of anti-boycott legislation on US trade and its overall relations with Israel and the Arabs.)

Ullman, Richard H., 'Human Rights and Economic Power: The United States Versus Idi Amin,' *Foreign Affairs* 56, 3 (April 1978), pp. 529–43.

United Nations Documents, *Declaration of the Conference of West European Parliamentarians on Oil Embargo Against South Africa, Brussels, 30–31 January, 1981*, February 1981.

United Nations Documents, *International Conference on Sanctions Against South Africa* 3 November 1980 (A/35/22/Add. 3; S/14156/Add. 3).

United Nations Documents, *International Conference on Sanctions Against South Africa*, Documents, 1981– , (A/Conf. 107/–).

United Nations Documents, *International Sanctions Against Apartheid South Africa, 1977–1980*, selected General Assembly and Security Council resolutions and conclusions of major international conferences and seminars, May 1980.

United Nations Documents, *Oil Sanctions Against South Africa*, First Special Report of the Special Committee Against Apartheid, General Assembly Official Records, 33rd Sess., Suppl. No. 22A (A/33/22/Add. 1), 1978.

United Nations Documents, *Papers Submitted to the International Conference on Economic Sanctions Against South Africa held in London from 14–17 April 1964*, 17 August 1964.

United Nations Documents, *Report of the International Seminar on Oil Embargo Against South Africa held in Amsterdam from 14 to 16 March, 1980*, 18 April 1980.

United Nations Documents, *Sanctions Against South Africa: Compilation of Declarations and Resolutions of Conferences and Seminars Organized or*

Co-sponsored by the Special Committee Against Apartheid, August 1977-February 1981, 1981.

United Nations Documents, Sanctions Committee, *Special Report* (S/AC 15/WP. 177/Add. 3/Rev. 1), 14 November 1975.

United Nations Documents, Sanctions Working Group, *Implementing an Effective Oil Embargo Against South Africa: The Current Situation*, August 1980.

UN Security Council, *Annual Reports of the Committee Established in Pursuance of Resolution 253 (1968) Concerning the Question of Southern Rhodesia* (cited as the UN Sanctions Committee); *Third Report* (S/9844), 15 June 1970; *Fourth Report* (S/10229/Add. 1/Annex II), 16 June 1971; *Fifth Report* (S/10852/Add.1), 31 December 1972; *Sixth Report* (S/11178/Add. 1), 9 January 1974; *Seventh Report* (S/11594/Add. 2/Annex II), 2 April 1975; *Eighth Report* (S/11927/Add. 1/Annex II), 6 February 1976; *Ninth Report* (S/12265), cited in SCOR, 32nd Yr., Special Supplement no. 2.

UN Security Council, Sanctions Committee, *Special Report* (S/AC.15/WP.177/Add.3/Rev.1), 14 November 1975.

United States House Committee on Foreign Affairs, Subcommittee on International Organizations and Movements, *Sanctions as an Instrumentality of the United Nations: Rhodesia as a Case Study*, Washington, DC: Government Printing Office, 1972.

United States House Committee on Foreign Affairs, Subcommittee on International Organizations and Movements, *Data and Analysis Concerning the Possibility of a U.S. Food Embargo as a Response to the Present Arab Oil Boycott*, 93rd Congress, 1st session, Washington, DC (21 November 1973).

US Congress, House of Representatives, Committee on Foreign Affairs, *The Middle East: New Hopes, New Challenges*, Hearings before the Subcommittee on the Near East and South Asia, 93rd Cong., 2nd sess., 9 April–27 June 1974, Washington, DC: Government Printing Office, 1974. (Testimony on the Arab oil embargo.)

US Congress, House of Representatives, Committee on Foreign Affairs, *Discriminatory Arab Pressure on U.S. Business*, Hearings, Subcommittee on International Trade and Commerce, Committee on International Relations, 94th Cong., 1st sess., 6 March–11 December 1975, Washington, DC, 1976.

US Congress, House of Representatives, Committee on Foreign Affairs, Committee on International Relations, *The Rhodesian Sanctions Bill*, Joint Hearings before the Subcommittees on Africa and International Organizations, 95th Cong., 1st sess., 1977.

US Congress, House of Representatives, Committee on Foreign Affairs, *Economic Sanctions Against Rhodesia*, Hearings, Subcommittees on Africa and on International Organizations, Committee on Foreign Affairs, 2 April–21 May 1979, Washington, DC, 1979.

US Congress, Senate, Committee on Foreign Relations, *Sanctions Against Rhodesia – Chrome*, Hearings before the Subcommittee on African Affairs, 92nd Cong., 1st sess., 1971.

US Congress, *Arab Boycott: Hearings on S. 69 and S. 92 before the Subcommittee on International Finance of the Senate Committee on Banking, Housing and Urban Affairs, 95th Cong.*, 1st sess. (1977). (Hearings related to Export

Amendments in their final form. Includes a compilation of available statistics on the Arab boycott's impact on business concerns in the US.)

US Congress, *Discriminatory Arab Pressure on U.S. Business: Hearings Before the Subcommittee on International Trade and Commerce of the House Committee on International Relations*, 94th Cong., 1st sess. (1975). Contains review of other transnational boycott activities.)

US Congress, *Discriminatory Overseas Assignment Policies of Federal Agencies: Hearings Before a Subcommittee of the House Committee on Government Operations*, 94th Cong., 1st and 2nd sess. (1976). (Examines the extent of US compliance with the Arab boycott demands.)

US Congress, *Effectiveness of Federal Agencies' Enforcement of Laws and Policies Against Compliance, by Banks and other U.S. Firms, with the Arab Boycott: Hearings Before a Subcommittee of the House Committee on Government Operations*, 94th Cong., 2nd sess. (1976) (2 parts).

US Congress, Senate, Committee on Foreign Relations, *Importation of Rhodesian Chrome*, Hearings before the Subcommittee on African Affairs, 93rd Cong., 1st sess., 1973.

US Congress, Senate, Committee on Banking, Housing, and Urban Affairs, Subcommittee on International Trade, *Hearings: Arab Boycott*, 95th Congress, 1st session (1977).

US Congress, Senate, *Trade Sanctions Against Rhodesia*, Hearing Committee on Foreign Relations, 12 June 1979, Washington, DC, 1979.

US Congress, Senate, *Embargo of Phosphate Exports to the Soviet Union*, Hearing, Committee on Commerce, Science, and Transportation, 19 February 1980, Washington, DC, 1980.

US Department of Commerce, *Export Control, 83rd Quarterly Report*, Washington, DC: Government Printing Office, 1968.

U.S. Foreign Aid, Its Purposes, Scope, Administration, and Related Information, New York: Greenwood Press, 1968. (Analyses the purpose, scope, administration, cost and effectiveness of the various foreign aid programs in which the US has been engaged since 1941.)

'U.S. Legislation of Foreign Investments and the Arab Boycott,' and 'Boycott of Banking and Underwriting Firms,' and 'U.S. Anti-Boycott Legislation and Action, 1975,' *Middle East Review* 7 (Winter 1975/76), pp. 22–6.

'U.S. Trade Sanctions against Uganda: Legality under International Law,' *Law and Policy in International Business* 11 (1979), pp. 1149–91.

Vagts, Detlev, 'Coercion and Foreign Investment Rearrangements,' *American Journal of International Law* 72 (January 1978), pp. 17–36.

Viner, J., *Dumping, A Problem of International Trade*, Chicago: University of Chicago Press, 1923.

Vinson, J. Chal, *Referendum for Isolation: Defeat of Article Ten*, Athens, Ga.: University of Georgia Press, 1969. (Discusses increased interest in sanctions after 1900 and examines the League's debate on their use.)

Vinson, J. Chal, 'Sanctions,' in Alexander de Conde (ed.), *Encyclopedia of American Foreign Policy*, New York: Charles Scribner's Sons, 1978, pp. 924–35.

Walczak, J. R., 'Legal Aspects of the U.S.S.R. Grain Embargo,' *Denver Journal of International Law and Politics* 10 (Winter 1981), pp. 279-97.

Walinsky, Louis, J., 'Coherent Defense Strategy: the Case for Economic Denial,' *Foreign Affairs* 61, 2 (Winter 1982/3), pp. 272-91.

Wallensteen, Peter, *A Study of Economic Sanctions*, Uppsala, 1968 (mimeo).

Wallensteen, Peter, 'Characteristics of Economic Sanctions,' in William D. Coplin and Charles W. Kegley (eds), *Multi-Method Introduction to International Politics*, Chicago: Markham Publishing Company, 1971. (Originally printed in *Journal of Peace Research* 5, 3 (1968), pp. 248-67.)

Walters, R. S., 'Soviet Economic Aid to Cuba, 1959-1964,' *International Affairs* 42 (January 1966), pp. 74-86.

Webster, Sir Charles, *Sanctions: The Use of Force in an International Organization*, London: The David Davies Memorial Institute of International Studies, March 1956.

Weigand, Robert, 'The Arab League Boycott of Israel,' *Michigan State University Business Topics* (Spring 1968), pp. 74-80.

Weintraub, Sidney, *et al.*, *Economic Coercion and U.S. Foreign Policy*, Boulder, Colorado: Westview, December 1981. (Examines six case studies of economic coercion during the term of President Johnson and concludes that such methods do work.)

Wendzel, Robert L., 'Embargoes or Boycotts,' *International Politics: Policymakers and Policymaking*, New York: John Wiley, 1981, pp. 243-50.

Widmer, Hans, *Der Zwang im Völkerrecht*, Leipzig: Robert Noske, 1936. (Contains a good historical review of the problem of sanctions since the establishment of the League of Nations.)

Wild, Payson Sibley, Jr., *Sanctions and Treaty Enforcement*, Cambridge, Mass.: Harvard University Press, 1934.

Wiles, Peter, 'Economic War and the Soviet-Type Economy,' *Osteuropa Wirtschaft* (March 1965), pp. 27-42.

Wilezynski, J., 'Strategic Embargo in Perspective,' *Soviet Studies* 19 (July 1967), pp. 74-86.

Wilkins, John R., 'Legal Norms and International Economic Development: The Case of the Cuba Shipping Restriction in the United States Foreign Assistance Act,' *California Law Review* (October 1967), pp. 977-1019.

Williams, Benjamin H., 'The Coming of Economic Sanctions Into American Practice,' *American Journal of International Law* 37 (July 1943), pp. 386-96.

Williams, John F., 'Sanctions Under the Covenant,' *British Year Book of International Law* (1936), pp. 130-49.

Williams, J. L., 'U.S. Regulation of Arab Boycott Practices,' *Law and Politics of International Business* 10 (1978), pp. 815-86.

Williams, Michael and Michael Parsonage, 'Britain and Rhodesia: The Economic Background to Sanctions,' *World Today* 29 (September 1973), pp. 379-88.

Williams, Roth (pseudonym of Konni Zilliacus), *The League, the Protocols and the Empire*, London: Allen & Unwin, 1925.

Willrich, M. and M. A. Conant, 'International Energy Agency: An Interpretation and Assessment,' *American Journal of International Law* 71 (April 1977), pp. 199-223.

Wilson, Clifton E., 'The Use and Abuse of International Law,' in Neal D. Houghton (ed.), *Struggle Against History: U.S. Foreign Policy in an Age of*

Revolution, New York: Simon & Schuster, 1968. (Questions the legality under the UN Charter of the US quarantine of Cuba during the missile crisis and the economic embargo.)

Wilson, G. G., 'Sanctions for International Agreements,' *American Journal of International Law* 11 (1917), pp. 387-9.

Wilson, G. G., 'Boycott,' *International Law Situations* (1932), pp. 89-135.

Wilson, H. R., *For Want of a Nail: The Failure of the League of Nations in Ethiopia*, New York: Vantage, 1959.

Wittkopf, E. R., 'Foreign Aid and United Nations Votes: A Comparative Study,' *American Political Science Review* 67 (September 1973), pp. 868-88.

Wolf, Charles, *Foreign Aid: Theory and Practice in Southern Asia*, Princeton, New Jersey: Princeton University Press, 1960.

Wolf von Amerongon, O., 'Economic Sanctions as a Foreign Policy Tool?', *International Security* V (Fall 1980).

Woolcock, Stephen, 'East-West Trade: U.S. Policy and European Interests,' *The World Today* 38, 2 (February 1982), pp. 51-9. (Examines the reasons for the divergence between the US and European approaches to East-West trade.)

Wright, Quincy, 'The Legal Status of Economic Sanctions,' *Amerasia* (February 1939).

Wright, Quincy, 'Permissive Sanctions Against Aggression,' *American Journal of International Law* 36 (1942), pp. 103-6.

Wright, Quincy, 'The Cuban Quarantine,' *American Journal of International Law* 57, 3 (July 1963), pp. 546-65.

Wrong, Dennis, 'Oil, the Marines, and Prof. Tucker,' *Dissent* (Spring 1975), pp. 111-13.

Wu, Yuan-Li, *Economic Warfare*, Englewood Cliffs, New Jersey: Prentice-Hall, 1952.

Zacklin, Ralph, *The United Nations and Rhodesia, A Study of International Law*, New York: Praeger, 1974.

Zimmern, Alfred E., *The Economic Weapon in the War Against Germany*, New York: George H. Doran, 1918.

Zimmern, Alfred E., 'The League's Handling of the Italo-Abyssinian Dispute,' *International Affairs* 14 (November-December 1935), pp. 751-68.

Zvereva, L., 'Some Results of the Economic Boycott of Egypt by Arab States' (in Russian), *Narodi Azii i Afriki* 4 (1981), pp. 109-15.

Index